TOMORROW'S PEOPLE AND NEW TECHNOLOGY

T0384230

As we witness a series of social, political, cultural, and economic changes/disruptions this book examines the Fourth Industrial Revolution and the way emerging technologies are impacting our lives and changing society.

The Fourth Industrial Revolution is characterised by the emergence of new technologies that are blurring the boundaries between the physical, the digital, and the biological worlds. This book allows readers to explore how these technologies will impact peoples' lives by 2030. It helps readers to not only better understand the use and implications of emerging technologies, but also to imagine how their individual life will be shaped by them. The book provides an opportunity to see the great potential but also the threats and challenges presented by the emerging technologies of the Fourth Industrial Revolution, posing questions for the reader to think about what future they want. Emerging technologies, such as robotics, artificial intelligence, big data and analytics, cloud computing, nanotechnology, biotechnology, the Internet of Things, fifth-generation wireless technologies (5G), and fully autonomous vehicles, among others, will have a significant impact on every aspect of our lives, as such this book looks at their potential impact in the entire spectrum of daily life, including home life, travel, education and work, health, entertainment and social life.

Providing an indication of what the world might look like in 2030, this book is essential reading for students, scholars, professionals, and policymakers interested in the nexus between emerging technologies and sustainable development, politics and society, and global governance.

Felix Dodds is Adjunct Professor at the Water Institute at the University of North Carolina, US and Associate Fellow at the Tellus Institute Boston, US. He is the author/editor of over 20 books, including *Stakeholder Democracy* (Routledge, 2019), *Negotiating the Sustainable Development Goals* (Routledge, 2016 with Ambassador

David Donoghue, Jimena Leiva Roesch) and *The Water, Food, Energy and Climate Nexus* (Routledge, 2016 with Jamie Bartram). In 2019 he was a candidate to head the United Nations Environment Programme.

Carolina Duque Chopitea is the Co-founder and Head of Analytics at Brandformers.io, a digital marketing agency headquartered in Panama. She holds a Master's Degree in Business Analytics from Hult International Business School (San Francisco) and a degree in Political Science and Environmental Studies from the University of Victoria, Canada. With her multidisciplinary background working in the public and private sectors, Carolina works with brands and organisations to help them realise their full potential by blending data with creativity.

Ranger Ruffins is a Master's student at the University of North Carolina, US at Chapel Hill (UNC), pursuing a degree in City and Regional Planning. Her area of focus is land use and environmental planning, with a specific interest in resilience in the face of natural hazard disasters and the ability for cities to adapt to the effects of a changing climate. She earned her BA from the UNC in Environmental Studies in 2016. After graduating, Ranger worked in New York City as the Environment Program Assistant at The Overbrook Foundation, working on grant development for the foundation's environment portfolio.

"I simply love *Tomorrow's People and New Technology*. Teasingly playful, inquisitive rather than just another turgid tome trying to be politically correct and accurate with each forecast, the authors' bandwidth is wonderfully broad, the insights incisive, and the writing welcoming. This book is a speculative triumph. It invites us into an imaginative world of endless fascination and ingenuity, at once allying suspicions that the future belongs only to the smart machines we have created and are in the process of letting loose."

Richard David Hames, *Executive Director,*
Centre for the Future

"Many have dubbed the years between 2020 and 2030 the 'decade of action and ambition' where vast transformations need to be achieved if we are to meet both SDG and Paris climate goals. That can seem daunting and challenging to individuals who feel they don't have agency or the capability to make a difference, but *Tomorrow's People and New Technology* provides an engaging and accessible blueprint for how technology can play a crucial role in helping individuals to change their lives to make a big difference. Funny and thought-provoking, it is a great read!"

Kirsty Schneeberger, *MBE, Chair UK*
Environmental Law Association

"Humanity has understood the necessity to change the course of development. Nations have made their pledges in the form of SDGs and climate goals. The word progress has been reevaluated. To what extent we can succeed in this fundamental transformation in such a relatively short time, the jury is still out, but the clock is ticking. It is a remarkable book bringing closer to our daily lives what is at stake and how technological shift can and will influence our journey. Excellent reading for all who plan to spend the rest of their lives in the changing future."

Ambassador Csaba Kőrösi, *Director of the*
Office of the President of Hungary, former Co-chair
of the UN Open Working Group on Sustainable
Development Goals

"No one has written more or provided a larger lens through which we can view the subject of sustainable development than has Felix Dodds, whether alone or in collaboration with very interesting co-authors. *Tomorrow's People and New Technology* issues an invitation to consider the future through the 2030 development agenda and the life it might engender. It poses the pertinent questions – How will technology be the primary driver of society, economy and way of life? Will it help us to realize the great value of our humanity? Will we see the technology as our partner in achieving sustainable development? Will its use be equitable in improving quality of life globally so that no-one is left behind? What sort of world do we want and how will technology help bring it into being? These questions are not academic. COVID-19 has accelerated the use of technology and we must answer these questions – now. Agree or disagree with the authors but read their answers."

Ambassador Liz Thompson, *Permanent Mission of Barbados to the United Nations*

"In 2015 governments agreed to both the Sustainable Development Goals and the Paris Climate Agreement, creating a pathway to securing a viable future on this planet. Even with renewed political will, however, delivering on the transformations called for will call for innovation at many levels. This book therefore offers key insights by looking to 2030 and exploring the impact of a number of new technologies on our lives and on delivering on these two multilateral agreements. *Tomorrow's People and New Technology* recognizes both that the changes that we all will experience over the next ten years will be enormous, and that massive shifts are required to turn our economies and societies around. It tries to help people understand how these technologies might impact positively on their lives and by doing so makes those changes seem less threatening. The book also recognizes the challenges will be different in different parts of the world and explores how these could potentially increase inequality. Finally it highlights for the reader some of the policy challenges these new technologies would bring. Required reading at the intersection of climate, SDGs, innovation, and disruption."

Paula Caballero, *(Mother of the SDGs) former Director for Economic, Social and Environmental Affairs in the Ministry of Foreign Affairs of Colombia*

"Though many books describe tech and AI's impact on our future, few paint an intimate and detailed picture of how our lives – at home, work, and with friends – will be completely reshaped by the innovations that are just beginning to take root today. *Tomorrow's People and New Technology* is a fascinating forecast at life by 2030 and the ways in which we must change to harness technology's promise in every facet of our daily lives."

Maria Figueroa Kupcu, *Partner and Head of New York Office, Brunswick Group; Chair, Institute for Global Leadership, Tufts University*

"In 2021, the last thing people needed was another doomsday book. *Tomorrow's People and New Technology* is written in an accessible and fun style and illustrates how frontier or 4IR technologies can improve our daily life and help achieve the Sustainable Development Goals (SDGs) and the Paris

Climate Change Agreement, allows people that are usually not concerned about these international issues far from their daily life, to not only be aware but reflect on them. It brings it home! Potential negative impacts are brought only at the end allowing for a more educated societal debate about these issues, including the monetization of our attention through these ever-omnipresent platforms. Kudos for this putting this book out there and getting the debate going on needed national and international policies needed to make sure these frontier technologies help us achieve the SDGs not further increase inequalities and polarization."

Chantal Line Carpentier, *Chief, New York Office of UNCTAD*

"More often than not, we see technology as something that is happening to us – that is, ordinary people are impacted in both positive and malign ways without agency or voice. In addition to helping us understand the scope of emerging technologies, *Tomorrow's People and New Technology* calls on the reader and individual to be proactive and help shape trends in ways that support the sustainable development agenda and our immediate social lives."

Gavin Power, *former Executive Deputy Director, UN Global Compact*

"The world has committed to the SDGs and the Paris Agreement, which civil society and multilateral stakeholders had strongly advocated for. This is the decade of action, which will decide whether we can secure a sustainable future for humankind and our planet.

In Bonn, we have known Felix Dodds as a long-term ally in the engagement for sustainable development and also a great visionary. With *Tomorrow's People and New Technology,* he and his co-authors have created a very inspiring and simply good read about our potential future world in 2030 – a world with blurring digital, physical and biological boundaries. The positive vision of emerging new technologies is a valuable instrument that can help us recognize and embrace opportunities and potentials to achieve a sustainable development for our societies while leaving no one behind.

I hope that this book, which is also an invitation to take a pro-active approach, will attract a large number of readers. Given our commitment to a fair and liveable planet in 2030, it is great motivation to have this vivid and captivating image at hand – and in the back of our minds."

Katja Dörner, *Mayor of Bonn, Germany's United Nations City*

TOMORROW'S PEOPLE AND NEW TECHNOLOGY

Changing How We Live Our Lives

Felix Dodds, Carolina Duque Chopitea, and Ranger Ruffins

With cartoon art by John Charles, inks
by Lee Townsend, and lettering by Nikki Foxrobot

Routledge
Taylor & Francis Group

LONDON AND NEW YORK

from Routledge

First published 2022
by Routledge
2 Park Square, Milton Park, Abingdon, Oxon OX14 4RN

and by Routledge
605 Third Avenue, New York, NY 10158

Routledge is an imprint of the Taylor & Francis Group, an informa business

British Library Cataloguing-in-Publication Data
A catalogue record for this b ook is available from the British Library

Library of Congress Cataloging-in-Publication Data
Names: Dodds, Felix, author. | Duque Chopitea, Carolina, author. | Ruffins, Ranger, author.
Title: Tomorrow's people and new technology: changing how we live our lives/Felix Dodds, Carolina Duque Chopitea and Ranger Ruffins; with cartoon art by John Charles, inks by Lee Townsend, and lettering by Nikki Foxrobot.
Description: New York, NY: Routledge, 2022. | Includes bibliographical references and index. |
Identifiers: LCCN 2021020647 (print) | LCCN 2021020648 (ebook) | ISBN 9780367492908 (hardback) | ISBN 9780367492885 (paperback) | ISBN 9781003045496 (ebook)
Subjects: LCSH: Industrial revolution–History–21st century. | Sustainable development–History–21st century. | Environmental policy. | Economic policy. | Social change.
Classification: LCC HD2321.D553 2022 (print) | LCC HD2321 (ebook) | DDC 338.09–dc23
LC record available at https://lccn.loc.gov/2021020647
LC ebook record available at https://lccn.loc.gov/2021020648

ISBN: 978-0-367-49290-8 (hbk)
ISBN: 978-0-367-49288-5 (pbk)
ISBN: 978-1-003-04549-6 (ebk)

DOI: 10.4324/9781003045496

Typeset in Bembo
by Deanta Global Publishing Services, Chennai, India

This book is dedicated to those who search for a better and more sustainable world for everyone.

CONTENTS

ILLUSTRATIONS

Figures

Tables

Boxes

Cartoons

ABBREVIATIONS

ABC	Atanasoff-Berry Computer
AI	Artificial intelligence
AWG	Atmosphere water generator
AR	Augmented reality
BLM	Black Lives Matter
BYOT	Bring Your Own Thermostat
BIPV	Building-integrated photovoltaics
CNN	Cable News Network
CO$_2$	Carbon dioxide
CWT	Carlson Wagonlit Travel
CSD	Circuit Switched Data
CRISPR	Clustered regularly interspaced short palindromic repeats
CAD	Computer aided design
CBD	Convention on Biological Diversity
CBHR	Corporate Human Rights Benchmark
DARPA	Defense Advanced Research Projects Agency
E.F.F.E.C.T.	Effective Focused Fast Exceptional Creative Training
ENIAC	Electronic, Numerical and Integrator Computer
EPA	Environmental Protection Agency
EU	European Union
FIFA	Fédération Internationale de Football Association
4IR	Fourth Industrial Revolution
GMOS	Genetically modified organisms
GPS	Global positioning system
GHG	Greenhouse Gas
GDP	Gross domestic product
HBO	Home Box Office

IOGAN	Identifying Outputs of Generative Adversarial Networks
IPCC	Intergovernmental Panel on Climate Change
IEA	International Energy Agency (IEA)
ILO	International Labour Organization
IRENA	International Renewable Energy Agency
ITU	International Telecommunications Union
IOT	Internet of Things
IOMT	Internet of Medical Things
IHR	International Health Regulations
LNG	Liquefied natural gas
MAAS	Mobility as a Service
NBA	National Basketball Association
OLED	Organic light-emitting diode
ODG	Osterhout Design Group
PWC	PricewaterhouseCoopers
RBI	Restaurant Brands International
STEM	Science, technology, engineering, and math
SMAC	Social, mobile, analytics and cloud
SMS	Short message service
SDGS	Sustainable Development Goals
UHC	Universal Health Coverage
UCLA	University of California, Los Angeles
UAE	United Arab Emirates
UN	United Nations
UNEP	United Nations Environment Programme
VR	Virtual reality
WEF	World Economic Forum
WHO	World Health Organization
WWW	World Wide Web

ABOUT THE AUTHORS

Meesha Brown serves as President of PCI Media. Meesha has an unwavering commitment to education as the fundamental means to empower people to realise their undeniable human rights and create lasting cultural change. As the first woman and person of colour to lead PCI Media, Meesha is passionate about ensuring that PCI Media's work fully embodies the principles of diversity, equity, and inclusion.

Meesha has 20 years of experience in education and communication spaces. She has worked with a range of partners spanning government, NGO, and private sector agencies to see to the education of children and adults and to produce award-winning media. Meesha's work has touched and changed the lives of millions of people.

In 2015, Meesha produced #ISurvivedEbola, a global public health campaign. The campaign saved lives by empowering over 10 million people to take measures to protect themselves and others from contracting the deadly Ebola virus.

Meesha began her professional career in public education. During her tenure as Director of Literacy for New York City Public Schools, she led changes in education policy, impacting outcomes for 1.1 million students. Meesha then worked with national organisations and state departments of education to scale the implementation of more effective teaching techniques.

Additionally, Meesha has over two decades of extensive experience in capacity building, partnership management, community engagement, facilitation, and learning design.

Meesha has skilfully managed PCI Media's program portfolio across 70 countries, 30 languages, and numerous partners on issues including immunisation, nutrition, violence against women and children, and climate resilience.

Meesha sits on the Boards of Calvert Impact Capital, the David and Dovetta Wilson Scholarship Fund, and Reimagine.

Meesha holds a BA in Education with a specialisation in Reading from the University of Texas, US and studied in the Urban Policy MSc program at the

New School. Meesha is one of 11 children from West Texas and has experienced first-hand the transformative power of education from a place of love, not loss. Meesha is dedicated to the work of sharing this gift with all people.

Felix Dodds is an Adjunct Professor at the University of North Carolina and an Associate Fellow at the Tellus Institute. He was the co-director of the 2014 and 2018 Nexus Conference on Water, Food, Energy, and Climate. In 2019 he was a candidate for the Executive Director of the United Nations Environment Programme (UNEP).

Felix was a member of an informal expert group for the President of the UN General Assemblies Brookings Report: 'Links in the Chain of Sustainable Finance: Accelerating Private Investments for the SDGs, including Climate Action' (2016).

He has written or edited over 20 books; his last book was *Stakeholder Democracy: Represented Democracy in a Time of Fear*. His other books have included the Vienna Café Trilogy, which chronicles sustainable development at the international level. The first *Only One Earth* he cowrote with the father of Sustainable Development Maurice Strong and Michael Strauss, the second *From Rio+20 to the New Development Agenda* with Jorge Laguna Celis and Ambassador Liz Thompson and the last one *Negotiating the Sustainable Development Goals* with Ambassador David Donoghue and Jimena Leiva Roesch.

Felix was the Executive Director of Stakeholder Forum for a Sustainable Future from 1992 to 2012. He played a significant role in promoting multistakeholder dialogues at the United Nations and proposed to the UN General Assembly the introduction of stakeholder dialogue sessions at the United Nations Commission on Sustainable Development. In 2011, Felix was listed as one of 25 environmentalists ahead of his time.

Also, in 2011 he chaired the United Nations DPI 64th NGO conference 'Sustainable Societies Responsive Citizens', which put forward the first set of indicative Sustainable Development Goals. From 1997 to 2001 he co-chaired the UN Commission on Sustainable Development NGO Steering Committee.

Carolina Duque Chopitea is the Co-founder and Head of Analytics at Brandformers. io, a digital marketing agency headquartered in Panama. Originally from Panama and raised in the Argentinian Patagonia, Carolina moved to North America to pursue her studies. She holds a Master's Degree in Business Analytics and a Master's in International Business from Hult International Business School in San Francisco, US, and an undergraduate degree in Political Science and Environmental Studies from the University of Victoria, Canada.

Carolina has experience working in the private and public sectors. She first developed professionally at the Panama Mission to the United Nations in New York, where she dedicated her time to the Mission's engagement with the Sustainable Development Goals. She also worked as a fundraiser for a variety of NGOs, and held a position at the International Fund for Agricultural Development (IFAD) in New York, where she worked in partnership development and supported the team in the development of the 2021 Food Systems Summit.

She transitioned into the private sector where she worked as a Marketing Analyst for a software development company in San Francisco and later as a Marketing Analytics Manager at Reciqlo, a circular economy company that transforms glass into solid amendments and construction materials. During the pandemic of 2020 Carolina decided to pursue her dream of being an entrepreneur and co-founded Brandformers to help brands transform so they can thrive in the digital economy. Today, with her multidisciplinary background working in the public and private sectors, Carolina works with brands and organisations to help them realise their full potential by blending data with creativity.

Ranger Ruffins is a Master's student at the University of North Carolina, US at Chapel Hill (UNC), pursuing a degree in City and Regional Planning. Her area of focus is land use and environmental planning, with a specific interest in resilience in the face of natural hazard disasters and the ability for cities to adapt to the effects of a changing climate.

Ranger earned her BA in Environmental Studies in 2016, from the University of North Carolina where she grew interested in the nexus between environmental challenges, social justice, and human well-being. To bridge these interests, Ranger studied Global Development Studies in Uganda for a semester where she researched the industrial impact on wetlands in Jinja and the effects on rights-based sustainable development.

After graduating, Ranger worked in New York City as the Environment Program Assistant at The Overbrook Foundation, working on grant development for the foundation's environment portfolio. During her time at Overbrook, Ranger worked with several community-based organisations, tackling climate justice within their communities. She gained a deeper understanding of how the impacts of climate change intersect all aspects of society, especially those with minimal adaptive capacity. This inspired her to pursue a Master's degree in Planning to greater explore the multifaceted challenges that climate-based hazards pose to the built environment. She is particularly interested in advocacy planning and using this approach to strengthen hazard mitigation and resilience plans to support the needs of those most vulnerable and least able to adapt to the impacts of climate change.

FOREWORD

Meesha Brown

Who are tomorrow's people and how will they live their lives? The future of humanity and the infinite possibilities for future ways of being has always been a consistent place of imagination for great thinkers. And because of innovative and futuristic (at the time) inventions like the printing press, radio, and television – the imagined futures conjured by our species' greatest imaginers spread into the collective consciousness. In some ways we are all futurists.

But it is often the case that the future we imagined isn't quite what actually unfolds. I must admit that when watching my favourite characters on Star Trek (The Original Series and The Next Generation) beam themselves from one location to another and engage in virtual experiences, I believed someday I would also experience those things. However, I did not expect that the first version of teleportation would be Zoom or that I would need goggles for simulation exercises, or what we currently call VR.

As the authors of this book point out – the future is already here. Seismic changes are already underway that are impacting every facet of human life. Even if it were desirable to halt progress (it is not), there is no hope of returning to the before times or maintain the status quo. Over the next decade, the way people across the globe, inhabit personal and professional spaces, travel, eat, socialise, learn, and even how they experience intimacy will transport us to a different world (most likely) right here on earth.

With every great transformation comes great opportunity and great risk. The world is always changing, but we are living in a time of unprecedented revolution across multiple spheres. The ways in which we understand and interact with ourselves and others, our relationships to work and government and the ways we organise our lives and leisure will never be the same again.

While it is clear that our current state of affairs leaves much to be desired. If the introduction of this new technology develops favourably, this will be a very good thing for all of humankind.

Indeed, the technological advancements that are ushering in what the authors of this book refer to as the Fourth Industrial Revolution have the potential to carve a path to environmental sustainability – most importantly zero carbon emissions, but also water conservation and sustainable food systems and cities. Longer lifespans, healthier living and lifelong education at no cost are within our reach. Big data and robotics have the potential to minimise human error, solve problems before they exist, and provide unprecedented access and avenues for inclusion for people with disabilities.

But it cannot be left to chance that the emerging future the version of the future we want and that the benefits of tomorrow are equitably distributed. The greatest risk for tomorrow is that we build it upon the inequitable foundation of today. We live on a physically fragile planet plagued by rising inequity, intensifying social tension, and geopolitical recalibration. We know that the governing and economic systems of yesterday were designed to exclude and exploit and are also wholly unable to deal effectively with in technologies and currencies. If we have any hope of harnessing the current winds of change to create a sustainable and equitable world, we must commit to more than another technological revolution. We must be intentional about the social and cultural revolution that we also need.

What this timely and important work makes clear is that now is the time for individuals that find themselves at decision making tables to reimagine what is possible and what is desirable.

Should developing nations invest any longer in yesterday's technologies and energies or should they boldly leapfrog to tomorrow's solutions?

Could technological transitions be planned in a way to rebalance the economic position and potential of low- and middle-income countries?

How do we balance the power of AI with human privacy and agency?

And perhaps most importantly, how can we avoid programming the biases and inequities of today into our tomorrow?

Certainly, at this time traditional capital and human investments like formal education and job training are needed, but this moment calls for something more.

The period of rapid and exponential change we are about to encounter will require a completely new schematic for living. The lives we live today will be in just a few short years largely unrecognisable. Truly, the only constant is change, but most people don't like change much at all. Consider the dramatic spike in feelings of isolation, anxiety, and depression reported during the stay-at-home orders during the COVID-19 pandemic. This experience teaches us that people need support to make sense of and feel agency in the wake of dramatic changes in social norms and behaviour that impact the way they live, work, socialise.

As we step into the glittering future world of tomorrow, we must think about how best to support the transition for all of humankind. While those in Silicon Valley may be already riding in driverless electric cars, some communities are still travelling largely by gasoline engines, or in some cases by foot. How does one conceive of quantum computing when Internet connection is a luxury? I believe the ability to collectively grapple with these questions and others will determine if the future rises to its utopian possibility or degrades into a dystopian nightmare.

Starting now, everyone must be intentionally included in the conversation. Entertainment-education and other narrative interventions are a cost-effective and well-received way to erase barriers to change by speaking to everyone in the two most important languages – the universal human language of story and each of our mother tongues.

With the flood of misinformation surrounding the existence of COVID-19, its severity, and COVID vaccines we have a common first-hand experience of how lack of knowledge, cultural histories, and/or anti-science attitudes can lead to behaviours that interfere with progress and despite the best that technological solutions have to offer, inhibit or even roll back social and medical progress.

Imagine this same scenario played out in relationship to robot farmers, breakthrough nanotechnology and bio medicine, or education. In order to avoid potentially violent resistance, the cultural conversation about what the future will look like cannot be limited to a small group of highly educated, well-resourced and connected individuals.

Designing an equitable future means investing in Communications for Development and Communications for Social Change initiatives like those we produce at PCI Media.

Watching the crew of the USS Enterprise helped me to think about a future very differently. Intentionally produced entertainment media can continue to be a powerful tool to educate global populations about the new world they and their children will inhabit, empower them to engage with new technologies and decisions affecting their use, and inspire them to embrace the promise and possibility that our collective future holds.

INTRODUCTION

Felix Dodds, Carolina Duque Chopitea, and Ranger Ruffins

> In 2030 we will be ageless, and everyone will have an excellent chance to live forever. 2030 is a dream and a goal.
>
> (Esfandiary, 1977)

We write this book knowing that many have made predictions before us and many will make them after us. History is full of incorrect predictions, which is clearly expressed by the one we open this introduction with.

> The future is like an event horizon over which 'the new' constantly cascades. Some of the events that matter require preconditions. Some emerge in wholly unexpected ways. The key is to constantly scan for those different potentials that matter so that can be pushed from potential to reality most efficiently.
>
> *(Lawrence, 2019)*

This book looks at the Fourth Industrial Revolution and how emerging technologies may impact the future, and what the world might be like in 2030. It offers some positive windows into that world. It is also intended to provide 'food for thought' about the potential negative impacts of emerging technologies, hopefully arming readers with information that they might use to shape their lives or influence policy makers.

We recognise that throughout this book we mostly discuss emerging technologies from the perspective of developed nations, yet we also take some time to reflect on how disruptive technologies may impact and be adopted in other parts of the world. We situate this book in the context of 2030 because this is the date by which nations have agreed to address societies' biggest challenges and create a more sustainable and inclusive world: 2030 is a significant date for

DOI: 10.4324/9781003045496-101

delivering the 17 Sustainable Development Goals (SDGs),[1] the Paris Climate Agreement (PCA),[2] and most likely an important year to look back and take account on our progress as a society. The Climate Agreement commits governments to keep the rise in global temperature well below 2 degrees C (3.6 degrees F) compared to pre-industrial time and to be carbon neutral by 2050.

Our goal with this book is not only to help the reader understand emerging technologies and how can they impact their lives, but also how these technologies fit within the 2030 Agenda for Sustainable Development and where they can have a positive or negative impact on delivering these global agreements.

Firstly, here in the introduction we describe the aims of the book, what it is about, and why discussing emerging technologies and their impacts on the lives of ordinary people is essential to better understand the possible implications of the Fourth Industrial Revolution.

Secondly, this book briefly looks at some mega-trends and identifies several groundbreaking and emerging technologies that have the possibility to redefine the human experience: From how we cook and shop to how we socialise, learn, and work. The technologies we focus on are artificial intelligence, big data and analytics, biotechnology, augmented reality and virtual reality, the Internet of Things, blockchain, self-driving transportation, quantum computing, and new energy sources.

Tomorrow's People and New Technology takes a positive approach to these new technologies while raising questions for the reader to think about their implications for the present and future. While recognising that governments and industry are where decisions are taken, people do have the ability to impact on that depending on how their voice their opinions, what they decide to buy, and how they live their lives.

Tomorrow's People and New Technology will frame the landscape that we will be living in 2030 as one where there are choices policymakers, consumers, and individuals will need to make today regarding the use of groundbreaking technologies which will shape these technologies as they are being adopted. In short, it invites the reader to take a proactive approach rather than a reactive one when faced with technological adoption. Finally, as our world is in a period of unprecedented change, this book situates these emerging technologies in the context of a world trying to address key issues such as a global pandemic, climate change, growing inequality, and the Sustainable Development Goals.

BOX 0.1: THE FAMILY REFLECTED IN THIS BOOK

Through the book we will engage a family as protagonists to ask questions about the world in 2030 and what the policy and lifestyle implications are.

Our imaginary family is made up of five people in a mixed African American Latino family. Emma and her partner Antonio, both in their 40s' Emma's mother in her 70s; and two children, Maya, who is 10, and Carlos, who is 15.

Emma is a software engineer working on data analytics for a company and her partner Antonio is a manager in a solar photovoltaics company. Emma's mother, Victoria, lives in Ecuador and worked at a real estate company and still does some work virtually to support selling houses. Maya at ten is already running an online virtual reality fashion channel and Carlos is a gamer.

Chapter 1: A brief history of the industrial revolutions

Chapter 1 takes on a historical approach to answer the question: How did we get here? This chapter briefly walks the reader from the First to the Fourth Industrial Revolution, explaining what their implications were, and what they meant for the world and lives of ordinary people. It then places particular importance on the Fourth Industrial Revolution as this is humanity's present reality. This chapter discusses how these revolutions have built on each other and provides the bedrock to understanding and contextualising the following chapters.

Chapter 2: The world we live in

Chapter 2 digs deeper on the Fourth Industrial Revolution, but not as a 'concept' rather as a reality for people. This chapter looks at the world in 2021, as we move from the Third to the Fourth Industrial Revolution. It looks at where various technologies are in 2021 in terms of development and adoption. It gives a broad understanding of how customers, citizens, and companies are interacting, using, and shaping these technologies. It also discusses where we are in terms of the Sustainable Development Goals and the Paris Climate Agreement in 2021, current trends and tension in the social and political systems, and their association with these technologies. Finally, this chapter moves to set the rest of the book in 2030, setting it as the present time for the rest of the book. To do this, the authors are making several assumptions based on the world today and combine both reality and fiction.

Chapter 3: Home life

Chapter 3 looks at how these technologies are affecting the way we live at home. This chapter points out the technologies which will have the greatest impacts in our home lives from AI to big data and 3-D printing. It gives an opportunity to discuss how AI will make homes 'smarter' and how IOT will help control home appliances through electronically controlled Internet-connected systems. I will also provide an opportunity to explore how robotics will change the home. This chapter will focus on how 'home life' has and will become more convenient and efficient through the adoption of these technologies and has given people more time to focus on other tasks. However, it also looks at the possible implications of having a highly Internet-connected home that produces tremendous amounts of data that is then shared with companies.

Chapter 4: Travelling around

Chapter 4 provides an opportunity to look at the technologies that will impact on us travelling. This will include one which is getting great attention and investment: Self-driving cars and possible flying cars as well (the Jetsons here we come!).

Apart from looking at self-driving cars in 2030, the chapter also discusses other forms of mobility and those technologies that are tangential to but associated with travel such as hotels, airports, and space tourism. In short, this chapter looks at how mobility has changed in the world and highlights what kinds of mobility-compatible energy sources will be in place by 2030. Finally, this chapter discusses the infrastructure – both physical and social – required by anticipated mobility systems.

Chapter 5: Education, working life, and health

Chapter 5 takes the reader on a journey that explores how education, working life, and health will be in 2030. Globalisation, demographic changes, and the adoption of technologies significantly redefine the workplace and present many challenges. But many opportunities also arise. Therefore, this chapter provides an opportunity for the reader to understand how technologies like AI and automation, data analytics, virtual reality, and blockchain, among others have shaped the workplace and how these technologies are changing the way we are educated and trained for the workplace. It will look at how our education system might adapt as AI and other technologies impact on our learning. Will we see teachers replaced by AI in many different forms, such as within a robot but also engaging with the student to identify in more depth their requirements as a student – tailoring the learning to the individual? It can make available to everyone the best thinkers' and scientists' material as we move forward – even if they are dead.

Chapter 6: Entertainment

Chapter 6 discusses how entertainment will be in 2030. This takes a brief look at how technologies change TV, sports, music, gambling, sex, and more. Particularly, it looks at how data analytics, AI, augmented and virtual reality, and blockchain shape the entertainment industry. How 3-D printing and new energy sources can also enhance the delivery of reducing CO_2 and enhancing the experience of the consumer. This chapter examines the lives of consumers and discusses the implications of technologies as people look to fill leisure time. It looks at the impacts of new forms of entertainment, and how those forms build, change, or destroy our communities.

Chapter 7: Social life

Chapter 7 explores how social life will change in 2030. It discusses how tech-nologies have continued to shape the way we interact with each other, from how we make friends to how we date. This chapter also looks at the impact of biotechnologies on human society, its advantages in terms of disease prevention and cure, and its ability to create 'superhumans'. It discusses some of the ethical implications that these technologies have when it comes to humans' social lives. Where will Facebook, Twitter, Instagram, TikTok, Netflix, Spotify be in 2030? This chapter as well discusses the relationship between the real and virtual world as their boundaries become more and more blurry.

Chapter 8: Living around the globe

Chapter 8 looks at technological adoption in different regions of the world. We acknowledge that technological adoption and the impacts of the Fourth Industrial Revolution will be felt differently in different places. To bridge this gap, this chapter explores how the different technologies and industries discussed throughout this book are impacting other regions of the world, and the implica-tions of these technologies for the lives of people around the globe. From how we live at home or travel, to how we work, learn, and socialise, this chapter takes you on a journey around the globe that puts current global inequalities and technological adoption rates into context, and speculates about how these may evolve in the next ten years.

Chapter 9: Beyond 2030

Chapter 9 provides some concluding thoughts on the possible state of the world in 2030. It then invites the reader to think of our world beyond this. This chap-ter will discuss if we were able to meet deadline for the implementation of the Sustainable Development Goals and where we are in fighting climate change. It discusses the remaining challenges and opportunities as the world heads into 2050, a planet with 10 billion people.

Acknowledgements

John Charles for the cartoon art and inks by Lee Townsend and lettering by Nikki Foxrobot. Patrick O'Hannigan for copyediting and general comments from Andrew Binns, Ian Care, and Liz Thompson. From the Routldge team thanks to John Baddeley, Hannah Ferguson and Jayanthi Chander. Specific com-ments were made for different chapters. **Introduction:** Gary Lawrence, Paul Peeters; Chapter 1 **The history of industrial revolutions:** Chris Spence, Margaret Brusasco Mackenzie; Chapter 2 **The world we live in:** Mette Bloch Hansen; Chapter 3 **Home life:** Robin Dodds, Ashley Gill, Mette Bloch Hansen, Mairi Kershaw, Maria Figueroa Kupcu, Gary Lawrence, Charles Nouhan, Chris

Spence; Chapter 4 **Travelling around:** Angela De Sapio, Hans Friederich, Danielle Gaillard-Picher, Harold Goodwin, Geoffrey Lipman, Chris Lyle, Paul Peeters; Chapter 5 **Education, health, and working life:** Merri Dodds, Mette Bloch Hansen, David Horan, Mairi Kershaw, Don Koch, Rick Norris; Chapter 6 **Entertainment:** Sapna Batish, Ashley Gill, Chris Spence, David E Willmes; Chapter 7 **Social life:** Steven Higgins, Elizabeth Christenson; Chapter 8 **Living around the globe:** Naysa Ahuja, Hana AlHashimi, María Fernanda Diez, Tobias Ogweno, Kilaparti Ramakrishna, Kiara Worth, Uchita de Zoysa; Chapter 9 **Beyond 2030:** Charles Nouhan.

Notes

1 The seventeen Sustainable Development Goals cover: SDG1: No Poverty; SDG2: Zero Hunger; SDG3: Good Health and Well-being; SDG4: Quality Education; SDg5: Gender Equality; SDG 6: Clean Water and Sanitation; SDG7 Affordable and Clean Energy; SDG8 Decent Work and Economic Growth; SDG9 Industry, Innovation and Infrastructure; SDG 10 Reduce Inequality; SDG 11: Sustainable Cities and Communities; SDG 12: Responsible Consumption and Production; SDG 13 Climate Action; SDG 14: Life Below Water; SDG15: Life on Land; SDG 16: Peace and Justice Strong Institutions; SDG 17: Partnerships to achieve the Goals. A full list is in Annex 1 with their targets.
2 The Paris Climate Agreement Aims to decrease global warming described in its Article 2, 'enhancing the implementation' of the UNFCCC through:
   • Holding the increase in the global average temperature to well below 2 °C above pre-industrial levels and to pursue efforts to limit the temperature increase to 1.5 °C above pre-industrial levels, recognising that this would significantly reduce the risks and impacts of climate change.
   • Increasing the ability to adapt to the adverse impacts of climate change and foster climate resilience and low greenhouse gas emissions development, in a manner that does not threaten food production.
   • Making finance flows consistent with a pathway towards low greenhouse gas emissions and climate-resilient development.

References

Esfandiary, M.F. (1977) Telespheres. *Popular Library.*
Lawrence, G. (2019) In reviewing this introduction.

1

A BRIEF HISTORY OF THE INDUSTRIAL REVOLUTIONS

Introduction

Today, many of us wake up and look at our phones, navigate the Internet for news, turn on the lights in our rooms, take a shower, and have breakfast, perhaps preparing eggs that were produced in faraway farms. Most of us wear clothes and drive cars that have been mass-produced in factories. Beyond 'country of origin' labels, we don't know where these factories are or how our goods got to us.

There are thousands of different occupations around the world, from businesspeople, bankers, financial analysts, data scientists, and engineers to architects, construction workers, project managers, consultants, writers, journalists, community organisers, truck drivers, cashiers, receptionists, farmers – you name it, and someone somewhere likely makes a living out of it.

New and emerging careers evolve as the pace of change increases. Even the nature of how essential jobs deliver their goods and services is changing. We are also seeing jobs disappear as new changes take root. Over the preceding three industrial revolutions we have created technologies and occupations to satisfy ever-changing human needs. Job loss and job gain have tended to balance, but it is not clear that will still be the case for this Fourth Industrial Revolution.

A history of human innovation

The history of the industrial revolutions has been one of human ingenuity expressed through creativity, innovation, courage, hard work, intellect, and passion. It is the history of love for progress, but it is also a history of greed, inequality, violence, and unfairness. Depending on where you live in the world, you may be experiencing multiple industrial revolutions at the same time, even though in developed countries the various revolutions have tended to build on

DOI: 10.4324/9781003045496-1

each other. A sustenance farmer in Senegal may be still taking food to market with a donkey and cart but may have electricity in his or her village from solar panels or own a mobile phone.

Imagine prior to the First Industrial Revolution you live in a world with no Internet, no electricity, no running water, no toilet, and no waste disposal systems. No cooking stove or ovens, no strawberries in the winter, little or no access to education, and certainly no modern medicine or antibiotics. You still travel by horse or foot. Your family and friends, like 80 per cent of the world population, are engaged in farming. The remainder of the population carefully crafts goods by hand. Your standard of living is not much better than thousands of years ago. All the advancements we enjoy today have their roots in the First Industrial Revolution and the subsequent industrial revolutions that have truly shaped the world we live in.

Of course, not everyone has benefitted equally from the developments brought by these revolutions. Neither every person nor every country in the world reaps the benefits of the industrial revolutions equally, yet everyone has been impacted by them.

In his book, *The Great Transformation*, Karl Polanyi coins the term 'social dislocation' to explain the process in which previous social tendencies were undermined, and society moved from a premodern economy mostly based on redistribution and reciprocity to a market economy driven by industrialisation and increasing state influence (Polanyi, 1944). He explains that the expansion of capitalism fundamentally changed humans' economic relations as land, labour, and money became commodities subordinated to the laws of the market, resulting in significant social dislocations. Polanyi claims that social dislocations often created spontaneous movements to protect the foundations of societies.

This idea of 'social dislocations' that Polanyi applies to the emergence of market capitalism and the movement from the commons to private ownership echoes the social dislocations that have taken place throughout industrial revolutions and the subsequent social movements that have emerged to protect society from abrupt change.

The history of capitalism and the Industrial Revolution, and their respective evolutions, are different, yet highly interconnected. The industrial revolutions have not only been characterised by their developments and technological advancements but also by the social upheavals, unrest, and anxiety that they created.

The term 'Industrial Revolution' was popularised by English writer Arnold Toynbee in the late 1880s. Toynbee's lectures on the Industrial Revolution, published in 1884, were the first and most influential attempts to historicise the transition to a machine-based economy, particularly in Britain (Wilso, 2014). This term was later used to describe not one but four distinct periods of industrial revolution throughout history.

Klaus Schwab, founder and executive chairman of the World Economic Forum (WEF), describes an industrial revolution as the emergence of:

> New technologies and novel ways of perceiving the world [that] trigger a profound change in social and economic structures.
>
> *(Schwab, 2017A)*

Simply put, industrial revolutions are the intersection of change between emerging technologies and the way humans live and perceive life.

According to the Merriam-Webster dictionary, a *revolution* is a sudden, radical, or complete change, often in society and the social structure, frequently accompanied by violence. And *industrialisation* is the process by which an economy is transformed from a primarily agricultural focus to one based on the manufacturing of goods. Individual manual labour is often replaced by mechanised mass production, and craftsmen are replaced by assembly lines. Characteristics of industrialisation include economic growth, a more efficient division of labour, and the use of technological innovation to solve problems as opposed to dependency on conditions outside human control (Investopedia).

It is hard to overstate the significance of the First Industrial Revolution – starting around 1760 to 1820. Up until that point, civilisation had made almost no economic progress for most of its existence, and suddenly there was a spike in social and economic progress. For most of human history, the economic growth rate was about 0.1 per cent per year, which allowed for a gradual increase in population but no growth in per capita living standards (Silver, 2012).

The Industrial Revolution was marked by increased production brought by machines and characterised by new energy sources, particularly steam power and the rise of coal and creation of factories.

The Second Industrial Revolution – the Technological Revolution – was the age of mass production; it was a phase of rapid standardisation and industrialisation characterised by the mass introduction of electrical power, among others.

The Third Industrial Revolution was the move from analogue and mechanical devices to digital ones bringing with it semiconductors, mainframe computing, personal computers, and the Internet – this was the Digital Revolution.

The Fourth Industrial Revolution, the one we are currently living in, is a period that is changing the way we live, work, and relate to one another. It is driven by technological advances and built upon the previous revolutions. This period is characterised by the blurring boundaries between the physical, digital, and biological worlds and it is increasing the pace of change to an extent not previously seen.

All these revolutions brought major societal transformations with significant implications for the average person. During these periods, particularly in what is now known as the developed world, people went from mostly working the land to working in factories, from the countryside to cities, from production to mass production, from paper to personal computers, and from personal computers to smartphones and personalised assistants in our digital devices, all in the last three hundred years.

Economic development has grown exponentially: More changes to human society and the environment around us have taken place in the last three centuries than in the previous 15,000 years of human history.

This chapter digs deeper into each of these revolutions. It discusses topics like how they emerged, what drove them, and who was impacted the most. The goal of this chapter is to give the reader some historical context of human economic and technological development, and the tools to better understand the significance of these revolutions.

This chapter will focus particularly on the Fourth Industrial Revolution, and the changes and technologies emerging from this period. It will seek to answer what technologies are currently emerging and why are they worth talking about.

The revolution of revolutions: The First Industrial Revolution and the steam engine

The latter half of the 18th century saw the emergence of the First Industrial Revolution; the age of steam and factories that changed the course of humanity forever. The First Industrial Revolution refers to a transition to a new manufacturing process that began in Britain and spread to the rest of the world. This period transformed mostly rural, agrarian societies into industrialised, urban ones, and goods began to be produced in large quantities by machines in factories.

Scholars continue to debate why the Industrial Revolution sparked in Britain as opposed to other parts of the world. But broadly speaking, Europe and particularly Britain had the political, social, and economic conditions that allowed for the birth of this revolution. Some of the factors that may have contributed to the revolution are the culture of science and invention of Europe at the time that fostered the creation of revolutionary technologies. In Britain this was accompanied by freer political institutions that encouraged innovation and protect property rights, creating incentives for investors, resulting in Britain becoming the cradle of the revolution.

The First Industrial Revolution resulted in increased production brought about using machines and characterised by new energy sources, particularly coal and steam.

Before the revolution, world industries were generally small-scale and relatively unsophisticated. For example, most textile production was centred on small workshops and involved thousands of individual manufacturers (White, 2009).

The textile industry in Britain was at the forefront of this revolution, adapting innovations like the flying shuttle, the spinning jenny, the water frame, and the power loom to make weaving more efficient. Producing cloth became much faster and required less human labour. Tasks that were previously done by hand by hundreds of individual and independent weavers were brought together in a single cotton mill, and as a result, factories were born. The rise in demand for

goods, particularly textiles, combined with increased production capacity to create the perfect ingredients for kickstarting a revolution.

The steam engine was a revolutionary source of energy in this period. In the
1770s, it powered the machines used to pump water out of mine shafts (History,
n.d.). Improvements to the steam engine allowed miners to dig deeper and
extract more coal, making it a cheap and plentiful energy source.

The steam engine spread across most of Britain like the flu, shaping industries
like flour, paper, and cotton mills, not to mention ironwork, distilleries, and
construction (think canal building). Many industries became heavily reliant on
this source of energy. Demand for coal increased significantly because it was
used to run the factories that produced manufactured goods. Coal also powered
transportation via railroads and steamships. It is still used today to produce electricity and steel. Pollution from industrial-scale coal and natural gas are standing
legacies of the Industrial Revolution.

To date, we still struggle with these energy sources, because their burning
emits greenhouse gases that get trapped in the atmosphere, contributing to climate change and putting the future of humanity at risk.

The first person to show scientific evidence of climate change was amateur
American scientist Eunice Foote. Her experiments in the mid-1800s warned of
the Earth's greenhouse effect:

> An atmosphere of that gas would give to our earth a high temperature; and
> if as some suppose, at one period of its history the air had mixed with it a
> larger proportion than at present, an increased temperature … must have
> necessarily resulted.
>
> *(Foote, 1856)*

At the same time, life in the countryside was also changing. Inventions, like the
iron ploughs drawn by horses, began to displace wooden ploughs, thus making
some farmers redundant. As a result, an oversupply of cheap agricultural labour
led to unemployment, hence driving many to the cities in search of work, where
they supplied employees for the large-scale labour-intensive factories then on the
rise (White, 2009).

Even though this migration increased the population of cities, rural areas
also began to change as cities started expanding and the rise of large factories
turned smaller towns into major centres over a few decades (History, n.d.). Not
only increased demand and production capacity were necessary for the Industrial
Revolution, but also the previous technological advances in the agricultural sector that led to rural unemployment and drove labour to the industrial centres.
These factors created the perfect conditions that set the stage for the most significant economic events in human history.

This period marked not only the rise of the factory but also innovations in the
transportation and communications sectors. Britain's road networks were substantially improved in this period. Due to the growing demand for coal and other

raw materials, many mine owners and industrial speculators began financing networks of canals. They also improved roads and railroads to link their mines more effectively with the industrialised centres (White, 2009).

Steam-powered ships were widely used to power the transport along Britain's rivers and canals as well as across the Atlantic. By the 1830s, the stagecoach journey from London to Edinburgh was significantly shortened from nearly two weeks to two days (White, 2009). The price of travel also fell dramatically, leading to greater possibilities for movement of labour (Brusasco, 2021). Locomotives began to transport freight (and passengers) between the industrial hubs of Manchester and Liverpool (History, n.d.).

Communication tools also began to flourish in this period. In 1837, William Cooke and Charles Wheatstone patented the first commercial telegraphy system, used for railroad signalling (*The Telegraph*, n.d.).

Banks and finance also rose in this period: a stock exchange was established in London in the 1770s, and the New York Stock Exchange was established in the 1790s (History, n.d.). This period also gave rise to the father of the modern economy, Scottish philosopher Adam Smith, who in 1776 published *The Wealth of Nations*, in which he promoted an economic system based on the free market, private ownership of means of production, and lack of government interference. Smith also advocated the protection of workers which capitalism has alas *not* included. Here the well-known metaphor, 'the invisible hand' of the market was born, to refer to the unforeseen forces of the markets that in a free-market economy will reach supply and demand equilibrium. He insisted that rational actors behaving in their self-interest under freedom of production and consumption fulfil the best interest of society. This is when capitalism met industrialisation, and the implications for human economic development are unprecedented.

No revolution comes unpunished. By default, revolutions signify a radical change. The First Industrial Revolution was no different; it dislocated the foundations of 18th-century societies, resulting in societal consequences and uprisings.

Workers acquired new and distinctive skills as craftspeople became machine operators. Despite sweeping social progress like the growth of cities, development of the middle class, and increased wealth, the revolution brought severe consequences to some social sectors.

The early industrial economies that drove this period were also associated with the exploitation of workers and poor living conditions. This period saw the birth of sweatshops where workers were increasingly exposed to dangerous conditions while working very long hours, and many human rights were violated. Even with the increasing economic progress and improvement for the middle and upper classes, poor and working-class people continue to struggle. Rapid and unplanned urbanisation led to overcrowded cities that suffered from pollution, poor sanitation, and a lack of clean drinking water (History, n.d.).

Massive industrialisation also sparked social movements that continue to shape our society today. Technological advances and automation displaced workers, resulting in widespread discontent and the insurgence of anti-industrialisation movements. One of the most well-known opposition groups that emerged from this period were the Luddites. Even today, the name 'Luddite' is used to refer to people who dislike technology.

The Luddites originated among the textile workers of Nottingham, England, and they opposed further industrialisation, insisting that machines would displace them from their jobs and render their skills obsolete even if they also required new skills and created jobs. To show their opposition, Luddites broke machines, burned factories, and started riots. The Luddites are often depicted as only a violent anti-industrialisation movement. Nevertheless, they also showed an early expression of working-class political awareness that demanded workers' protections.

Increasing discontent with the inhumane working conditions and living standards powered the trade union movement. Workers were paid very low wages and worked long hours in factories with little or no safety standards. Trade unions (labour unions in the US) were created first in 1824, when they coalesced around demands for better wages and working conditions. Out of these first campaigns, child labour laws were born, and regulations about health and safety at work began to address some of the negative new circumstances that industrialisation was having on the lives of the working class. Just as the Luddites did, the union movement also fostered violent uprisings. Nevertheless, modern working standards, including minimum wage, overtime pay, health benefit plans, eight-hour workdays, and weekends off were shaped by union insistence on collective bargaining.

The Second Industrial Revolution: The age of science and mass production

Despite the great advances that came with the First Industrial Revolution, the world was still quite different from what it is today; there was no electricity, no cars, and no telephones, yet the First Revolution was the foundation for the Second. Approximately 40 years after the disruption brought by the Industrial Revolution, in the 1870s, a second period of change was brewing.

The Second Industrial Revolution, also known as the Technological Revolution, was characterised by a period of rapid standardisation and industrialisation between the late 19th century and early 20th centuries. Underpinning this was the rapid expansion of railroads and telegraph lines after the 1870s that allowed for unprecedented movement of people and ideas, until movement was interrupted in 1914 by World War I.

This was also a period of growth in the populations of cities and an expansion of factories as workplaces for more and more people. There were significant advances in the creation of steel and chemicals, as science began to be applied in manufacturing processes. Most importantly, this revolution gave us petroleum, the energy source that is crucial for modern human life as we know it.

The combination of large-scale iron and steel production, together with increased knowledge of chemicals and science, the widespread use of machinery, the telegraph, petroleum, and the beginning of the telephone all blended together to help fuel mass production of manufactured goods.

This period witnessed advances in manufacturing and agriculture. Transportation also became more accessible to more people through trains and automobiles. The ability of ideas to be shared much quicker became possible via newspapers, radio, and telegraphs (Niller, 2019).

The late 1800s witnessed great inventions. For example, Thomas Edison produced the phonograph and the light bulb (Pacheco, n.d). The masses' adoption of the light bulb and electricity more broadly have significantly improved human life and powered economic progress. Electricity has become central to human life, and many would even argue that it is a human right. These inventions also formed the foundation for the vacuum tubes that powered early computers, which would soon thereafter spark the Third Industrial Revolution.

The impact of Edison's invention and the use of artificial light have permeated every aspect of human life, from our homes, restaurants, factories, and streets to our phones, computers, and refrigerators. It would be unimaginable for us today to live in a world without electricity, the light bulb, or artificial light.

It is remarkable to imagine how an invention like the light bulb can thrive in an environment where there is technically no physical infrastructure to support it; the light bulb was born in a time that there were no power plants, electrical wiring, or electrical grid to support this invention. But humans saw the great potential of the light bulb in advancing human development and so its creation triggered a massive engineering and logistics movement to bring electricity to cities and homes worldwide.

Communications technologies also improved significantly. In 1866, the first transatlantic underwater telegraph cable was installed. Only ten years later, Scottish-born inventor Alexander Graham Bell patented the first commercial telephone and established the Bell Telephone Company (History, 2010). Innovations in papermaking also took place, and the current paper machines that create paper in large quantities at a high speed were invented (Vale, 2016). This development led to the availability of cheaper paper, and with it greater distribution of books and newspapers. This period also witnessed the rise of the fountain pen, the mass production of pencils, and the rise of steam rotary printing presses that produced newspapers for the masses.

The Second Industrial Revolution also introduced the first internal combustion engine powered by gasoline, giving birth to automobiles and then other forms of transportation. This invention was one of the biggest advancements seen since the introduction of the steam engine. The first internal combustion engines could only power small vehicles, but improvement and evolution paved the way for mass mobility, from automobiles and airplanes to locomotives and massive ships that triggered the mass movement of people, good, and services around the world.

The internal combustion engine improved living standards for many and revolutionised manufacturing, paving the way for the modern production line.

Today the impact of the combustion engine can be felt in every corner of the world, and it brought great advancement to humanity. Nevertheless, advances of the Second Industrial Revolution created a paradox that today threatens human existence on the planet. The use of petroleum for energy production and to power engines is responsible for emitting millions of tonnes of greenhouse gasses into the atmosphere annually, and if not addressed on time, it will jeopardise life on the planet as we know it.

Like its predecessor, the Second Industrial Revolution was powered by new energy sources, but it was also driven by remarkable human ideas that gave birth to the modern organisational methods for operating large-scale businesses, first among them the assembly line.

The assembly line revolutionised business and allowed for the mass production of standardised goods. American automotive pioneer Henry Ford introduced the assembly line after realising that the complex job of assembling many parts into a single finished product could be broken down into a series of smaller, simpler tasks (The Henry Ford, n.d.).

This concept significantly sped up production and reduced cost because each worker was only required to assemble one or two parts. Henry Ford's goal was to make automobiles for the masses, and the Ford Motor Company was the first to apply line manufacturing to the mass production of affordable cars. The company became a leader in the automotive industry. At its peak, it employed 40,000 workers in a factory in Michigan (Niller, 2019). As Ford's cars begun to take to the street, he claimed that customers could have cars of 'any colour so as long as it is black'. This quip by Henry Ford became famous, and it very well describes the times: to mass-produce something, you needed to standardise production of it.

Moreover, during this revolution, improvements in public health and sanitation significantly reduced mortality rates due to infections and diseases. Public health initiatives such as the construction of the London sewage system and laws that regulated water supplies emerged in the 1860s. Also, crop failure no longer implied famine and malnutrition for rural areas, because they were now connected to large markets through transport and infrastructure.

Mass production and standardisation led to an economic and productivity boom. Living standards improved significantly in industrialised countries, and the prices of goods fell dramatically (Vale, 2016).

Cheaper goods and standardisation also caused social dislocations; once again job displacement and unemployment were on the rise as workers were replaced by more efficient machines, and many factories, ships, and other forms of fixed capital were becoming obsolete as owners failed to catch up with the new energy sources and innovations of the time.

During the 1920s productivity spiked, resulting in cheaper goods and hence putting many businesses in constraints. This period saw a booming economy and an increase in consumerism, particularly in the US, where it came to be known as the 'Roaring Twenties'. The 1920s also witnessed rising inequality, which reached its peak in 1929, right before the Great Depression.

At the time, in the US, the top 0.1 per cent richest adults' share of total household wealth was close to 25 per cent (Keshner, 2019). Shortly after the Second Industrial Revolution, a period of economic hardship was felt around the world, hitting the US the hardest. On 29 October 1929, on what is known as 'Black Friday', Wall Street crashed, unleashing the Great Depression. The Depression devastated the US economy: a third of all banks failed, unemployment rose to 25 per cent, and homelessness spiked. Meanwhile, international trade collapsed, and housing prices plummeted (Amadeo, 2020). The 'Roaring Twenties' was over, and it took the market many years to recover.

Many argue that the Great Depression was partly caused by the staggering inequality levels of the late 1920s, and that inequality is often a sign of economic bubbles in asset pricing (PBS, 2014; Keshner, 2019). Others say that to some degree, the Great Depression brought staggering income inequality to a halt. Yet research suggests that it actually increased income gaps, with the top earners' income dropping by 4 per cent and the bottom household income dropping by 20 per cent (Keshner, 2019).

Today, once again, inequality is on the rise, posing a great threat to economic stability. According to the Census Bureau, it is at its highest level in five decades. As the global COVID-19 pandemic ravages the world economy, issues of inequality are increasing while entering the Fourth Industrial Revolution.

The Third Industrial Revolution: The rise of a digital society

Even though the First and Second Industrial Revolutions significantly advanced society, making many people richer and more urban with a higher standard of living, the world they affected was still very different from ours today. Beginning in the 1950s, the Third Industrial Revolution encompassed the move from mechanical and analogue devices to digital ones. This was the Digital Revolution, a period that saw the rise of semiconductors, mainframe computers, personal computers, the Internet, smartphones, and exponential growth in connectivity. Televisions that used to tune with an antenna were replaced by Internet-connected tablets.

It is often said that throughout history, war and conflict have triggered significant innovations as civilisations had to innovate to retain a cutting edge advantage against their enemies. This period proved no different.

Although the Third Industrial Revolution started in the 1950s, it was rooted in technological advancements made throughout World War II. Both the World War and its 'Cold War' aftermath were devastating, but it should also be noted that we ultimately owe digital computers and the Internet to those events. World War II was a driving force behind computing. During this period, engineers and mathematicians realised that using a Boolean system (that is, a binary system of 0s and 1s) instead of analogue approaches would greatly simplify computer programming (Levy, 2013).

The Third Industrial Revolution increased personal productivity, automated mundane tasks, introduced changes in the workforce, and advanced globalisation. Advances in computing enabled new ways of generating, processing, and sharing information; this was the beginning of the Information Era.

Given the increased use of electricity that took place throughout the Second Revolution, the binary system easily resembles the two possible states of an 'on' and 'off' switch. This not only simplified computer design but gave rise to the digital computers we are so familiar with today. The Atanasoff-Berry Computer (ABC), created in 1937, was an early digital computer. It was followed by the Colossus (1943) and the ENIAC (1945), which was the first programmable general purpose digital computer (Cengage, 2020; Freiberger, n.d.). By the 1940s and 1950s, the binary system began to be incorporated into the first-generation digital computers.

Digital technologies started with a fundamental idea: Computers and how to network them, which ultimately became the Internet.

Advancement in digital computers was accompanied by the invention of silicon transistors. These replaced the vacuum tubes that, up until the 1950s, had been used in computers. Beginning in the mid-1960s, these vacuum tubes were replaced by the silicon transistor which made it possible to produce less volatile devices that were more efficient, reliable, durable, economically viable, and much smaller than previous computers (Bestofmedia Team, 2011).

Silicon transistors were introduced and paved the way for the development of advanced digital computers (PBS, 1999). The introduction of the silicon chip powered the Digital Revolution, and today it permeates almost everything we use.

Silicon was the driver of modern tech, and since the invention of the transistor, California's 'Silicon Valley' has become a formidable technology hub. In the late 1970s, so much silicon was being produced for the fast-growing companies using silicon to manufacture transistors that the Santa Clara Valley unofficially changed its name (Waters, 2015). There, silicon was abundant and cheap; it complemented a widespread willingness to innovate.

Thanks to the transistor, Silicon Valley and its surrounding areas experienced a wave of technological innovation, with companies like HP and Apple beginning to offer personal computers. Today, silicon transistors still power your computer, your smartphones, TVs, and even some electric cars. The invention of the early transistors and the integrated circuits that followed them still powers most modern tech.

Then came the Internet.

Since the invention of the printing press, no other invention has revolutionised communication and knowledge as much. The Internet took digital computing to the next level, advancing communication beyond the previously imaginable.

In 1969, ARPANET, the predecessor of what we know as the Internet, was created as an artefact of the US Defense Department's Advanced Research Project. The first successful connection was between the Stanford Research

Institute and a programmer at the University of California, Los Angeles (UCLA). Initially, its purpose was to improve communication within the military and for scientists. Out of this military-driven dilemma of 'inter-net-working', the concept of the Internet was born. In 1974, a new and more independent packet-switching protocol known as the TCP/IP, the 'Internet Protocol' was developed, allowing computers to send and receive information in the network (Rosenzweig, 1998). By 1983 ARPANET had adopted TCP/IP, and from that union the 'network of networks' began to take shape (Andrews, 2019).

The potential of the Internet as a powerful tool for communication was quickly realised. Just a few years after the innovation of the IP, in 1989, Sir Tim Berners-Lee invented the World Wide Web. With it came HTML, HTTP, and URLs – a set of protocols and a language that has allowed us to create web pages, use browsers, and share links (WWW Foundation, n.d.).

Tim Berners-Lee pushed to ensure that HTML and the underlying code for web creation were open source, meaning available on a royalty-free basis. This decision made the World Wide Web (WWW) and the Internet itself a hub of creativity, collaboration, and innovation. The idea of open source and collaboration remains very much alive within the programming community and it speaks directly to the spirit of the WWW as a platform for communication, knowledge sharing, creativity, and human innovation.

Back in the 1990s, the Internet was a revolutionary tool. Today it's still revolutionary. Without the Internet, the WWW and the spirit of open source, many advances in AI, analytics, and programming languages would not be possible.

Even in 2020, amid a global pandemic, the Internet and the tools and apps it brought with it has allowed many of us to stay connected in a time of social isolation. Hundreds of cities have been put on lockdown, but cyberspace has been thriving and given us economic resilience. The Internet has proved to be a place of comfort. Many of us get to connect with our loved ones through webcams and play games with our friends online. Lucky workers got to preserve their jobs if they were easily moved online.

The importance of the Internet in our modern world cannot be overstated. It has become an essential tool for communication, learning, advocacy, research, and business. It has been used for harm, but also a tool that has sparked unprecedented large-scale social movements.

In the space of 70 years, the digital world has become crucial to the functioning of society. Digitalisation and the Internet facilitate organisation and the dissemination of information. These technologies can also help make the world a more fair, peaceful, and just place by democratising education and information.

Yet, the Internet is also a double-edged sword. The Internet can and has been an outlet for mass misinformation dissemination and it has threatened privacy. This has become much clearer in 2020 with Internet porn, anomie fostered by platforms like Twitter, Facebook, Parler, and fake news while once respectable journalism finds itself behind paywalls.

Despite the promising opportunities brought by the Internet and the adoption of digital technologies, the Digital Revolution's reach has been unequal around the globe. Its arrival has displaced many people from their jobs and rendered some skills redundant. However, it has also created new jobs, skills, and opportunities.

The Third Industrial Revolution played a significant role in shaping the current century. Even though it remains unclear whether this revolution has come to a halt to give space for the next, it is quite clear that we are entering a new Industrial Revolution, one that is taking advantage of the Internet and digitalisation to innovate in imaginable ways.

The Fourth Industrial Revolution: Blurring digital, physical, biological boundaries

It is unclear when exactly the Third Industrial Revolution finished and gave space for the Fourth. However, the later one built on its predecessor, significantly expanding the digital realm, and introducing changes in how we live, work, and relate to one another.

As a term, the 'Fourth Industrial Revolution' found traction in 2016, when Klaus Schwab, founder and executive chairman of the World Economic Forum, popularised it. According to Schwab, a technological revolution is underway:

> characterized by a fusion of technologies that is blurring the lines between the physical, digital, and biological sphere.
>
> *(Schwab, 2016)*

The Fourth Industrial Revolution represents new ways in which technologies are becoming central and embedded within societies. This includes, but is not limited to, genome editing, improvements in artificial intelligence, breakthrough materials, and new approaches to governance such as blockchain (Davis, 2016).

Schwab has pointed out three main reasons why the world is going through another industrial revolution, and how this differs from the Third: *velocity, scope, and system impact*. He argues that the speed of technological innovation has no historical precedent, because the Fourth is evolving at an exponential rather than linear pace. This revolution is impacting almost every industry and aspect of human life. And these technological changes and advancements foresee the transformation of production, management, and governance systems (Schwab, 2016).

Nevertheless, while it seems obvious that we are at the horizon of a new revolution, the Fourth Industrial Revolution is arriving while the Third is still spreading and maturing across countries and organisations, particularly in the developing world.

Even aspects of the Second Industrial Revolution are yet to arrive in some parts of the world. What is interesting, however, is that some new technologies can bypass older ones (Davis, 2016). Meaning that even though these revolutions built upon each other and were fundamental for their successors when it comes to societal adoption, this does not necessarily follow.

To put things into perspective, over 70 per cent of the world population have mobile devices, yet over 55 per cent of people, that is, 4.2 billion people, lack safely managed basic sanitation services, an advancement that arrived for many with the Second Industrial Revolution (Silver, 2019; WHO, 2019).

Promised advances from the First and Second Industrial Revolution have not delivered for some people, but they are simultaneously experiencing some aspects of the Third and even the Fourth revolutions. As such, the world not only faces social inequalities but a 'technological divide' in which technological innovation and adoption have not been evenly distributed within and between countries.

Like the other revolutions, the Fourth brings many societal advantages, particularly for consumers that are increasingly able to afford the digital world and new technologies are emerging to fulfil their ever-changing needs. However, this revolution can also deepen global inequality, particularly as emerging technologies and their applications disrupt the labour market (Schwab, 2016).

Automation, advancements in artificial intelligence, and big data, among others, could make millions of people professionally 'redundant'. As historian Yuval Noah Hariri puts it: 'Big data algorithms might create a digital dictatorship in which all power is concentrated in the hands of a tiny elite while most people suffer not from exploitation, but from something far worse – irrelevance' (Harari, 2018). The displacement of workers by automation might exacerbate the gap between returns to capital and returns to labour (Schwab, 2016).

It is speculated, however, that 65 per cent of children entering primary school today will work in jobs or industries that do not yet exist (McLeod and Fisch, 2010). Even to date, the most in-demand occupations did not exist five or ten years ago, and this rate of change is most likely to accelerate (WEF, 2016). As such, we must be prepared for this wave of change, ensuring that people have the necessary access to education to fill the labour market demands.

As with the other revolutions, technological advances can destroy jobs, but also can create millions more. In this sense, however, it is impossible to tell if this will be the case for the Fourth Industrial Revolution. There is a heated debate around these assumptions.

> Nevertheless, what seems plausible is that talent, more than capital, will represent the critical factor of production. This will give rise to a job market increasingly segregated into 'low-skill/low-pay' and 'high-skill/high-pay' segments, which in turn will lead to an increase in societal tensions.
>
> *(Schwab, 2016)*

Most notably, the jobs being created in the late Third and early Fourth Industrial Revolution tend to require higher levels of education and specialised study, while those being destroyed involve physical or routine tasks. This premise puts education and the right to education at the centre of the Revolution.

Take, for example, Amazon: They have created thousands of jobs for people working in their warehouses and delivering packages, yet many of these people can be replaced by automation and drone delivery services.

Inequality and lack of access to education is the greatest threat to the Fourth Industrial Revolution. As mentioned earlier, inequality is at an all-time high in over five decades, and many argue that the pandemic has 'accelerated times' and push us faster and deeper into the Fourth Industrial Revolution. As such, inequality becomes an essential issue to address, especially as an ever-increasing number of people work remotely and new skills are needed.

It is important for societies to be proactive in addressing the possible consequences of the Fourth Revolution: From the digital divide to workers' redundancy or better still re-education, to the concentration of intellectual capital and innovation in the hands of a relative few.

Companies, citizens, and particularly governments are struggling to keep pace with the Fourth Industrial Revolution. From what has been discussed so far, it is clear that individuals should develop skills such as interpreting and analysing data, to successfully compete in the Fourth Industrial Revolution. Yet companies are also struggling to grasp its effects. This revolution is having a major impact on business and how they operate. Businesses are seeing the introduction of technologies that create new ways to serve customers and disrupt the value chain. New business models like the 'sharing', 'gig', and 'on-demand' economy combined with changes in consumer pattern behaviour are significantly impacting business (Schwab, 2016, 2017).

What is more, governments will also endure the changes that the Fourth Industrial Revolution is fostering. Currently, technology is often missing from the average policymaker's 'toolkit' (Schulze, 2019). Politicians tend to take a reactive approach to technological development, leaving companies unregulated and without guidance, putting citizens at risk.

Governments' bureaucratic and long-standing institutions will need to redefine themselves to properly serve citizens of the 21st century. According to Schwab, the systems in place for policy and decision-making have their roots in the Second Industrial Revolution, when politicians had time to study a specific issue and develop the necessary responses (Schwab, 2016). Even at the current pace of innovation and technological advancements, this framework is outdated.

Just as companies and individuals need to reinvent themselves to stay competitive, governments will also need to do so to stay relevant and effectively serve people in the Fourth Industrial Revolution. The digital world and the technologies that are emerging during the Fourth Industrial Revolution provide the tools that can help governments to stay relevant and enable citizens to directly engage with them.

As with the other revolutions, this revolution is driven by emerging technologies, and even more interesting (as Klaus Schwab noted), these technologies contribute to the blurring of the physical, digital, and biological worlds. Some of these technologies have fully emerged from this period; however, many of them have their roots in other revolutions and have been taken to new levels of sophistication during the Fourth. This book focuses mostly on the impacts of some technologies emerging from this period, because the authors believe these are the ones at the forefront of the Fourth Industrial Revolution. They have the capacity to redefine society the most.

Artificial intelligence (AI)

AI has been around since the 1950s, but in the last few years, with the rise of the Internet and improved computer power and capabilities, there has been a surge in AI development and usage, showing promising advances. AI is the science and engineering of making 'intelligent' machines and computer programs built from man-made algorithms that utilise data to perform logic-based tasks (McCarthy, n.d.). Simply put, AI enables computers to 'think' like humans, by using data and previous experience to recognise patterns, process information, draw conclusions, and make recommendations.

AI is an umbrella term under which techniques like machine learning, deep learning, natural language processing, robotics, and machine vision fall. One of the most widely used of these technologies is machine learning, particularly by the business sector, and it is a term we surely want to be familiar with if we want to be empowered and shape the future of AI in our lives. Machine learning (ML) relies heavily on statistics and provides computers with the ability to learn from experience without being programmed explicitly for that. The idea is that ML allows computers to learn automatically and adjust accordingly. For example, you can teach a machine to recognise what a car is. Machine learning itself has three main subsets: Supervised learning, unsupervised learning, and reinforcement learning.

AI and its advancements play a central role in the Fourth Industrial Revolution. AI is already revolutionising home and work life, the entertainment industry, the way we produce goods, shop, commute, learn, and relate to one another – even how we fall in love, with AI now driving online dating such as Match.com.

Big data and analytics

Big data is a term that denotes the increasing volumes of data being produced, both structured and unstructured. These datasets are so large that traditional data processing applications fall short in trying to manipulate or make sense of them, which means new techniques are required to manage datasets of that scale. Big data is characterised by three 'Vs': volume, variety, and velocity (Oracle, n.d.).

Ever-increasing volumes of data that contain greater variety are being generated with growing velocity (Oracle n.d.). There are approximately 2.5 quintillion bytes of data created each day, and that pace is accelerating with the growth of new technologies like the Internet of Things (IoT) (Northeastern University, 2016; Marr, 2018). To put such a huge number into perspective, a quintillion has 18 zeros. If laid flat, 2.5 quintillion pennies would cover the Earth five times (Yappn, 2017).

Advances in data collection, storage, and processing have made all this possible. By 2018, 90 per cent of online data had been created in the last two years alone (Marr, 2018). The rising levels of data collection bring with it two main challenges, namely, data quality and data privacy.

As AI continues to develop, data, big data, and analytics become crucial for training AI systems. AI in turn also becomes crucial for big data analytics because it can automate parts of the analytics process to make the data useful. AI and data build on each other in a positive feedback loop. The increased availability of data from IoT, smartphones, computers, and other devices and our ability to process it into insights is the baseline to revolutionise how we live, travel, work, and socialise. Data pushed us closer to the Fourth Industrial Revolution because it holds the key to move from mass standardisation to mass personalisation. Data is intrinsically entangled with most, if not all, the emerging technologies that characterise this era.

Quantum computing

As previously discussed, computers had a long run before they became fast and portable. Yet their evolution continues. Emerging computational technologies are making computers even smarter, enabling them to process vast amounts of data faster than ever before. Quantum computing now in development can make computers more powerful than they are today. These new computer capabilities can significantly improve AI, creating and solving complex data models in seconds, and speed up the discovery of new materials (McGinnis, 2018).

Quantum computers take advantage of the ability of subatomic particles to exist in more than one state simultaneously. As such, quantum computing uses qubits instead of bits (0-1) to perform computations. However, unlike bits, qubits can store much more information because they can exist in any superposition of several values. Quantum computers are still mainly under development, but if they prove workable, they will be revolutionary (Marr, 2017). Because they operate under different principles than those that govern existing computers, they are well-suited to solving complex mathematical problems (Katwala, 2020).

The Internet of Things (IoT)

Broadly speaking, the IoT refers to objects that are connected to the Internet. It is the use of sensors in objects like toothbrushes, kettles, scales, and engines. In short, IoT is the network of physical objects from consumer to industrial devices that collect and communicate data through embedded technology. Often this data is collected and sent to a cloud, where it is analysed and used for insights, automation, product improvement, and more. In the simplest sense, IoT devices help determine what is going on in the physical world and connect it to the digital realm (Gartner, 2018).

As such, IoT encompasses the larger context in which we leverage and manipulate the data that comes from technology-embedded devices. IoT is not only about smart things but also about their ability to collect data and the systems in place to analyse it, automate, and optimise it.

As a network technology, the development and adoption of IoT will largely depend on interoperability between the systems created by competing companies in that development space. In other words, the success of IoT devices will depend on vendors' ability to create systems that can communicate and share services with each other. Critical issues, such as vendor lock-in, or the impossibility of communication across platforms can prevent the emergence of IoT on a large scale. Therefore, sensors and platforms developed by different companies need to communicate with one another, and companies creating ecosystems around their standards will need to enable third-party participation to encourage the growth of the IoT ecosystem (Noura, Atiquzzaman & Gaedke, 2019).

Not everything connected to the Internet and with an IP address is IoT. Essential to understanding what is and what is not IoT is the premise of 'communication'. IoT devices do not require human interaction to communicate and send data (Duffy, 2014). For example, smartphones, laptops, and game consoles are not part of the IoT world. But in turn, IoT devices are 'things' that contain embedded technology with a unique identifier enabling them to connect and communicate to the Internet, to your smartphones, and other IoT devices.

IoT is a revolutionary technology that has the potential to impact consumers and significantly impact business, particularly industrial ones. As a result of Internet-connected devices, we will be able to sense what is going on in the physical world to a much greater degree. We could manage the world and people to a greater extent. Prior to the arrival of IoT, companies relied on predictive analytics to tell you, for example, when airplane engines need an oil change. IoT not only has the potential to tell you when that will be needed, but also point out failures or changes in the engine before they take place (Gartner, 2018). As you can imagine, this will have a significant impact on, for example, avoiding plane crashes caused by mechanical failures.

Augment and virtual reality

Augmented reality (AR) is the use of technology to superimpose information, including images, sound, and text on the physical world. One of the most well-known examples of AR is the Pokémon GO app game. In the game, players are located and 'catch' Pokémon that pop up in the real world. AR uses computer sensors and algorithms to determine the position and orientation of camera, and then render 3-D graphics as they would appear from the viewpoint of the camera, superimposing the computer-generated images or sounds over the user's view of the real world (Bardi, 2019). In short, augmented reality adds to the real world through a device rather than replacing it.

In contrast, virtual reality (VR) fully immerses a user into a digital world. VR is the use of computer technology to create immersive experiences in a simulated environment. Instead of viewing a screen, users are immersed and able to interact with 3-D worlds and simulations (Bardi, 2019). Today the most common form of VR is through the head-mounted display (HMD), which users use to immerse themselves in alternative realities.

Virtual reality has the capacity to revolutionise our understanding of the world. For example, it can revolutionise how we build cities, houses, and buildings, it can revolutionise education and work by creating virtual workspaces, it can be used for high-risk job training, for shopping, and even how we play video games and socialise.

As the Fourth Industrial Revolution pushes us to the crossroad between the physical and digital realm, VR and AR have become an integral part and driving force of this revolution.

Mobility and autonomous technology

Emerging technologies in mobility can significantly change the sector as we know it. The way people and goods move from one point to another is changing. This change has been brought by converging technological and social trends such as 'the rapid growth of carsharing and ridesharing; the increasing viability of electric and alternative powertrains; new, lightweight materials; and the growth of connected and, ultimately autonomous vehicles'. The result is the emergence of a new ecosystem of mobility that could offer:

> Faster, cheaper, cleaner, safer, more efficient, and more customized travel.
> *(Corwin & Pankratz, 2017)*

One of the most impactful trends is emerging around autonomous technologies. These self-driving objects have the potential to revolutionise the way we move around, trade goods worldwide, and shape the future of cities.

By definition, autonomous technology can drive a vehicle without active physical control or monitoring by a human operator (DMV, n.d.). This category primarily includes self-driving cars and trucks, but also the next generation of self-driving planes and trains. Every year it feels like we are closer to this reality, yet the technology and infrastructure to put self-driving cars on the streets and get planes to land themselves without oversight by a pilot is not quite there yet. A 2016 article in *Business Insider* claimed that:

> 10 million self-driving cars will be on the road by 2020.
> *(Piper, 2019)*

Companies like General Motors, Tesla, Waymo, Toyota, and Honda claimed they will be making self-driving cars by 2020 (Piper, 2019). Yet here we are, and they have not rolled out to the streets in anything like those forecast numbers. But we are getting closer to being in the back seat for a close look at how self-driving vehicles are likely to revolutionise our lives.

3-D printing technology

3-D printing or 'additive manufacturing' is the process of making a three-dimensional solid object from a digital file. In an additive process like 3-D printing, an object is created by laying down successive layers of material until the object is complete. 3-D printing facilitates the production of complex shapes using less material than traditional manufacturing methods (3D Printing, n.d.). It allows manufacturing businesses to print their parts at a lower cost and faster than before with easily customisable features. You can see why this is a revolutionary technology: It can significantly disrupt the value chain.

If 3-D printers go mainstream, and people adopt them in their homes, it will revolutionise how we produce and deliver goods and services. Instead of having Amazon deliver to you, you could just print things at home. In the retail space, for example, 3-D printing poses a big risk to physical stores and intellectual property.

New energy sources

When we refer to new energy sources in this book, we mean both emerging forms of energy production and the improvement of energy sources already in place, particularly renewable ones. This encompasses but is not limited to solar, wind, geothermal, wave, hydroelectrical, hydrogen gas, carbon capture and sequestration, space technology, and next-generation nuclear power. The energy sector (including capture, storage, and transmission) is growing, spurred by the falling cost of renewable energy technologies and improvements in battery storage capacity (McGinnis, 2018).

Our current energy system relies heavily on fossil fuels, which over time cause our climate to drastically change, putting human survival at risk. As such, our long-term sustainability as a species will rely on our ability to exploit new, clean sources of energy. This future very likely could see the rise of decentralised energy production, redesigning the way we buy and sell energy. Decentralised energy resources (DER) could help us mitigate climate change and bring energy to those who not yet have it.

Biotechnology

Simply put, biotechnology is the mix of science and engineering with biology. It has been around for hundreds of years, yet recent discoveries and technological advancements are bringing biotechnology into the spotlight and making us question what it means to be human. Biotechnology is the use of biology to make products for a range of uses, including pharmaceuticals, materials, genetically modified organisms, and more efficient industrial manufacturing processes (Academy, n.d.).

The discovery of CRISPR (clustered regularly interspaced short palindromic repeats) could transform medicine, agriculture, and other areas central to human life (Plumer, Barclay, Belluz & Irfan, 2018). Advancements in biotechnology combined with the emergence of big data that can give us lifestyle information and real-time data about people, which can further the impact that biotechnology will have in our lives. Innovations in nanotechnology could help us reduce genetic defects, treat cancer, resurrect extinct species, and enable a range of other imaginable benefits or dangers. As the evolution of biotechnology accelerates, ethical questions become apparent. Biotechnology is giving humans 'God-like' powers and potentially the possibility to redefine what it means to be human. It is a great responsibility.

Blockchain

Blockchain was born in 2008, the brainchild of an anonymous person or group using the name Satoshi Nakamoto. It is a shared, immutable ledger for recording transactions, tracking assets, and building trust in a network (IBM, 2020). Basically, it is a database shared in a peer-to-peer network of computers that verifies transactions. Blockchain is a technology that permanently records transactions that cannot be erased later, but only updated, thereby keeping a never-ending historical trail. In this sense, blockchain brings implications to how we transact, store data, and move assets. Blockchain facilitates peer-to-peer electronic transactions and interactions without a trusted third party required to prevent double spending. It also uses cryptographic proof instead of a central trust, effectively putting trust in the network rather than a central institution such as a bank. To date, the most famous form of blockchain technology has been that of cryptocurrencies such as Bitcoin, yet it has many other uses, including usage for asset management, payments, supply chain maintenance, and energy efficiency.

Conclusion

Reviewing the history of the industrial revolutions exposes the evidence of how technologies can irreversibly change the trajectory of societies. Understanding this history is an essential step in evaluating how we got here, and what actions should be taken in order to shape these revolutions rather than have them shaping us. This review revealed how the industrial revolutions are ultimately driven by the individual and collective choices of people, from the invention to adoption, and opposition to technologies. Ultimately the effect of these revolutions is truly felt when consumers and citizens adopt and employ the technologies and cultural changes in their daily lives. In this way, the revolutions are not about the technologies themselves but about how they change human life, for better or worse.

The First Industrial Revolution proved to be the bedrock for the following ones, it was a period of rapid industrialisation and urbanisation. However, it was also a period of growing inequality and poor living conditions for many. The Second Industrial Revolution saw the advent of many revolutionary technologies, including the automobile and the electric light bulb as well as the increased use of petroleum. The Third Industrial Revolution gave rise to the world we are so familiar with today: A world with the Internet and computers. And now we face a period of unprecedented change as we go deeper into the Fourth Industrial Revolution, a development that is changing the way we live, work, and relate to one another, a time characterised by blurring boundaries between the physical, digital, and biological worlds.

Since the First Industrial Revolution, we have undergone unprecedented change as a society. Yet our changes and advancements have also come at the expense of natural resources and other species. The First Industrial Revolution gave rise to increased pollution, but since the second half of the 20th century, humanity has witnessed a surge in human activity that has significantly impacted and changed the Earth's systems.

Human economic activity has profoundly changed our relationship to nature. The increased growth in human economic activity is known as the 'Great Acceleration'. First recorded in the mid-20th century, and continuing today, the phrase refers to the increased human economic activity due to its industrialisation that is leaving an imprint on our planet, both in terms of a larger carbon dioxide footprint and activities influencing ocean, atmospheric, and land patterns (IGBP, n.d A). Many scientists support the theory that we have entered a new geological era, the Anthropocene, which is described as a time where human impact on the planet has been the dominant influence on climate and the environment, including climate change (IGBP, n.d. B).

The current period, the Fourth Industrial Revolution, possesses not only challenges of technological change and inequality but also a range of other social and environmental challenges. Consequently, this book argues that it is imperative that we enter the Fourth Industrial Revolution with the Paris Agreement and the 2030 Agenda for Sustainable Development and its Sustainable Development Goals at heart, because those agendas were created precisely to tackle the environmental and social issues we face.

Some say that the current global pandemic is exacerbating the development of the Fourth Industrial Revolution, particularly as working from home and social distancing blur the boundaries between the physical and the digital even more. COVID-19 also exposed our dependence on digital technology and the need for in particular two different types of workers: The essential ones, and those with high skills, making many other workers redundant.

The pandemic also brought to light inequalities within and among countries around the world. Most of the policies adopted around the world, like lockdown, were mostly 'developed' nations-centric. These types of policies do not take into full account the informal economy and other challenges that developing economies face. It is hard to know what will happen post-pandemic, but it is clear that all economies will be significantly impacted (if not by the pandemic itself, then certainly by political response to it). What we know is that it is a time of unprecedented challenge where suddenly it feels that the fabric of society is changing and only a few are economically secure.

References

3D Printing. (n.d) What is 3D Printing? *3D Printing.com.*

Academy, K. (n.d) Intro to Biotechnology. *Khan Academy.*

Amadeo, K. (2020, July 29) The 9 Principal Effects of the Great Depression. *The Balance.*

Andrews, E. (2019, October 28) Who Invented the Internet? *History.*

Bardi, J. (2019, March 26) What is Virtual Reality? [Definition and Examples]. *Marxent's 3D.*

Bestofmedia Team. (2011, August 24) Computer History 101: The Development of the PC. *Tom's Hardware.*

Brusasco-Mackenzie, M. (2021) Peer Review Comments.

Cengage. (2020, September) Computer, Digital. *Encyclopedia.com.*

Corwin, S., & Pankratz, D.M. (2017, November 16) Forces of Change: The Future of Mobility. *Deloitte.*

Davis, N. (2016, January 19) *What is the Fourth Industrial Revolution?* World Economic Forum. Available online at https://www.researchgate.net/publication/341447257_The_4th_Industrial_Revolution_Implications_for_School-based_Agricultural_Education

DMV. (n.d) *Key Autonomous Vehicle Definitions.* State of California Department of Motor Vehicles. Available online at: https://www.dmv.ca.gov/portal/vehicle-industry-ser vices/autonomous-vehicles/autonomous-vehicle-definitions/

Duffy, J. (2014, June 26) 8 Internet Things that are not IoT. *Network World.*

Foote, E. (1856) Circulstances affecting the heat of the sun's rays, Scientific America. Available online at: https://books.google.co.uk/books?id=6xhFAQAAMAAJ&pg=PA382#v=onepage&q&f=false.

Freiberger, P.A. (n.d) Atanasoff-Berry Computer. *Britannica.*

Gartner. (2018, February 1) Dale Kutnick from Gartner with Nick Senior VP at Gartner. *Gartner.*

Harari, Y.N. (2018) *21 Lessons for the 21st Century.* New York: Random House.

History. (2010, February 9) First Transatlantic Telegraph Cable Completed. *History.*

History. (n.d) Industrial Revolution.Available online at: Industrial Revolution: Definitions, Causes & Inventions - HISTORY

IBM. (2020) Blockchain for Dummies. IBM. Available online at: Blockchain For Dummies®, 2nd IBM Limited Edition (larkinblockchain.consulting)

IGBP. (n.d A) Great Acceleration. *Global International Geosphere – Biosphere Programme.*

IGBP. (n.d B) Anthropocene. *Global International Geosphere – Biosphere Programme Change.*

Katwala, A. (2020, March 5) Quantum Computers Will Change the World (if they Work). *WIRED.*

Keshner, A. (2019, February 24) America's 1% hasn't had This Much Wealth since Just before the Great Depression. *Market Watch.*

Levy, S. (2013, November) The Brief History of the ENIAC Computer. *Smithsonian Magazine.*

Marr, B. (2018, May 21) How Much Data Do We Create Every Day? The Mind-Blowing Stats Everyone Should Read. *Forbes*.

Marr, B.B. (2017, July 4) What is Quantum Computing? A Super-Easy Explanation For Anyone. *Forbes*.

Mcleod, S., & Fisch, K. (2010) Shift Happens. *The Guardian*.

McCarthy, J. (n.d) What is AI? / Basic Questions. *John McCarthy Stanford*.

McGinnis, D. (2018, December 20) What is the Forth Industrial Revolution? *Salesforce*.

Niller, E. (2019, 25 January) How the Second Industrial Revolution Changed Americans' Lives. *History*.

Northeastern Univeristy. (2016, May 16) How Much Data We Produce Each Day? *Northeasetrn Univeristy Graduate Programs*.

Noura, M., Atiquzzaman, M., & Gaedke, M. (2019) Interoperability in Internet of Things: Taxonomies and Open Challenges. *Mobile Networks and Applications*, 24, 796–809.

Oracle. (n.d) What is Big Data? *Oracle*.

Pacheco, C. (n.d) Has Rapid Industrial Development Been a Blessing or a Curse for Americans? *Industrial Development: The Second Industrial Revolution*.

PBS. (1999) Transistorized! *PBS*.

PBS. (2014) 1930s High Society. *PBS – History Detectives*.

Piper, K. (2019, July 15) It's 2020. Where are Our Self-Driving Cars? *Vox*.

Plumer, B., Barclay, E., Belluz, J., & Irfan, U. (2018, December 27) A Simple Guide to CRISPR, One of the Biggest Science Stories of the Decade. *Vox*.

Polanyi, K. (1944) *The Great Transformation: The Political and Economic Origins of Our Time* . Boston, MA: Beacon Press.

Rosenzweig, R. (1998) Wizards, Bureaucrats, Warriors, and Hackers: Writing the History of the Internet. *The American Historical Review*, 103(5), 1530–1552.

Schulze, E. (2019, January 17) Everything you Need to Know about the Fourth Industrial Revolution. *CNBC*.

Schwab, K. (2016, January 14) *The Fourth Industrial Revolution: What It Means, How to Respond*. World Economic Forum. Available online at: The Fourth Industrial Revolution: what it means and how to respond | World Economic Forum (weforum.org)

Schwab, K. (2017A) *The Fourth Industrial Revolution*. Geneva: World Economic Forum.

Silver, L. (2019, February 5) *Smartphone Ownership is Growing Rapidly Around the World, but not Always Equally*. Pew Research Center. Available online at: Pew-Research-Center_Global-Technology-Use-2018_2019-02-05.pdf (pewresearch.org)

Silver, N. (2012) *The Signal and the Noise: The Art and Science of Prediction*. London: Penguin Group.

The Henry Ford. (n.d) *Henry Ford: Assembly Line*. The Henry Ford Organization. Available online at: Henry Ford: Assembly Line - The Henry Ford

The Telegraph. (n.d) The First Electric Telegraph in 1837 Revolutionised Communications. *The Telegraph*.

Vale, R. (2016, July 21) *Second Industrial Revolution: The Technological Revolution*. Richmond Vale Academy.

Waters, B. (2015, January 12) The History of Silicon Valley. *Medium*.

WEF. (2016) Chapter 1: The Future of Jobs and Skills.

White, M. (2009, October 14) The Industrial Revolution. *British Library*.

WHO. (2019, June 18) *1 in 3 People Globally Do not have Access to Safe Drinking Water – UNICEF, WHO*. World Health Organization. Available online at: 1 in 3 people globally do not have access to safe drinking water – UNICEF, WHO

Wilson, D.C. (2014) Arnold Toynbee and the Industrial Revolution: The Science of History, Political Economy and the Machine Past. *History and Memory*, 26(2), 131–161. Available online at: Arnold Toynbee and the Industrial Revolution: The Science of History, Political Economy and the Machine Past on JSTOR

WWW Foundation. (n.d) *History of the Web.* World Wide Web Foundation. Available online at: History of the Web – World Wide Web Foundation

Yappn. (2017, February 8) How Much is 2.5 Quintillion? *Medium.*

2

THE WORLD WE LIVE IN

Introduction

The political backdrop for this book is, as we said, the 17 Sustainable Development Goals (SDGs) and their 169 targets (United Nations, 2015), and the Paris Climate Agreement (UNFCCC, 2015). We will look at ten disruptive industries: Artificial intelligence, big data and analytics, biotechnology, augmented reality and virtual reality, the Internet of Things (IoT), blockchain, 3D printing, self-driving transportation, quantum computing, and new energy sources. By doing so, we are looking at the societal changes that will help or hinder the implementation of the goals and the Paris Climate Agreement.

Many governments recognise that the impact of climate change is getting worse each year. The Paris Agreement sought commitments to try to stabilise temperature rise at no more than 2 degrees Celsius relative to pre-industrialisation. At present, based on governments' commitments, the temperature rise will be between 2.5 to 2.8 degrees Celsius.

Already across the world there has been an increase in devastating storms, extended droughts, erratic cold and heatwaves, and impacts of rising sea levels. These are the consequences of climate change, all of which the Intergovernmental Panel on Climate Change (IPCC) predicted, and which the governments did not take enough warning from. It reminds us of the fable of the boiling frog. The premise of the fable is that if you put a frog into hot water it will jump out, but if you put it into normal temperature water and increase the temperature slowly it will not see the danger and will be cooked to death. Let us hope that isn't humanity.

In 2019, Greta Thunberg became the voice for young people taking up and highlighting the cause of climate change through school and university strikes. A new term (climate emergency) came into common use in the media

DOI: 10.4324/9781003045496-2

CARTOON 2.1 Frogs in hot water

while national and local governments across the planet passed resolutions in support of recognising the 'climate emergency'. As of December 2020, over 1,800 jurisdictions in 33 countries have declared a climate emergency (Climate Emergency Declaration, 2020). All this was part of an increasing global pressure on governments to take action on climate change as they prepared for the Glasgow Climate Summit originally planned for November 2020. At the end of 2019, a new emergency emerged, that of the COVID-19 pandemic. It started in China and by April had been felt in nearly every country. As the COVID-19 pandemic emerged, the Climate Summit was postponed a year to November 2021 as was the linked Convention on Biological Diversity (CBD). (Dodds, 2020).

We know as of March 2021 that China informed the World Health Organization (WHO) on 31 December 2019 of the possible outbreak. Finally, WHO declared it a pandemic on 11 March 2020.

The World Health Organization had already warned all countries on 10 January 2020:

> As provided by the International Health Regulations (2005) (IHR), countries should ensure that:

> - Routine measures, trained staff, appropriate space, and stockpile of adequate equipment in place at points of entry for assessing and managing ill travelers detected before travel, on board conveyances (such as planes and ships) and on arrival at points of entry.

- Procedures and means are in place for communicating information on ill travellers between conveyances and points of entry as well as between points of entry and national health authorities.
- Safe transportation of symptomatic travelers to hospitals or designated facilities for clinical assessment and treatment is organised.
- A functional public health emergency contingency plan at points of entry in place to respond to public health events. The impacts have been drastic with stay-at-home orders in some countries and parts of those countries.

(WH0, 2020)

The pandemic has had a huge impact in every country, with nearly three million deaths by the end of April 2021 and over 120 million cases.

The responses have been different around the world and the result of this has seen too many people die because others would not heed the call for wearing masks and following health instructions.

The beginning of 2021 saw a number of COVID-19 vaccines being made available and by the time this book comes out some developed countries will have vaccinated those that want it, and a form of normality will be returning for them. That normality will be different because of the pandemic and we will try and address this in the coming chapters. It will also be different in developing countries which will receive the vaccine much later, another example of inequality in the world.

In September 2019, the United Nations had held its first high-level meeting on universal health coverage. The event under the theme 'Universal Health Coverage: Moving Together to Build a Healthier World', focusing on accelerating progress towards universal health coverage (UHC), looking at financial risk protection, accessing the quality of essential health care services and access to safe, effective, quality, and affordable essential medicines and vaccines for all. The political declaration agreed only three months before COVID-19 was first communicated by WHO, which said:

> Strengthen efforts to address communicable diseases, including HIV/AIDS, tuberculosis, malaria, and hepatitis as part of universal health coverage and to ensure that the fragile gains are sustained and expanded by advancing comprehensive approaches and integrated service delivery and ensuring that no one is left behind.
>
> *(United Nations, 2019)*

At the World Economic Forum (WEF) held less than two weeks after the first WHO advisory went out on 21–24 January 2020, WEF identified 'health systems under new pressures' as one of the top five critical worldwide risk factors. So, governments were warned but had not taken any action. The WEF report said:

Health systems around the world are at risk of becoming unfit for purpose. New vulnerabilities resulting from changing societal, environmental, demographic, and technological patterns threaten to undo the dramatic gains in wellness and prosperity that health systems have supported over the last century. Non-communicable diseases – such as cardiovascular diseases and mental illness – have replaced infectious diseases as the leading cause of death, while increases in longevity and the economic and societal costs of managing chronic diseases have put healthcare systems in many countries under stress. Progress against pandemics is also being undermined by vaccine hesitancy and drug resistance, making it increasingly difficult to land the final blow against some of humanity's biggest killers. As existing health risks resurge and new ones emerge, humanity's past successes in overcoming health challenges are no guarantee of future results.

(WEF, 2020)

The other four critical risks are also relevant to this book, and were:

- Climate threats and accelerated biodiversity loss.
- An unsettled world.
- Risks to economic stability and social cohesion.
- Consequences of digital fragmentation.

(WEF, 2020)

This has surely been a wake-up call that humanity is facing its own sustainability as a species and that we are becoming more at risk; we are now understanding that there are now increasing links between the issues that face us.

If we address climate change this can help us considerably because the change in climate and the loss of biodiversity is exacerbating the spread of disease. Climate change can make things worse because as climate change increases it also creates a more unsettled world and risks economic stability and social cohesion. And even if they do help us address our problems technological fixes are not enough.

Disruptive industries: Where we are in 2021?

The emerging changes brought by the Fourth Industrial Revolution are already being felt. These ten disruptive technologies we focus on here are, in our view, the engine of this revolution. We will assess how they are impacting our lives in 2021, before stepping off to consider how they will affect our lives by 2030 and our ability to meet our global commitments to the SDGs and Paris.

Artificial Intelligence

> Success in creating Artificial Intelligence (AI) would be the biggest event in human history. Unfortunately, it might also be the last, unless we learn how to avoid the risks.
>
> *(Hawkins et al., 2014)*

AI is about the creation of intelligent machines that work with us and make our lives better. AI has at its centre three major pillars: Machine learning (ML), natural language processing (NLP), and robotics.

Currently, the most widely used applications of AI, particularly ML, are in business analysis and behavioural analytics. This results in advertising and product recommendations. Google uses it in its search engines, predictive analysis, and clinical research. It is also increasingly available to people through open-source libraries like scikit-learn or TensorFlow; by Google, you can access and use the algorithms for analysis.

AI, as the quote from Stephen Hawkins indicates, worries some of the top scientists. Your image of AI may be from the *Terminator* movies you have seen. In those films, humans had built an artificial intelligence defence network known as Skynet (Tesla's system is called Starlink). According to the *Terminator* movie franchise, the AI network becomes self-aware and then initiated a nuclear holocaust. This was followed by the AI trying to destroy what is then left of humanity.

In 2021, that is not where we are. Yet!

It is true, however, that Audi, Mercedes-Benz, Toyota, Volvo, and of course Tesla are already leading the way using AI for the development and use of self-driving and self-parking vehicles. The AI in cars is called reinforcement learning (RI) which is part of machine learning that has grown out of gaming. The objective of AI is to maximise the total reward. So, for a car you are looking at safety, low pollution, comfort, ride time, and obeying the rules of the road. It would try and ensure that the positives are all achieved to their maximum.

Already, AI in traffic cameras can read number plates and can also help in the flow of traffic in a city.

The power of AI can also be found when we are calling for Uber or Lyft rides. AI enables Uber to address a cluster of business challenges:

> Many of the hard problems we work on can benefit from machine learning, such as improving safety, improving ETAs, recommending food items, and finding the best match between riders and drivers.
>
> *(Such et al., 2019)*

AI in our homes has been built around recognising our speech patterns with the use of Cortana (Microsoft), Siri (Apple), and perhaps the most used, Alexa

(Amazon). These AI implementations allow several voice tasks, including asking to play particular music, adding events to your diary, calling someone, searching the Web for something, and ordering products on the Web.

Cleaning our homes can now be undertaken by iRobot 'Roomba' vacuum cleaner becoming one of the first robots in homes. It uses AI to scan a room and look for obstacles, and then works out the best way to clean that room.

Samsung and LG in 2020 unveiled home refrigerators that have AI that scans the refrigerator interior and can tell its owners what they are short on and even suggest meals based on what it finds. These smart refrigerators link to your smartphone. Their touchscreen-equipped doors can be used as a bulletin board or can link to your Samsung TV.

These new fridges are finding themselves already part of murder mystery novels with the 2018 Jacqueline Frost *'Twas the Knife Before Christmas: A Christmas Tree Farm Mystery*. In the novel the prime suspect was found innocent because she was chatting on her fridge Internet while watching a food programme with other chefs. This placed her nowhere near the murder —saved from jail by her fridge.

In response to the COVID-19 pandemic, China and other countries used drones to spray public spaces with disinfectants. According to the WEF, a drone spray can be 50 per cent more effective than a spray done manually by individual people.

Drones are starting to be experimented with in delivering goods to our homes and this will increase substantially over the next decade as Amazon and other online companies accelerate the use of them as a person-less way to deliver goods. Drones are also being used by police forces to reduce crime by gathering data. We are not yet into the realm of the *RoboCop* film of them patrolling the community. Yet!

Even journalism is using AI. In May 2020 Microsoft sacked its journalist for their homepages on MSN website and the Edge browser. They have been replaced by stories that will now be generated by AI.

> One staff member who worked on the team said: 'I spend all my time reading about how automation and AI is going to take all our jobs, and here I am – AI has taken my job'.
>
> The individual added that the decision to replace humans with software was risky, as the existing staff were careful to stick to 'very strict editorial guidelines' which ensured that users were not presented with violent or inappropriate content when opening their browser, of particular importance for younger users.
>
> *(Waterson, 2020)*

In what is colloquially known as 'drone journalism', some of the stories we are now reading in newspapers or see on television are put together with images or other data from drones.

FIGURE 2.1 The Sophia robot (© ITU/R.Farrell)

Sophia the Robot, developed by Hanson Robotics and launched in 2016, is so far the most human-looking robot. The Sophia robot uses visual data processing and facial recognition software to imitate human expressions. Like Alexa, it can answer questions and enter into basic conversation and is designed to get smarter over time. 'Sophia' is marketed as a potential companion for elderly people, and as an assistant for events.

Augmented reality and virtual reality

> Augmented Reality/Virtual Reality refers to computer-generated simulations that integrate the real world (AR) or are entirely self-contained (VR). AR applications let you move around in the real world. With VR, you have to remain in the same location because you cannot see your surroundings [in a headset].
>
> *(PC, 2020)*

Spending in 2019 on augmented reality (AR) and virtual reality (VR) jumped by nearly 15 per cent compared to 2018 from US$17.8 billion to US$20.4 billion in 2019 (Slesar, 2019). This increase is expected to only get steeper as we move through the next decade and the use of AR/VR gets better and expands.

'The use of VR is most known in gaming: Fantasies involving violence are likely to be more damaging in an immersive setting than they are in a video', Thomas Metzinger, a philosopher at Johannes Gutenberg University in Germany, told New Scientist. 'There is a danger of people getting used to not only observing but also carrying out such acts, because they are embodied in an avatar' (Paris and O'Dowd, 2020).

One of the VR applications that people are becoming more aware of is that of helping with buying or selling a house. When buying a house, considerable time is spent by the realtor and prospective buyers going around to see houses. With a VR headset, a potential buyer can walk through a listed house and see what it looks like. It can also let the buyer change the colour of walls, move or change furniture, even change room configurations by knocking walls down or putting them in. Helping to design houses that are more environmentally friendly is a game changer for the industry.

VR is now also part of some people's sex life (they are known as 'digisexuals', meaning – in McArthur's (McArthur, 2017) paraphrase – 'people whose primary sexual identity comes through technology'). VR is starting to give people an unrestricted ability to test out all their fantasies. It has been suggested that immersing in a VR experience will offer in the future as satisfying a sexual experience as those with human partners (McArthur and Twist, 2019).

The sex industry is a major technology accelerator, creating virtual worlds and multi-player environments for those participating. The film *Total Recall* gives an idea of where this might be going for VR. In the film we saw Douglas Quaid (Arnold Schwarzenegger) visit 'Rekall', which is a company that plants false memories into people's brains. They can then imagine they are on Mars engaged in whatever they wish. Is this somewhere we may be going in the industry over the next ten years? Probably not, but it may not be sci-fi by 2050.

As far as AR is concerned, perhaps the most recognised use that most people have experienced is 'Pokémon GO'. The game exploded around the world in 2016 and its success was based on combining the real world with Pokémon characters. As we write this book, Niantic Labs is bringing out a next generation of multiple player AR technology. This will enable a friend to be able to go on an adventure with you where you see and interact in the same space. According to Diana Hu, Niantic's director of AR Platform:

> Pokémon Go Buddy Adventure feature will not only allow you to interact with your Pokémon via the AR camera, it will also provide Trainers with a shared experience of seeing their real-world friends interacting with their buddy Pokémon in real time.
>
> *(Statt, 2019)*

Another AR example the reader will likely be aware of is the Instagram and Snapchat Snap Camera or Zoom's video filter; these enable people to overlay on their face an AR filter using the different lenses. As a result, people turn themselves into whatever they want as they are talking to friends. It can put bunny ears on and even turn subjects into what looks like talking toilet paper rolls.

Zoom meetings were the rage in 2020 and 2021 and you could choose great backdrops or a filter that represented you as an animal. This was made famous by Rod Ponton, a Texas lawyer who appeared at a court hearing with a cat filter on which he could not turn off. The hearing went viral and an exchange with the judge that went:

> 'Mr. Ponton, I believe you have a filter turned on in your video settings', Ferguson perceptively noted.
> 'Can you hear me, judge?' Ponton replied.
> 'I can hear you. I think it's a filter', the judge responded.
> Ponton agreed and explained the situation: 'I don't know how to remove it. I've got my assistant here and she's trying to remove it but, uh … I'm prepared to go forward with it'.
>
> *(Moye, 2021)*

Outside of the entertainment world, AR and VR are especially useful applications for medical training. Some hospitals are already using AR for teaching the ins and outs of anatomy. AR enables students to look inside the human body without physically having to open it up. By doing this, it is helping to save lives and create higher skilled jobs.

As cars have more AI integrated into them, it helps them with lane assistance and parking assistance. Car industry manufacturers such as Porsche have developed help for remote service engineers by using Osterhout Design Group (ODG) smart glasses to guide a mechanic through repair scenarios.

In schools, AR and VR help teach children in a fun way through immersive learning. The VR use is nearly always in a classroom to travel with an app to a particular place, while AR use is when students are on a field trip. Some augmented castle field trips are already available.

> Using the Metaverse app, teachers created an augmented field trip at Palamidi castle in Nafplio Greece, in which students dressed for the middle ages and solved augmented reality puzzles and challenges based on a story that had taken place at the castle during that time period.
>
> *(Metaverse, 2017)*

Big data and analytics

'Information is the oil of the 21st century, and analytics is the combustion engine'. Peter Sondergaard, Senior Vice President, Gartner (Marr, 2018).

Big data and analytics rely on three key elements, those being:

1. Volume: the amount of data generated.
2. Velocity: how fast that data can be generated.
3. Variety: how the data is structured.

As discussed in the previous chapter, we have collected most of the world's data in the last two years. Yet this data means nothing if we are not able to processes it, analyse it, and derive insights from it. The availability of data, as well as our capacity to make it useful, is the core of the Fourth Industrial Revolution.

To date, big data powers most of the AI and ML learning applications we know. Our ability to find the right data and processes it will be crucial for the further advancement of AI and autonomous cars, for example. The development of AI is intrinsically dependent on our ability to collect and process data. In turn, AI helps us be more efficient at processing this data and so is a mutually reinforcing loop.

When we shop online, our data is being collected; then companies are buying our purchasing history, or even our search history. This enables them to target us with ads to buy their products based on this history.

Platforms such as Amazon, Spotify, and iHeartRadio are collecting our musical interests. Built on this data, they create playlists they think we will like, while of course also trying to sell us that music – preferable as a download on their platform.

TV watching has already changed with the entry of Netflix, Hulu, and Amazon, into not only showing programmes but also producing them; in 2020 these were followed by Disney, Apple, and a number of the traditional TV broadcasters that are linked to existing films and series such as NBCUniversal (Peacock) and Paramount+ (CBS).

These companies are using the information on what their viewers watch to identify programmes they may want to create and give recommendations for what they should next watch. The viewing history will also tell them which actors are popular and even which directors appeal to certain demographics. One surprising byproduct of this has been the positive impact on some actors who were finding it difficult to get work through traditional means. As the platforms have seen them as popular, they have gained new work and exposure. An example would be an actor like Brendan Fraser, who has gained a new lease on life with the TV programme *Doom Patrol*. This development is also refreshing old production houses such as Bollywood:

> Online platforms such as Netflix and Amazon Prime have opened up new revenue streams for Bollywood's less active or defunct production houses that are grappling with declining sales from satellite TV rights. The platforms are acquiring rights to stream older classics as well as new titles.
>
> *(Jha, 2017)*

In the area of health care, big data and analytics have enabled doctors to give more focused health care and to be aware of new treatments. We now use apps to check our diabetes, our heart rate, our nutrition, and even how far we have walked. This helps us and our doctors to monitor health in real time.

With the COVID-19 virus, big data helps monitor the impact of the pandemic and where there are big clusters of the virus. This then enables the health services to move resources to where they are most needed more quickly and so save lives. Investment in big data in health care is expected to reach US$34.27 billion by 2022. Savings, according to a McKenzie report, would be in the region of ten times as much in the US alone (Kayyali et al., 2013).

Track and trace introduced during 2020 is an attempt to trace those that someone infects and to keep the impact of any re-emergence of COVID-19 in a community to a limited number.

Big data places an increasing role in helping the police look at where crime is happening and what kind of crime it is. Police departments can then allocate extra resources to those areas. Perhaps it is not yet as advanced as in the film *Minority Report* where the police arrested you before you committed the crime.

Using the global positioning system (GPS), drivers can know when roads have traffic jams or are closed, so they might take a different route. City transport systems can use their traffic light system to move traffic quicker. Big data provide the source to be able to analyse bus and metro train routes to see which the popular times and routes are so they can reallocate stock to the more popular destinations. Tourism departments in government can track people entering the country and which tourist venues they visit. This can help with dealing with crowding and with designing advertising to promote the 'less-travelled destinations' so spreading the visitors across more tourist venues in the high season. This smart approach to transport will not only reduce CO_2 but pollution in general from vehicles.

Social media platforms such as Facebook, Twitter, and Instagram, and dating platforms like Match and Tinder use big data to recommend news and adverts based on a person's interests or to match together people who might be compatible as partners.

Social media platforms are also being used to inform first respondents using a big data programme so that when a disaster hits, such as hurricanes, floods, and fires to collect tweets, photos, and can show first respondents where the most critical areas are.

Biotechnology

> Synthetic biology is an example of a dual-use technology: it promises numerous beneficial applications, but it can also cause harm. This has led to fears that it could, intentionally or unintentionally, harm humans or damage the environment.
>
> *(Karoui et al., 2019)*

There have been serious concerns raised about the use of unrestrained biotechnology. These have focused mostly in the public eye around the use of biotechnology in production for so-called 'bioengineered foods' and what the reader will know as 'genetically modified organisms' (GMOs).

Controversy usually focuses on the mixing of growing GMO crops in proximity to non-GMO crops and contaminating the non-GMO crops (via unintended cross-pollination) with little regard for the possible impact on humans and animals. Concerned citizens and organisations felt that there had not been enough scientific research and public consultation on GMO crop safety and or potential impacts on biodiversity, including insects, animals, and human health.

Monsanto (bought by Bayer in 2016) was one of the leading GMO producers. It had farmers signing agreements that they could only use the seeds they buy for that year they buy them. Farmers accused Monsanto of being 'seed police' and checking farm records to see if farmers complied with Monsanto policies. The aim of Monsanto was to force farmers who use GMO crops to buy them every year, thus overturning an age-old practice of using any leftover seeds the following year.

Monsanto also developed what became known as 'terminator seeds'. As the crop grew, the resulting seeds were sterile and therefore would require farmers to buy again every year. In 1999, after huge public pressure, Monsanto pledged not to commercialise this practice. The industry pushing a GMO rollout has been a case study of how not to do it. Concern over this has stoked reaction from both nonprofits and scientists:

> Greenpeace has been campaigning against Kellogg's with the help of 'FrankenTony', a monstrous version of the tiger used by Kellogg's in the marketing of their products, while Friends of the Earth were selling Frankenfoods T-shirts in the spring of 2000. The metaphor seemed to resonate in a wide variety of contexts.
>
> *(Hellsten, 2003)*

With projected growth in the world population of nearly a billion more people by 2030, and as more people move out of absolute poverty, there is going to be an increase in the demand for food. There are different estimates on when we will not have enough food to feed people because of these demands. Sara Menker, CEO of Gro Intelligence, has suggested that by 2027, there will also be an increase in pests due to climate change. Can biotechnology play a role here? And if so, under what rules?

As global citizens we seem to be less concerned about the use of biotechnology in drugs and vaccines than we are with food.

'There are more than 400 biotech drug products and vaccines currently in clinical trials targeting more than 200 diseases, including various cancers, Alzheimer's disease, heart disease, diabetes, multiple sclerosis, AIDS and arthritis' (Biotechnology Innovation Organization, 2020).

Biotechnology is also helping to make some manufacturing cleaner producing plastics from corn, which means that corn crops take carbon dioxide out of the atmosphere as they grow. The result is that they do not add greenhouse gases to the atmosphere when they are disposed of, if done within a circular economy model. But it is in danger of creating a conflict of plastics v food as land use is used to develop plastics.

Biotechnology is also used in environmental cleanups where through bioremediation it reduces contaminants.

In homes, you can find biotechnology in the detergents we use for cleaning clothes, where it replaces phosphates with a detergent enzyme that helps make rivers less polluted. The result is society trying to achieve cleaner air and water.

The use of biotechnology in DNA fingerprinting has also made us safer by helping law enforcement agencies find more criminals.

Internet of Things (IoT)

[The] Internet of Things is transforming the everyday physical objects that surround us into an ecosystem of information that will enrich our lives. From refrigerators to parking spaces to houses, the Internet of Things is bringing more and more things into the digital fold every day, which will likely make the Internet of Things a multi-trillion-dollar industry in the near future.

(Marr, 2018)

The Internet of Things (IoT) is a network of smart devices which was first discussed in the early 1980s. Bizarrely, the first Internet-connected device was a lonely Coke vending machine at Carnegie Mellon University. The vending machine could report its inventory and whether the drinks were cold or not. Ideas have to start somewhere. If you consider that before Coca-Cola put Father Christmas in red, he was dressed in green – an interesting legacy for a fizzy drink company! Now they need to address issues such as their contribution to diabetes and plastic waste.

Issues of privacy and security have been major concerns for the IoT as it has developed; this has included what data we allow access to companies. As we give away a lot of our private information, we are also seeing a massive increase in identity theft. Identity theft doubled during the pandemic to 1.4 million in 2020 in the US (Skiba, 2021).

In addition, cybersecurity for companies has become huge as hacking into the networks of government agencies and corporations is becoming far too common. As the IoT grows, its security vulnerability will continue to be a critical and ongoing challenge.

In the late 2010s there was a real explosion in consumer IoT devices. Our homes are becoming more and more part of the IoT. In a house in 2020, you may find a smart TV, a cloud-based voice recognition system such as Amazon Alexa or Google Home, or an Internet-connected security system with a doorbell and the lights all linked to your phone. Your lawn care might even be done through a smart water system which tracks the weather information to see if your lawn needs watering.

Toys are also part of the IoT. Lego, which used to be just building blocks, now sells a Lego app-controlled Batmobile which children can control through an app on an Android or iOS device, usually a smartphone.

A new car would have the IoT as an integral part of the car, where the actual ecosystem of the car can be constantly reviewed remotely. As we have seen, led by Tesla, updates to that ecosystem can be made directly to the car without even going into a garage. In September 2017, during Hurricane Irma in Florida, Tesla:

> Issued an over-the-air update to drivers in the state that [unlocked] the full battery capacity of its 60 and 70 kilowatt-hour Model S and X vehicles. The update [provided] those trying to escape the path of the storm with an additional 30 to 40 miles above the typical range of the vehicle.
>
> *(Liptak, 2017)*

In 2019 there were 9.5 million IoT devices (IoT Analytics, 2019). Amazon the same year announced they were planning to launch 3236 satellites to improve connectivity. This will, when completed, connect an estimated 90 per cent of people on the planet. The UN Broadband Commission in 2018 states that:

> Global broadband targets to bring online the world's 3.8 billion not connected to the Internet. This is designed to bring the unconnected online so that they also can benefit from Internet as a resource.

> Therefore, in response the United Nations' Broadband Commission for Sustainable Development launches 2025 targets to support 'Connecting the Other Half'.
>
> *(UN, 2018)*

BOX 2.1: WHAT IS A CIRCULAR ECONOMY?

Looking beyond the current take-make-waste extractive industrial model, a circular economy aims to redefine growth, focusing on positive society-wide benefits (MacArthur Foundation, 2021).

To satisfy demand of the use of IoT devices, increased amounts of satellites will be deployed in space. As such, one problem that we are increasingly facing is 'Space Junk' (2,400 dead satellites and over 100 million bits of debris [European Space Agency, 2021]), but this book isn't addressing this. Again, a circular economy approach here would address this and place the responsibility on those who create the satellites to ensure they are collected at the end of their life and the parts reused. Although we are in Chapter 2, this piece of information is the last addition to the book. As we submit this chapter, Astroscale, a Japanese company, launched as an 'end of life' product a spacecraft that could collect and clean up space and enable satellite companies to deliver on the circular economy. It is built around a magnetic plate which would draw the old satellite in before putting it into an accompanying spacecraft (McFall-Johnson, 2021).

BOX 2.2: WHAT DO G'S MEAN?

The G for your phone means generation – we are just moving into the fifth generation technology.

1G was released in 1971 and was an analogue system in the 1980s exclusively for voice calls.

2G was released in 1991 with the first digital cellular networks in the early 1990s and allowed for short message service (SMS) and circuit switched data (CSD) technology which enabled data speeds up to 14.4 kBit/s.

3G was released in 2001 – there were a few developments between 2G and 3G which enabled a data transfer rate of around 100–150kBit/s.

4G was released in 2008 (the next generation came in in 2006) and saw speeds of 10 to 20 times that of 3G and a mobile data rate of 100 Mbit/s.

5G was released in 2019 and not only improved the rates of transmission of data (20 Gbit/s) but also network coverage and reliability.

6G might be in place by 2030 and could be achieving a data transfer of 1 Tbit/s.

5G will play a critical role as part of the ecosystem that enables the IoT to happen faster. It is this next generation of wireless communication technology that is being rolled out after testing in a number of countries. When in place it will drastically reduce the time needed for downloading data. The UN International Telecommunications Union (ITU) issued a report on the standards that the 5G networks should work to, referred to as the International Mobile Telecommunications (IMT)-2020 network (UN ITO, 2017).

Controversy has emerged around 5G in the two areas of security and health. In the area of health:

> Some 5G conspiracy theorists contend that the new network generates radiofrequency radiation that can damage DNA and lead to cancer; cause

oxidative damage that can cause premature aging; disrupt cell metabolism; and potentially lead to other diseases through the generation of stress proteins.

(Johnson, 2020)

In April 2020 in the UK, vandals set 50 cellphone masts in the UK on fire because of a conspiracy theory linking the coronavirus with 5G (Hamilton, 2020).

5G has more security concerns than previous mobile phone network technologies have had. This is because 5G enables access to a person's data on a scale never before had in one device. Security people are particularly worried in the case of two of the leading companies (Huawei and ZTE), both being Chinese companies (and therefore under the control of the Chinese government, as is customary there). According to former Secretary of State Mike Pompeo, when he argued against those companies being used by EU allies he said:

> 5G networks will soon touch every aspect of life, including critical infrastructure. Innovative new capabilities will power autonomous vehicles, artificial intelligence, smart grids, and other groundbreaking technologies. Thanks to the way 5G networks are built, it's impossible to separate any one part of the network from another.

He went on to say:

> 'With 5G capabilities, the Chinese Communist Party could use Huawei or ZTE's access to steal private or proprietary information'. Pompeo went on to urge America's European Union (EU) allies 'not to trust Chinese firms with critical networks'.

(Pompeo, 2019)

Mobility

> Imagine a world where everything that can be connected will be connected – where driverless cars talk to smart transportation networks and where wireless sensors can monitor your health and transmit data to your doctor. That's a snapshot of what the 5G world will look like.

(ITSSA, 2019)

Mobility is not the same as transportation; it differs in a very critical way. Transportation is about moving goods and people, while mobility is about the ability to freely move or be moved. So, what are the present mobility innovations that are defining the world in 2021?

In many cities and towns in developed countries over the last 10–20 years there has been an explosion in the use of bicycles, bike lanes, and greenways. This is due to a response by a section of the population wanting more liveable and smart cities.

This book focuses on the disruptive side of the next ten years, and while increased bicycle usage can't really be called disruptive, bicyclists may benefit from disruptive technologies applied to urban planning. There has been a growth in hiring bikes in many cities, making them available to everyone. Making it convenient. And pushing cities to be more bike friendly.

The motor scooter is also becoming more available in cities and is integrating an IoT approach, such as one new start-up, Superpedestrian:

> Software is continuously monitoring for things like water penetration, cut internal wires, battery cell temperature imbalances, braking issues and more. Superpedestrian's software is also able to quickly enforce local speed limits via geofencing.
>
> *(Dickey, 2019)*

The use of IoT has even moved to the level of skateboards in the last few years.

Planning plays a critical role in how a city operates. Cities are increasingly having the ability to be able to have a much clearer idea of transport patterns in real time via sensors and wireless communication. An example from Dublin, Ireland:

> 'Constantly in motion, cities generate enormous amounts of data that can help officials deliver a better quality of life for its citizens and build competitive advantage with the right tools', said Dr. Francesco Calabrese, IBM Research Manager, Smarter Urban Dynamics. 'Dublin is becoming a smarter city by harnessing Big Data, extracting actionable insights from its transport data and delivering these instantly to decision makers so they can improve traffic flow and awareness of how to prepare for their future transportation need'.
>
> *(Berst, 2016)*

There has been significant advancement in self-driving technology with Waymo from Google or Zoox. In 2019 Waymo, in a pilot study, transported 6,200 riders in its first month in California (Korosec, 2019).

Perhaps the most dynamic change has been that of the increasing use of electric vehicles and in particular, the role that Tesla has played in disrupting the car industry. Uber as well as Tesla is starting to do the same with lorries (or as Americans call them, 'trucks').

In September 2015, Tesla announced the Model 3. This was an electric car that was aimed at the general public with a price around US$35,000. Prior to this, Tesla was known as a luxury car manufacturer, but that changed.

The Model 3 would have a top speed of 130 mph and a range of 220 miles and be available in the last quarter of 2017. It was a game changer.

In 2017 other car manufacturers that had electric cars had very poor range. Table 2.2 looks at range and cost in 2017, when Tesla released the Model 3. The additional difference was that Tesla was developing the hardware – the Model 3,

TABLE 2.1 The range and price of electric cars in 2017

Model	Range (Miles)	MSRP (USD)
Mitsubishi i-MiEV	63	$23,500
Smart Fortwo Electric Drive	70	$27,750
Ford Focus Electric	76	$29,120
FIAT 500e	84	$32,995
Kia Soul EV	93	$32,250
Nissan Leaf	107	$31,000
BMW i3	114	$42,400
Tesla Model 3	220	$35,000
Chevrolet Bolt (Bolt EV)	238	$36,620

(Fleetcarma 2017)

TABLE 2.2 Selected applications of 3-D printing

Application	Examples of uses
Aerospace	Turbine blades, fuel nozzles, structural members
Medicine	Implants, instruments, prostheses
Defence	Field replacement parts, inventory reduction
Custom Manufacturing	Razor handles, sneaker soles
Prototyping	Structural electronics, fit/function validation
Education	Conceptual modelling, problem-solving, career readiness
Hobbies	Geometric designs, figurines, toys
Art	Jewellery, costume design, footwear

(Congressional Research Service, 2019)

which could incorporate the software and become a driverless car (another game-changing innovation).

The total global plug-in vehicles in 2019 reached 2,264,400 units of which the Tesla output was 367,500 electric vehicles. Due to attractive subsidies, the leader in new car sales for electric models is Norway with 56 per cent of all new car sales being electric, followed by Iceland at 24.5 per cent and the Netherlands at 15 per cent. In 2020 and 2021, other car manufacturers are trying to catch up with Tesla and have a new fleet of electric cars coming out, so the expectation is for this to only grow in the future.

Similarly, Uber disrupted the taxi business by enabling anyone to be a taxi driver in their own vehicle simply by using the Uber app on their phone. They took this innovation a step further by allowing people commuting to nearby locations to share the ride. Interestingly, Uber's business model relies on their ability to replace drivers by driverless cars.

The driver represents the single largest expense in non-autonomous ride-sharing at 80 per cent of the total per mile cost, according to estimates by research firm Frost & Sullivan. By removing the driver from the equation, fully autonomous vehicles dramatically lower the cost of a ride while boosting its addressable market. Already offering software as a service, Uber plans to take the bet further by making the cost of rides so low (between its fleet of human and robot cars) that vehicle ownership becomes obsolete.

(Shetty, 2020)

The use of driverless cars will reduce the number of traffic-related accidents and deaths. In 2018 Uber had about 3 million drivers in the 65 countries they operated in, of which 900,000 are located in the US (Sainato, 2019). If Uber is successful in their development and deployment of self-driving cars it means that these drivers will need to find other employment.

It isn't just in the area of cars that advances are being made. Lorries (trucks) and buses are also being converted into electric vehicles and, like the Tesla cars, into self-driving vehicles. As 5G is rolled out across the world this will impact will be felt even more.

Otto, a self-drive lorry company now owned by Uber, has made its first delivery in auto drive – 50,000 cans of Budweiser. At this point it is focused on long drives on the motorways. In the US, around 70 per cent of the freight is delivered by trucks. There are also about 400,000 truck crashes every year in the US, killing approximately 4,000 people (Truck Safety Coalition, 2020). So far, the long-haul trucking industry has not sustained any job losses, but in the future it well might: 'Robots could replace 1.7 million American truckers in the next decade' (Kitroeff, 2016).

New energy sources

Once the renewable infrastructure is built, the fuel is free forever. Unlike carbon-based fuels, the wind and the sun and the earth itself provide fuel that is free, in amounts that are effectively limitless.

(Gore, 2009)

The harnessing of energy was at the centre of the Industrial Revolution and is at the centre of the Fourth Industrial Revolution.

There is a revolution underway shifting our energy production from fossil fuels to new greener forms of energy. Renewable energy has been around for a very long time, yet faced several problems when it came to its storage, distribution, and efficient production. In the past it was simply not financially viable, and it appeared to spark little interest. The change towards greener energy production was initially accelerated by government recovery packages (i.e. stimulus money) from the 2008 financial crisis. Many of the key developed countries invested around 20 per cent of their recovery package to green technology and some even more. China was around 35 per cent and South Korea 80 per cent (HSBC, 2009).

Already in mid-2020 in the midst of the COVID-19 pandemic, some countries have indicated their recovery packages will embrace the Green New Deal. The first to do so in April 2020 was South Korea, and a coalition of political ministers and CEOs is now pressuring the EU to do the same. This coalition includes ministers from Austria, France, Italy, Luxembourg, and Sweden and the CEOs of Iberdrola SA, Unilever, Volvo Group, and EON SE (Bloomberg Green, 2020).

BOX 2.3: THE GREEN NEW DEAL

This concept was promoted first by Thomas Friedman:

> If you have put a windmill in your yard or some solar panels on your roof, bless your heart. But we will only green the world when we change the very nature of the electricity grid – moving it away from dirty coal or oil to clean coal and renewables. And that is a huge industrial project – much bigger than anyone has told you. Finally, like the New Deal, if we undertake the green version, it has the potential to create a whole new clean power industry to spur our economy into the 21st century.
>
> *(Friedman, 2007)*

The Green New Deal was picked up as an idea by the New Economic Foundation in 2008 when they set up a 'Green New Deal Group' which published in September 2008 the 'Green New Deal: Joined-up policies to solve the triple crunch of the credit crisis, climate change and high oil prices'. The idea was amplified when the United Nations Environment Programme began to promote the concept. In October 2008 the Executive Director of UNEP Achim Steiner launched the 'Global Green New Deal' which promoted green jobs as a way in the final crisis to boost the world's economy while moving towards a more sustainable world. Many countries did use their recovery packages to promote green jobs and industries. More recently it has been picked up by the European Union and the Democrat Party in the US.

If the Green New Deal is followed by other countries, then it will give another huge boost to renewable energy and other green technologies and it will be the killer blow for coal and the real end to the supremacy of oil.

The main renewable energy sources used in 2021 are solar, wind, geothermal, and hydroelectric. The emerging ones include tidal, wave, and hydrogen. In 2019 the International Renewable Energy Agency (IRENA) report said that solar, wind, geothermal, and other renewable energy sources have doubled in the past ten years the total renewable energy provided in the world (IRENA, 2020). This included in the US, where it stands at 21 per cent in 2020. According to IRENA, almost 75 per cent of all new electricity in 2019 was produced by renewable energy.

'The renewable-energy business is expected to keep growing, though more slowly, in contrast to fossil fuel companies, which have been hammered by low oil and gas prices' (Penn, 2020).

Small solar electricity systems: Although Tesla is known primarily for building cars, it also has other manufacturing divisions. Tesla's roofs launched in 2016 and have since significantly expanded productivity and efficiency. The difference between the use of solar panels and a solar roof is that a solar roof replaces your roof tiles and so is an integral part of your house. As a Tesla roof feeds into a Tesla Powerwall battery, it stores the energy for the house. Even when there is a traditional power outage, it can power critical items such as refrigerators, lights, and computers. Tesla is already starting development on version 4 of its roof tiles after having launched version 3 in 2020. With each launch, the price of solar roofs is coming down. If replacing a roof at the same time as installing it, a Tesla roof is nearly comparable in price to traditional roofing.

Small wind electric systems are also rising in popularity. These are already very useful in rural areas but are dependent on living in an area which has enough wind resources. To use a real estate mantra which is also true for wind power, 'location, location, location'. They can also help with water pumping, particularly in rural areas when people are off the water grid.

Geothermal energy is another growing renewable energy sector. It is produced by tapping into the heat below the surface of the earth. It can be used for heating and cooling and for electricity generation. It is already a significant part of the electricity for countries such as Kenya, New Zealand, the Philippines, and El Salvador. Geothermal energy is an untapped resource according to the US Department of Energy GeoVision report (2019), which estimates that it could provide up to 16 per cent of US electricity by 2050 (USDOE, 2019).

It should be underlined that in 2020 three in seven people still lack the fuel to cook, often using dirty cookstoves and fuels, which account for 3.8 million household deaths a year according to the World Health Organization (WHO). The move towards promoting solar cookers, though helping, is still low in its uptake (public acceptance). Solar cookers have many drawbacks, such as weather dependency and relative inefficiency because it takes longer to cook with them. Still, they represent a cooking alternative for those around the planet who still do not have access to electricity.

3-D printing

Three-dimensional printing makes it as cheap to create single items as it is to produce thousands and thus undermines economies of scale. It may have as profound an impact on the world as the coming of the factory did (...) Just as nobody could have predicted the impact of the steam engine in 1750 – or the printing press in 1450, or the transistor in 1950 – it is impossible to foresee the long-term impact of 3-D printing. But the technology is coming, and it is likely to disrupt every field it touches.

(The Economist, 2011)

The 3-D printing concept was first suggested by David E.H. Jones in his regular column Ariadne in the *New Scientist* in October 1974 (Jones, 1974). But it was (American inventor and businessman) Chuck Hull who produced the first 3-D printer in 1986. 3-D printing uses computer-aided design (CAD) or a digital 3-D model to produce the information to print a 3-D object.

The quote from *The Economist* above came from a leader on 10 February 2011 under the title 'Print me a Stradivarius – How a new manufacturing technology will change the world'. When 3-D printing arrived, enthusiasts expected that just as everyone had a printer at home to print in 2-D they would soon have a 3-D printer next to it.

The table below offers an overview of current 3-D printing applications.

At present the home use of a 3-D printer enables us to print some basic household goods. The reality is the development of 3-D printers at home has not yet realised the expectations of those enthusiastic pioneers. So far really basic items can be 3-D printed at home, such as desk organisers, measuring cups, cups, key rings, lamps, wine racks, book ends, and even chairs.

To find someone with a 3-D printer at home is still very unusual. Some of those who had them during the COVID-19 pandemic of early 2020 banded together to produce face masks for hospitals.

The 3-D printing of an actual house gained media attention in 2014 when Winsun, a company based in Shanghai, used 3-D printing to build ten houses in one day. Ma Yihe, President and Chief Executive Officer of Winsun, which had just built the first 3-D-printed office building in Dubai, said then:

> If you do not believe it is possible, we will print a prototype.
>
> *(Yihe, 2016)*

In 2021, there are companies in the US that are offering a printed house for as little as $4000. These can be printed in a day for small houses, which brings down the cost enormously.

Outside the home, 3-D printing has seeped into many parts of our lives and the economy. One of the most publicised uses was that of the US company Defense Distributed printing a 3-D gun, including an AK-47. They raised the funds for that project through crowdsourcing, intending to make the design freely available online. Within a year, they had a gun that could fire 600 rounds. Defense Distributed's CEO explained his motivation as follows:

> I believe in evading and disintermediating the state. It seemed to be something we could build an organization around. Just like Bitcoin can circumvent financial mechanisms. This means you can make something that is contentious and politically important – not just a multicolored cookie cutter – but something important. It's more about disintermediating some of these control schemes entirely and there's increasingly little that you can do about it. That's no longer a valid answer.
>
> *(Wilson, 2013)*

President Obama's administration banned the manufacture of 3-D-printed guns, but President Trump's administration relaxed those rules.

> Not everything 3-D printed is on the dark side. In addition to the medical face masks already mentioned, that became more common in the corona-virus pandemic, there has been some excellent developments in the health industry particularly in the area of artificial prosthetics and bioprinting organs.
>
> *(Garcia et al., 2017)*

By 2018, according to the Wohlers Report, there were 19,285 3-D industrial printers worldwide and 591,079 consumer 3-D printers sold.

Finally, as a contribution to delivering the SDGs and the Paris Climate Agreements, 3-D printing offers the potential for environmental efficiency, reduction in waste, and more efficient use of energy associated with the transportation of goods.

Quantum computers

> Quantum computers could spur the development of new breakthroughs in science, medications to save lives, machine learning methods to diagnose illnesses sooner, materials to make more efficient devices and structures, financial strategies to live well in retirement, and algorithms to quickly direct resources such as ambulances.
>
> *(IBM, 2020)*

Quantum theory explains the nature and behaviour of energy and matter at atomic and subatomic levels. Quantum computing is a developing technology based on the principles of quantum theory. The computers we use today are encoded with information-based bits that take the value of 0 or 1. Quantum computers use quantum bits taking subatomic particles which enable them to exist in more than one state simultaneously – this could mean being a 0 or a 1 at the same time. This flexibility massively increases the speeds at which computers can operate.

In 2019 Google made a huge breakthrough which showed the extent that quantum computing could reduce the time for actions.

> Today we published the results of this quantum supremacy experiment in the *Nature* article, 'Quantum Supremacy Using a Programmable Superconducting Processor'. We developed a new 54-qubit processor, named 'Sycamore', that is comprised of fast, high-fidelity quantum logic gates, in order to perform the benchmark testing. Our machine performed the target computation in 200 seconds, and from measurements in our

experiment we determined that it would take the world's fastest supercom-
puter 10,000 years to produce a similar output.

(Martinis and Boixio, 2019)

Quantum computers will not be desktop computers but will live in data centres
and are still in their very early development. This emerging technology isn't yet
delivering more than what Google managed, but research is on the cusp of delivering for other major companies such as Microsoft and Amazon Web Services,
which will help their business.

Final thoughts

This chapter, we hope, gives an overview of the 10 disruptive industries which we
will weave into the next chapters and show how they might be part of your life
by 2030. Some of them, such as AI, IoT, big data, and analytics will be reflected
in most of the chapters, while others, such as quantum computers, will not, but
are part of building blocks for behind 2030, and so we wanted to include them.

We also hoped to try and make these technologies more understandable
and therefore easier to see how they will play a role in our lives in the coming
chapters.

References

Berst, J. (2016) Smart Mobility: Dublin Uses Real-Time Data to Reduce Congestion.
SmartCitiesCouncil. Available online at: https://smartcitiescouncil.com/article/smart-
mobility-dublin-uses-real-time-data-reduce-congestion

Biotechnology Innovation Organization. (2020) Biotechnology Solutions for Everyday
Life. *Biotechnology Innovation Organization.* Available online at: https://archive.bio.org/
articles/biotechnology-solutions-everyday-life

Bloomberg Green. (2020) European CEOs, Ministers Start Campaign for Green
Recovery. *Bloomberg,* New York. Available online at: https://www.bloomberg.com/
news/articles/2020-04-14/european-ceos-ministers-start-campaign-for-green-
recovery

Climate Emergency Declaration. (2020) Climate Emergency Declarations in 1,482
Jurisdictions and Local Governments Cover 820 Million Citizens, Climate Emergency
Declaration. Available online at: https://climateemergencydeclaration.org/climate-
emergency-declarations-cover-15-million-citizens/

Congressional Research Service. (2019) 3D Printing: Overview, Impacts, and the Federal
Role. Congress, Washington, DC. Available online at: https://fas.org/sgp/crs/misc/
R45852.pdf

Dickey, R.M. (2019) Scooter Maker Superpedestrian Raises $20 Million as It Gears U to
Launch. *Techcrunch.* Available online at: https://techcrunch.com/2019/11/19/scooter-
supplier-superpedestrian-raises-20-million-as-it-gears-up-to-launch

Dodds, F. (2020) Is It Time to Postpone the 2020 Climate Summit? *Inter Press Service.*
Available online at: https://www.ipsnews.net/2020/03/time-postpone-2020-clim
ate-summit/

Fleetcarma (2017) 2017 Battery Electric Cars Reported Range Comparison. *Fleetcarma*. Available online at: https://www.fleetcarma.com/2017-battery-electric-cars-report ed-range-comparison/

Friedman, L.T. (2007). Thomas L. Friedman: The Power of Green. *The New York Times Magazine*. Available online at: https://www.nytimes.com/2007/04/15/opinion/15iht-web-0415edgreen-full.5291830.html

Garcia, J., Yang, Z., Mongrain, R., Leask, R.L., & Lachapelle, K. (2017) 3D Printing Materials and their Use in Medical Education: A Review of Current Technology and Trends for the Future. *BMJ Simulation and Technology Enhanced Learning*, 4(1), 27–40. Available online at: https://doi.org/10.1136/bmjstel-2017-000234

Gore, A. (2009) *Our Choice: A Plan to Solve the Climate Crisis*. Emmaus: Rodale Books.

Hawkins, S., Russell, S., Tegmark, M., & Wilczek, F. (2014) Stephen Hawking: 'Transcendence Looks at the Implications of Artificial Intelligence – But are We Taking AI Seriously Enough?' *Independent*. Available online at: https://www.ind ependent.co.uk/news/science/stephen-hawking-transcendence-looks-at-the-impl ications-of-artificial-intelligence-but-are-we-taking-9313474.html

Hamilton, I. (2020) Vandals Set 50 Cellphone Masts in the UK on Fire because of a Conspiracy Theory Linking the Coronavirus with 5G. *Business Insider*. Available online at: https://www.businessinsider.com/attacks-cellphone-towers-coronavirus-5g-conspiracy-2020-4

Hellsten, I. (2003) Focus on Metaphors: The Case of "Frankenfood" on the Web. *Journal of Computer-Mediated Communication*, 8(1), JCMC841. Available online at: https://ac ademic.oup.com/jcmc/article/8/4/JCMC841/4584272

HSBC. (2009) *A Climate for Recovery: The Colour of Stimulus Goes Green*. London: HSBC. Available online at: https://www.globaldashboard.org/wp-content/uploads/2009/HSBC_Green_New:Deal.pdf

Internet of Things Analytics. (2019) IoT 2019 in Review: The 10 Most Relevant IoT Developments of the Year. *IoT Analytics*. Available online at: https://iot-analytics.com/iot-2019-in-review/

International Renewable Energy Agency. (2020) *Renewable Energy Capacity Statistics 2020*. Abu Dhabi: IRENA. Available online at https://www.irena.org/-/media/Files/IREN A/Agency/Publication/2020/Mar/IRENA_RE_Capacity_Statistics_2020.pdf

IBM (2020) What is Quantum Computing? *IBM*. Available online at: https://www.ibm. com/quantum-computing/learn/what-is-quantum-computing/

ITSSA (2019) ITSSA Newsletter 09 July 2019. *ITSSA*. Available online at: http://itssa.or g/itssa-newsletter-09-july-2019/

Jha, L. (2017) Netflix, Amazon Give Ailing Bollywood Production Houses A New Lease of Life. *Livemint*. Available online at: https://www.livemint.com/Consumer/o 4poATPysJaFXNpuASIVWJ/Netflix-Amazon-give-ailing-Bollywood-production-houses-a-ne.html

Johnson, D. (2020) How Worried Should You Be About the Health Risks of 5G? How to Geek. Available online at: https://www.howtogeek.com/423720/how-worried-should-you-be-about-the-health-risks-of-5g/

Jones, H.E.D. (1974) Ariadne. *New Scientist*. Available online at: https://www.newscien tist.com/letter/mg23230991-100-1-editors-pick-3d-printing-you-read-it-here-first/

Karoui El, M., Flight-Hoyos, M., & Fletcher, L (2019) Future Trends in Synthetic Biology a Repot. *Frontiers*. Available online at: https://www.frontiersin.org/articles/10.3389/fbioe.2019.00175/full

Kayyali, B., Knott, D., & Kuiken Van, S. (2013) The Big-Data Revolution in US Health Care: Accelerating Value and Innovation. *McKenzie*. Available online at: https://www. mckinsey.com/industries/healthcare-systems-and-services/our-insights/the-big-d ata-revolution-in-us-health-care

Kitroeff, N. (2016) Robots Could Replace 1.7 Million American Truckers in the Next Decade. Los Angeles Times, LA. Available online at: https://www.latimes.com/projects/la-fi-automated-trucks-labor-20160924/

Korosec, K. (2019) Waymo's Robotaxi Pilot Surpassed 6,200 Riders in its First Month in California. *Techcrunch*. Available online at: https://techcrunch.com/2019/09/16/waymos-robotaxi-pilot-surpassed-6200-riders-in-its-first-month-in-california/

Liptak, A. (2017) Tesla Extended the Range of Some Florida Vehicles for Drivers to Escape Hurricane Irma. *THE VERGE*. Available online at: https://www.theverge.com/2017/9/10/16283330/tesla-hurricane-irma-update-florida-extend-range-model-s-x-60-60d

MacArthur Foundation. (2021) What is a Circular Economy? Available online at: https://www.ellenmacarthurfoundation.org/circular-economy/concept

Marr, B. (2018) 19 Astonishing Quotes About the Internet of Things Everyone Should Read. *Forbes*. Available online at: https://www.forbes.com/sites/bernardmarr/2018/09/12/19-astonishing-quotes-about-the-internet-of-things-everyone-should-read/#1deef0b4e1db

Martinis, J., & Boixio, S. (2019) Quantum Supremacy Using a Programmable Superconducting Processor. *Google Blog*. Available online at: https://ai.googleblog.com/2019/10/quantum-supremacy-using-programmable.html

McArthur, N., & Twist, M. (2017) The Rise of Digisexuality: Therapeutic Challenges and Possibilities. *Journal of Sexual and Relationship Therapy*, 32(3–4), Special Issue on Sex and Technology, Taylor and Francis Online. Available online at: https://www.tandfonline.com/doi/abs/10.1080/14681994.2017.1397950?src=recsys&journalCode=csmt20

McArthur, N., & Twist, M. (2019) Robots and Virtual Reality are the Future of Sex. *Independent*. Available online at: https://www.independent.co.uk/news/science/sex-love-robot-virtual-reality-digisexual-future-vr-relationships-a8773391.html

McFall-Johnson, M. (2021) A Magnetic Spacecraft that Can Attract Dead Satellites has Entered Orbit – A Test in a New Effort to Clean Up Space Junk. *Business Insider*. Available online at: https://www.msn.com/en-us/news/technology/a-magnetic-spacecraft-that-can-attract-dead-satellites-has-entered-orbit-a-test-in-a-new-effort-to-clean-up-space-junk/ar-BB1eSwID?ocid=BingNewsSearch

Metaverse. (2017) Create Magic in Your Classroom. *Metaverse*. Available online at: https://medium.com/metaverseapp/you-can-create-magic-in-the-classroom-951d068f365c

Moye, D. (2021) Lawyer Gets Stuck in Cat Filter Mode During Zoom Trial: 'I'm not a Cat!'. *Huffington Post*. Available online at: https://www.huffpost.com/entry/rod-ponton-im-not-a-cat-legal-zoom-meeting_n_6022e4a8c5b6f38d06e7a1de

Paris, F., & O'Dowd, P. (2020) A Strange New World: Has Virtual Reality Gaming Lived Up to Its Promise? *Wbur*. Available online at: https://www.wbur.org/hereandnow/2020/02/24/virtual-reality-orion-13-games

PCMag Encyclopedia. (2020) Augmented Reality/Virtual Reality. *PCMag*. Available online at: https://www.pcmag.com/encyclopedia/term/arvr

Penn, I. (2020) Oil Companies are Collapsing, But Wind and Solar Energy Keep Growing. *New York Times*, New York. Available online at: https://www.nytimes.com/2020/04/07/business/energy-environment/coronavirus-oil-wind-solar-energy.html

Pompeo, M. (2019) Europe Must Put Security First with 5G. *Politico*. Available online at: https://www.politico.eu/article/europe-must-put-security-first-with-5g-mike-pompeo-eu-us-china/

Sainato, M. (2019) I Made $3.75 an Hour': Lyft and Uber Drivers Push to Unionize for Better Pay. *The Guardian*, London. Available online at: https://www.theguardian.com/us-news/2019/mar/22/uber-lyft-ipo-drivers-unionize-low-pay-expenses

Shetty, S. (2020) Uber's Self-Driving Cars are a Key to Its Path to Profitability. *CNBC*. Available online at: https://www.cnbc.com/2020/01/28/ubers-self-driving-cars-are-a-key-to-its-path-to-profitability.html

Skiba, K. (2021) Pandemic Proves to be Fertile Ground for Identity Thieves. *AARP*. Available online at: https://www.aarp.org/money/scams-fraud/info-2021/ftc-fraud-report-identity-theft-pandemic.html

Slesar, M. (2019) Top 10 Applications of Augmented and Virtual Reality. Available online at: https://onix-systems.com/blog/top-10-applications-of-ar-and-vr-in-busi ness

Statt, N. (2019) Pokémon Go is Getting a Live AR Multiplayer Feature Called Buddy Adventure. *THE VERGE*. Available online at: https://www.theverge.com/2019/11/6/20950615/niantic-pokemon-go-live-multiplayer-ar-augmented-reality-buddy-adventure

Such, P.F., Rawal, A. Lehman, J. Stanley, O.K., & Clune, J. (2019) Generative Teaching Networks: Accelerating Neural Architecture Search by Learning to Generate Synthetic Training Data. *Uber Engineering*. Available online at: https://eng.uber.com/generative-teaching-networks/

The Economist. (2011) Print me a Stradivarius – How a New Manufacturing Technology Will Change the World. February 10th. *The Economist*, London. Available online at: http://www.economist.com/node/18114327?story_id=18114327

The European Space Agency. (2021) Space Debris by the Numbers. *The European Space Agency*. Available online at: https://www.esa.int/Safety_Security/Space_Debris/S pace_debris_by_the_numbers

Truck Safety Coalition. (2020) Truck Crashes. *Truck Safety Coalition*. Available online at: https://trucksafety.org/truck-crashes/

United States Department of Energy. *GeoVision Report, US DofE*. Washington, DC. Available online at: https://www.energy.gov/eere/geothermal/geovision

United Nations (2015) *Agenda 2030 for Sustainable Development*. New York: UN. Available online at: https://sustainabledevelopment.un.org/post2015/transformingourworld

United Nations International Telecommunications Union. (2017) *Minimum Requirements Related to Technical Performance for IMT-2020 Radio Interface(s)*. Geneva: UN ITU. Available online at: https://www.itu.int/dms_pub/itu-r/opb/rep/R-REP-M.2410-2017-PDF-E.pdf

United NationAvailable online at: UHC-Political-Declaration-zero-draft.pdf (un.org).

United Nations. (2019) "*Universal Health Coverage: Moving Together to Build a Healthier World*". New York: UN. Available online at: https://www.un.org/pga/73/wp-content/uploads/sites/53/2019/07/FINAL-draft-UHC-Political-Declaration.pdf

United Nations. (2018) *UN Broadband Commission for Sustainable Development 2025 Targets*. New York: United Nations. Available online at: http://www.broadbandcommission.org/Documents/publications/wef2018.pdf

United Nations Framework Convention on Climate Change (2015) *The Paris Agreement*. Bonn: UNFCCC. Available online at: https://unfccc.int/process-and-meetings/the-paris-agreement/the-paris-agreement

Waterson, J. (2020) Microsoft Sacks Journalists to Replace them with Robots. *Guardian*. Available online at: https://www.theguardian.com/technology/2020/may/30/micr osoft-sacks-journalists-to-replace-them-with-robots

Wilson, C. (2013) In Download this Gun: 3D-Printed Semi-Automatic Fires over 600 Rounds by Cyrus Farivar. *Ars Technica*. Available online at: https://arstechnica.com/tech-policy/2013/03/download-this-gun-3d-printed-semi-automatic-fires-over-6 00-rounds/

World Economic Forum. (2020) *Global Risks Report 2020: Executive Summary.* Geneva: WEF. Available online at: https://reports.weforum.org/global-risks-report-2020/executive-summary/

World Health Organization. (2020) WHO Advice for International Travel and Trade in Relation to the Outbreak of Pneumonia Caused by a New Coronavirus in China. Geneva: WHO. Available online at: https://www.who.int/news-room/articles-detail/who-advice-for-international-travel-and-trade-in-relation-to-the-outbreak-of-pneumonia-caused-by-a-new-coronavirus-in-china/

Yihe, M. (2016) Quoted in Winsun. *The Future of Construction.* Available online at: https://futureofconstruction.org/case/winsun/

Zoom Blog. (2020) A Message to Our Users. *Zoom.* Available online at: https://blog.zoom.us/wordpress/2020/04/01/a-message-to-our-users/

3
HOME LIFE

Introduction

> The best way to predict the future is to design it.
>
> *(Fuller, 2012)*

The future evolves at an increasingly uneven pace making it more difficult for culture and society to absorb before moving on. In Chapter 1 we showed that the time between the different industrial revolutions is shortening.

This book looks to where advances are happening in the next ten years and hopefully helps the reader to understand where there might be friction or questions that need to be asked. It also builds on where we are in 2021 (at the time it was written) to look at some of the predictions that are being made on how our lives will have changed by 2030 while supporting the 17 Sustainable Development Goals (see Annex 1) and the United Nations Framework Convention on Climate Change (UNFCCC) Paris Climate Change Agreement (see Annex 2).

Sustainable Development Goal 11: Make cities and human settlements inclusive, safe, resilient, and sustainable.

In relation to climate change the largest 100 cities (SDG11) in the world provide around 20 per cent of the overall carbon emissions (Miller, 2018). You could argue (as we do here) that by 2030, our cities will need to transform drastically if the countries of which they are a part hope to deliver on aspirations outlined by the UNFCCC Paris Climate Agreement.

DOI: 10.4324/9781003045496-3

Strengthen the global response to the threat of climate change by keeping a global temperature rise this century well below 2 degrees Celsius above pre-industrial levels and to pursue efforts to limit the temperature increase even further to 1.5 degrees Celsius. Additionally, the agreement aims to strengthen the ability of countries to deal with the impacts of climate change.

(UNFCCC, 2020)

Sustainable Development Goal 7: Ensure access to affordable, reliable, sustainable, and modern energy for all.

The Fourth Industrial Revolution has at its centre decentralised sustainable energy resources, and new sources of energy which can help achieve the Paris Climate Agreement.

In 2018, buildings contributed around 39 per cent of energy-related carbon emissions to the worldwide tally, according to the Global Status Report for Buildings and Constructions by United Nations Environment Programme (UNEP), the International Energy Agency (IEA), and the Global Alliance for Buildings and Construction (UNEP, 2019).

Sustainable Development Goal 9: Build resilient infrastructure, promote inclusive and sustainable industrialisation, and foster innovation.

Creating smart cities will be a recurring theme through the next few chapters. We aim to place this book at the epicentre of the Global North (the group of countries that are in Europe, North America, and the developed parts of Asia), where these new technologies are likely to be predominant.

In 1950 there were only two cities in the world that were megacities (over 10 million people); by 2019 that had grown to 33 cities and by 2030 the project will add an additional ten cities, including two in India (Hyderabad and Ahmedabad) and two in China (Chengdu and Nanjing); others in Asia will include Tehran, Ho Chi Minh City, Seoul; and in Africa, Dar-es-Salaam and Luanda (Thornton, 2019).

It is important to understand that most of the built environment (SDG9) for 2030 already exists. Therefore, retrofitting of existing buildings and infrastructure will be even more necessary than building smarter new construction.

Sustainable Development Goal 10: Reduce inequality within and among countries.

Think of an urban family living in the US in the year 2030. As with other industrial revolutions, changes described in these pages are likely to increase insecurity and inequality (SDG10) in society and between the Global North and the Global South (the group of countries that are in Africa, Latin America, and the developing parts of Asia). We address some of this as food for thought throughout the book, but particularly in Chapter 8: Living around the globe, where we try to give some insight into what the situation in the Global South might be.

Like the previous industrial revolution, the Fourth Industrial Revolution is changing family and urban life.

Family life is part of the fabric of our communities and our societies. But the median length of marriage in the US is now only 11 years and the typical American family has shrunk to around 1.93 children (Statista, 2020).

Another defining factor for how people are living in 2021 is that 72 per cent of the 83 million 'millennials' [born between 1981 to 1996], according to the US Census Bureau 2015, cannot afford to buy a house (Del Vallle, 2018). Single-person households have reached over 28 per cent in the US and even more in Denmark (45 per cent); the estimates are globally something like 34 per cent of people (Euromonitor, 2018).

The present housing stock was built for larger families and for ones that stayed together longer. This changing nature of how people lead their lives in the 21st century has seen some interesting new approaches to living spaces. One of these is the Tiny House Movement.

> Simply put, the trend towards tiny houses has become a social movement. People are choosing to downsize the space they live in, simplify, and live with less. People are embracing the tiny life philosophy and the freedom that accompanies the tiny house lifestyle. The tiny house movement is about more than simply living in a small space (although, a small house is certainly part of it).
>
> *(The Tiny Life, 2020)*

Another development has been that of the shared or co-living housing movement. Unlike the normal rental rooms that people have taken in houses for a long time, this is more about creating a community.

The shared housing movement addresses the high cost of renting and social isolation that a growing number of people are feeling, particularly in the cities. The shared housing concept is built around a person having a bedroom for themselves or them and their partner and then sharing with others in the building's common areas. These can include a kitchen, movie and games rooms, a gym, pool tables, or quiet work areas.

Housemates might collectively organise BBQs, comedy shows, weekly dinners, or snack and game nights. As a trend by 2030, this may become more of a norm; even in 2021 hotels have been moving to create in addition to hotel rooms shared housing sections of their hotels. To service these they have been creating shared more living space and amenities. The slogan for HubHaus, one of the companies set up to offer arrangements like this, is:

> Rent one of our rooms and find your tribe.

(Shier, 2018)

These shared living places will benefit from collecting data and analytics of those that aim to be resident. If you know the people have similar interests it may be easier to build a community that is more likely to be supportive or each other. We explore this more in depth in Chapter 4: Travelling around.

Another company, Ollie, sees its 'co-living' mission as providing the 4 C's 'Convenience, Comfort, Community, and Cost-savings'.

The founders of Airbnb revolutionised the travel and tourism industry. The original idea came from the co-founders initially putting an air mattress in their living room for someone to rent. By 2008 this had become what we know as 'AirBedandBreakfast' (Airbnb), offering vacation and short-term rentals. Airbnb, like other platforms using AI, is collecting our data and using it to suggest similar holiday venues we might like.

Property buyers and renters of 2030–2040 are likely to want all the benefits offered by newly built homes which have smart technology integrated within their fabric (Hammond, (2019).

Hammond for the Allianz Partners produced an insightful report 'World in 2040. The future of healthcare, mobility, travel, and the home'; in it he identified the difference between urban development based on demand or supply (Hammond, 2019).

The demand side includes urbanisation (941 megacities by 2030), demographic changes (ageing population, smaller households), sustainability, affordability (increased inequality), and digital economy (remote working). The supply side includes construction technology (drones) and methods (3-D printed houses), building technology (smart buildings), access and distribution (online markets), and supplier landscape (labour availability). It does raise the question: Is the future supply- or demand-driven? For example, are we looking for smart cities or providers of smart cities (Lawrence, 2020)?

Now let us explore the home of tomorrow and what it might include.

House-buying

In the US the first recorded sale of a house was in 1890. The present real estate market globally is estimated at over US$280 trillion.

Moving homes is thought to be one of the most stressful experiences we have in our lives and so anything that reduces that stress can only be good news – this is where blockchain comes in. What is changing is that:

> All parties involved in the process, including the buyer, seller, real estate
> agent, the buyer's bank, and the land registry, have their own digital identities.
>
> *(CB Insights, 2019)*

Blockchain technology will be used to ensure trust between buyers and sellers, reducing the need for intermediaries such as agents. A blockchain may become a way to ensure that what you are buying, including valuation and ownership is trustworthy. The creation of a digital token to represent land titles will make a unique and transparent history for land ownership.

Moreover, the current approval for a mortgage can take up to 60 days. A blockchain makes the transaction streamlined and limits the use of intermediaries. Through smart contracts that take place on a blockchain transaction, frictions will decrease, enabling real estate exchanges and contracts to take place without lawyers or real estate agents. It would enable a verified digital identity, reducing the need for due diligence.

> In the near future, it may be possible for a homebuyer to buy a home and
> complete the sale (along with escrow and title insurance) by clicking on
> a shopping cart on a website. A blockchain will ensure that the buyer
> gets the title or deed, and the seller gets the cash (via a cryptocurrency).
> A blockchain will also record the title or deed to the appropriate public
> records, such as a county in the United States or similar.
>
> *(Zilbert, 2018)*

More interestingly, virtual reality will significantly impact the process of home-buying. Through realistic renders and immersive 360-degree tours, VR companies could show realistic experiences of their constructions to potential customers. This could help people buy homes from a distance and provide a virtual experience of what the home looks and feels like. Most people buy or rent after not only viewing a dwelling but also the local neighbourhood. VR would allow them to walk around, see the shops, go to the local schools, etc. It might link to a virtual lounge in the local schools in which potential students and parents could ask questions about the school and what it has to offer while also walking through it virtually. VR with predictive algorithms can show how the neighbourhoods will likely mature. However, there should be a warning that VR can be highly manipulative for the unwary (Lawrence, 2020).

House building

> These super-smart houses and apartments will cost at least 60 percent less
> than today's equivalent homes and will be built and fitted out in just a
> couple of weeks. If local planning and zoning regulations are amended to
> make it possible.
>
> *(Hammond, 2019)*

The new house of tomorrow may be one that has been 3-D printed, perhaps from recyclable waste. They will be built more quickly and more cheaply. In 2021 the first 3-D-printed house hit the market with the construction technology company SQ4D. It put a 3-D-printed house (1,400 square feet) on the market for US$299.999. This price is 50 per cent below a house constructed in a traditional way in the same neighbourhood. SQ4D is producing homes that are 1900 square feet that take 48 hours to print over an eight-day period, printing onsite using less than US$6,000 in materials (SQ4D, 2021).

The inside of our houses will also change. In the rest of this chapter, we will take you through what that might look like.

The houses of 2030 will need to be more flexible as far as their usage is concerned. The COVID-19 pandemic in 2020/21 showed that more and more people could work at home, and so by 2030 a house will probably need to support both 'home office' and 'domestic use'. Non-load-bearing walls could become moveable to accommodate the different uses required in a house or flat. It may be that as you go out for a run in the morning, rooms reconfigure themselves from sleep to work mode before you get back.

Roofs and windows and energy use

The development of building-integrated photovoltaics (BIPV) may make the house of tomorrow carbon neutral, energy (SDG7) self-sufficient or even providing energy to the local grid. In Chapter 2 we looked at the development of solar roofs by Tesla in particular. Another BIPV innovation not available in 2021 that may become standard by 2030 is that of solar windows.

Battery development is accelerating and depending on where you are in the world – the homes of tomorrow may very well be mini generators of power for local businesses or older homes as more modern dwellings sell their excess power to the local grid. Backing this up, blockchain could secure digital transactions. By this we mean it would allow for the creation of secure peer-to-peer networks within a smart grid. They offer the chance to track and bill energy used as well as energy produced.

Creating a circular (see Chapter 2) economy for batteries and, for that matter, solar panels will be critical for 2030 as the availability of heavy metals becomes less. Perhaps both should be rented and not sold with the rentee having product liability.

'New transactions are linked to previous transactions by cryptography which makes blockchain networks resilient and secure. Every network user can check for themselves if transactions are valid, which provides transparency and trustable, tamper-proof records' (Andoni et al., 2019).

It is worth noting that currently blockchain uses for cryptocurrencies like Bitcoin takes a lot of energy in validating transactions and mining.

Bitcoin mining uses more electricity than 159 individual countries – including more than Ireland or Nigeria.

(Martinez, 2017)

More recently (2019) Bitcoin exceeded the Netherlands (111 TWc) in the amount of electricity consumption it used and data centres worldwide used 199 TWh (Rowlatt, 2021).

Although problems exist in addressing how to make transparent windows generate electricity, solar is also being developed that can be flexible, e.g. can wrap around existing structures and aboard both UV and infrared – so it can generate in the night as well as the day (Lawrence, 2020). The solution seems to be a future with true transparent solar windows may involve nanotechnology:

If windows can be designed with quantum dot technology, enough energy may be able to be harnessed from the sun while still letting light through the glass windowpane the quantum dots are housed in.

(Marsh, 2020)

Quantum dots (QDs) discovered in 1986 by Alexey I. Ekimov, a Russian solid state physicist, are tiny semiconductor particles a few nanometres in size. They have optical and electronic properties that are different from larger particles due to quantum mechanics. When they are illuminated by UV light an electron in the quantum dot is excited to a state of higher energy.

Also in development are solar blinds and these may be a good answer for existing houses. Such blinds could be programmed to follow the sun and adjust on the fly to get the maximum energy from their surface. Blinds will likely utilise the 2030 version of something like a Tesla Powerwall to ensure that energy storage is not a problem. Another development that may figure in new housing by 2030 is transparent 'wood'. Céline Montanari from the KTH Royal Institute of Technology:

We prepared a material that is multifunctional – it can transmit light very well and also it can store heat. We combined these two functions in a single material.

(Alexa, 2019)

A critical function of a good house in 2030 will be the energy management system it has. As well as looking at energy capture, a house in 2030 will look to be as energy-efficient as it can be. The development of the 'Bring Your Own Thermostat' (BYOT) is an attempt to manage the demand for energy. The first generation of learning thermostat was put on the market by Nest in 2011, first enabling homeowners to communicate via Wi-Fi to turn the temperature up or down. Smart thermostats enable the sensing of occupancy and adjust the thermostat accordingly. BYOT would allow utilities to reduce by a small amount people's temperature in a high demand period to deal with the demand.

New designs will create homes that are either providing surplus or at least close to 'zero net' as possible (meaning that production and consumption zeros out). In 2019, according to Move.com, the average cost of electricity and gas for a new home was US$265 a month (Williams, 2019). Houses of 2030 should bring big savings to a household, relative to that figure.

> In 2030, individual and community energy generation contributes to more than fifty percent of the energy mix in developed countries.
>
> *(Burston, 2016)*

By 'individual', Burston means individual houses becoming energy providers not just for themselves but being able to have an income by charging their excess to the local grid.

Increased use of IoT devices in homes will allow us to have a greater understanding of how energy is being used in the home. The use of IoT and data analytics will enable a home to be more energy-efficient and have the capacity to make them eco-friendly. IoT technology can be used to monitor heat in your house and adapt automatically – let us say based on your presence in the room. Data analytics will be used to improve energy efficiency and provide people with money-saving information and understanding of their energy usage.

House interiors

In the past you just bought the house and then decided how you wanted to furnish it by going to lots of furniture and electrical shops. In the future you will have the chance to design through a virtual reality headset. You will be able to place the proposed furniture through VR and even purchase it on the spot. Here you can look at the empty room and design its interior before you move in. There are design companies in 2021 which will already help you do this. It may be that you design something that you want in the room, which can then be 3-D-printed. By printing it you might lose the name recognition of a product, but you gain with custom fabrication and with it being cheaper. Companies may have two versions of a product, one where they make the actual product and the other where they license the creation through a 3-D printer.

Security systems

Depending on how the increased insecurity and the growing inequality in the world we live in is resolved or not, home security will become more important. Already in 2021, we have seen the advancement of security systems for homes linked to your phone – something that is also being used to monitor and modify your energy use. Today comparatively few people use their smartphones to turn their home temperature down or their lights off, but this number will only increase as more of the house is linked to the biometric profiles of their occupants (Hammond, 2019).

IoT working with blockchain can be used to increase the security in a smart home network. Creating a blockchain of devices in a home would require a hacker to gain access to 51 per cent of the individual devices where those devices are in many cases distributed around the county or even the world (Labbadi, 2019).

With more of us working from home, security protects not just physical property but also personal data and intellectual property. Our homes will need to ensure our work is not stolen or compromised. Strong security will need to be part of our IoT.

Security is also about data integrity throughout healthcare delivery in its various forms – we will deal with this in Chapter 5. The COVID-19 pandemic showed the need for (among other things) the development of antibacterial fabrics in the home. Alexandra Whittington, the 'foresight director' of Fast Future publishing, was quoted by journalist Peg DeMarco:

> The latest example I've seen is a scarf that can fight contagious illness and protect the respiratory system from air pollution. … Home fabrics that help

CARTOON 3.1 The mom and dad are relaxing and sitting on the couch each looking at their own devices (which look like iPads). While looking at their devices, the husband addresses his wife

CARTOON 3.2 The frame zooms in on Emma holding her iPad-like device and it just shows the image of a security label and privacy rating on the screen

keep pathogens away may be important in the case of a future pandemic or the expansion of antibiotic-resistant bacteria.

(DeMarco, 2019)

The bedroom of 2030

Sleep is one of the most important reasons for a bedroom and most people don't manage enough sleep. It is no wonder that the present market for sleep aids and medications is about US$28 billion (LaRosa, 2018).

Often a bedroom is also an entertainment area – many have a television for people to watch in bed or one that acts as a huge games console. This may of course add to the lack of sleep people manage to have.

The flat screens of today are likely to be replaced with access to projecting programmes on our walls.

In 2015, Google registered a patent that would enable a projection system to display images on a wall that was painted with photo-reactive paint.

The patent suggests that the proposed technology would be able to update the projected images often enough to support videos (rather than just still images), meaning the McFlys' (a *Back to the Future II* film reference) window television could one day become a reality. The patent also says that any surface could be coated in transparent photo-reactive paint, meaning you could theoretically turn an entire house into a television if you wanted to feel like you lived in a sports bar or art installation.

(Murphy, 2015)

By 2030 this will be not only 2-D and 3-D programmes that we can watch but also VR where we are immersed in the program ourselves. In Chapter 6: Entertainment, we will discuss how the use of VR and AR will become an integral part of our entertainment.

Intelligent beds contain sensors (IoT family) which will build on what we have seen with the development of intelligent mattresses such as the Sleep Number mattress, which senses your movement and adjusts the comfort of the bed to what you like. With your bed collecting data about how you sleep, this data can then be used for health purposes, for example, correcting sleeping patterns that are bad for you and helping you to improve your sleeping. By 2030 beds will have programmable temperature zones for the sheets and pillowcases. This will also reduce the need to heat or cool the whole house and so save energy and CO_2 emissions.

> Sustainable Development Goal 12: Ensure sustainable consumption and production patterns.

Electric drones will become the main delivery vehicle for many items, including food, clothes, and other household things we order online (SDG12) – reducing CO_2 transport emissions. Walmart have been trialling the use of driverless trucks to make deliveries from a 'dark store' (this is a store in which you cannot buy something) in Bentonville in Arkansas. This trial they hope to expand in 2021 to other locations. The vehicle has a safety driver in it, and it goes to locations where people can pick up their orders (The Verge, 2020).

> Sustainable Development Goal 2: End hunger, achieve food security and improved nutrition, and promote sustainable agriculture.

Drones are playing and will increasingly play an important role in food security – being able to collect and analyse data and look at any environment trends and the finite amount of arable land and water. In June 2020 the United Arab Emirates (UAE) launched the Food Security Dashboard using AI and data analytics which:

> Rapidly measure the five important indicators of food security including, the supply index; stock availability; local production; consumption levels; and the cost of vital commodities in the Emirate.

(Rizvi, 2021)

They are helping address crop losses due to the example of insects on growing pecan nuts by releasing ladybirds as opposed to using pesticides. At the same time supporting organic farming also produces a smaller carbon footprint and keeps our soil and water cleaner.

For some people owning clothes in 2030 may be completely different from today. It may be a mixture of approaches where in some cases 3-D printing the clothes at home or have them 3-D-printed at a hub and delivered on demand or overnight by drones. Perhaps we will not own our clothes in the future. Future closets will be:

> Both exciting fashion pieces on loan temporarily, and hyper customized basics tailored to the individual.
>
> *(Gill, 2020)*

This idea was birthed in 2009 with 'Rent the Runway', a company that aimed to enable people to have high-end clothes – normally outside their price range – but for a four- to eight-day period. By doing so the clothes were priced at around 10 per cent of the retail price. In 2019 'Rent the Runway' has spot #5 on CNBC's Disruptive Top 50 list. If by 2030 this becomes a more normal approach to clothes it will mean less space will be needed to store clothes while at the same time more opportunity for wearing different styles even on a modest budget.

Smart stylists of 2030 could be a 'thing' using AI to learn and understand what you like – perhaps better than you do – by also understanding your colours through your bathroom mirror (see below). Perhaps even linked to an AI wardrobe that helps you with your selection.

> Americans dispose of more than 68 pounds of clothes per person annually, and fast fashion only ignites this harmful chain reaction of churn and burn, leading to an acceleration of the textile industry's environmental consequences.
>
> The Environmental Protection Agency (EPA-USA) has declared several textile manufacturing facilities to be hazardous waste generators, and clothing and other textiles represent approximately 9 percent of municipal solid waste. The amount of discarded clothing tossed into landfills is projected to reach 35.4 billion pounds in 2019. The fashion industry's CO_2 emissions are also projected to increase by more than 60 percent to nearly 2.8 billion tons per year by 2030.
>
> *(Stirpe, 2018)*

In reaction to this projection many of the key fashion houses have set carbon emission reductions by 30–45 per cent. Like many consumables the clothes of 2030 can be recycled through a circular economy approach to fabrics.

Bluetooth technology has been used since 2014 to track our running or walking. Nike+ shoes include a sensor that links to your smartphone. For the joggers reading this book, there are some interesting developments in 2021 with spider silk. The silk can be coated with carbon nanotubes and can then monitor your heart rate. Perhaps it will be hard to create farm spider silk in significant amounts, but by 2030 other sensors will be used (Steven et al., 2013).

Children of tomorrow

> In fact, growing up with digital technology may be changing teen brain development in ways we don't yet know – and these changes may, in turn, change how teens relate to technology.
>
> *(Allen, 2019)*

Sustainable Development Goal 4: Ensure inclusive and equitable quality education and promote lifelong learning opportunities for all.

The children of our imaginary house in 2030 will want their rooms to be as up to date as children of any era. We will look in more depth at some of the entertainment and social life that people are experiencing much more in Chapter 6: Entertainment and Chapter 7: Social life, but a window to those chapters will be opened here.

Already the children of 2021 have in many cases created two lives they live: There is the normal non-virtual one which all children have always had, but now there is also this second virtual one.

Second life started where people create an avatar of themselves to meet other people and socialise in this virtual world. This can look nothing like them, and the personality created can be a complete fantasy. On the positive side, it can help shy children or those with disabilities to personalise their online learning experiences (SDG4) and increase their learning and engagement with a broader number of people. This virtual second life has taken on a broader definition so as to represent someone's online social profile which might also include Instagram, Facebook, Twitter, YouTube, Pinterest, and Snapchat. Both identities or personas bring with them problems that a child will try and navigate.

The pressure of this second 'online existence' has seen an increase in youth suicides. In a survey of Chicago children, the number one issue they worried about was gun violence (87 per cent); the second was bullying and cyberbullying (76 per cent). The third was poverty (74 per cent) and the eighth was social media (65 per cent) (Chicago Department of Public Health, 2019).

The roll-out of AR and VR, particularly for educational pursuits, will open children and youth to imaginary worlds that can be amazing places for learning. It may be that you can talk with historical figures such as John F. Kennedy or Martin Luther King about your civics project (see Chapter 5: Working life, education, and health).

Enjoying music is something we all enjoy, but even that may change. In 2020 due to an AI, an algorithm has enabled Frank Sinatra to sing a song written after he died – the Britney Spears song 'Toxic' (Robitzeki, 2020).

Instead of just watching a film like *Ice Age* or *Zootopia* the equivalent in 2030 may be interactive where you could see or be a character in the film. How much fun would that be? Of course, I am choosing a 'friendly' example – there will need to be parental control because the choice of characters could be very dark as well something which an AI system could oversee.

You do not want a young child using the system to see violent or sexually active characters. According to the American Psychology Association, the average age of children seeing porn is 13.37 years old, with the youngest being five (Perry, 2019). AI in the house of 2030 doubtless has parental controls. But outside the home, something like 77 per cent of all teenagers own a smartphone – what do you do? Through software, parents will also need to predetermine what pages they can navigate through more digital safeguard controls. This could extend to even screen time – once you exceed it in a day your phone goes off, except for emergency calls (Google, 2020).

Another interesting product that will need some parental control software and that is in development in 2021 is that of perception-changing contact lenses which enable someone to:

> Display anything your smartphone can, such as social media pages, satellite navigation, and video chat.
>
> *(Stephens-Borg, 2019)*

Will kids' rooms look much different in 2030? Probably not much in colour and décor, but they will be enhanced as far as access to AR and VR is concerned. The ability to access fashion through 3-D-printed clothes will not necessarily diminish peer pressure about wardrobe choices or relieve anxiety about growing up and what others will think of you – it may actually increase.

Many toy manufacturers are now aiming to make their products recyclable. Mattel – well-known for brands such as Fisher-Price's, products Barbie, and Hot Wheels – announced in 2019 that it had:

> set its sights on ensuring all of its products are made from and packaged in 100 percent recycled, recyclable or bio-based materials within the next decade (by 2030) with children able to get their hands on its first sustainably made toys early next year.
>
> *(Holder, 2019)*

Some toys may be 3-D printable at home and children may learn very early how to develop changes to 3-D printing programmes to make their toys more unique.

In April 2020, the three largest toy manufacturers Mattel, Hasbro, and LEGO announced their intention to phase out plastic by 2030 or before. (Katanich, 2020).

At the end of this chapter, we look at robotics in the home, but it would be important to mention here that an AI can also be a 'friend' to a growing child who is more reclusive, filling a role that in the past might have been given to an imaginary friend.

Ian Pearson, a Sunderland football club supporter (there must be a few), and futurist suggests that a family might find that their daughter might respond if popular cartoon character Peppa Pig:

> could sit with her at dinnertime and keep her amused when she's putting up with you talking at her. She (Peppa Pig) could encourage her that the broccoli isn't actually poison and it might be fun trying it; [She] could interact with her and offer some positive encouragement.
>
> *(Bulger, 2017)*

A future bathroom

> Now, it may not look like it's changed much, but in 2030 – like most other things in our house – will have become a smart toilet. That means it measures 10 properties of your urine, including glucose, and it looks for health problems before they present themselves.
>
> *(Chen, 2019)*

The bathroom of tomorrow will keep water use to a minimum.

> Sustainable Development Goal 6: Ensure availability and sustainable management of water and sanitation for all.

In 2018 over 2 billion people were living in countries experiencing high water stress (UN, 2018). Some estimates suggest that if current trends continue, by 2030, demand for water (SDG6) will exceed supply by 40 per cent, impacting both developed and developing countries alike (UNEP, 2016).

These projections for 2030 make water one of the critical issues that people around the world will face. This will impact our cities, workplaces, and homes.

Houses of 2030 will integrate saving water into their designs through big data and IoT giving us new insights into how to manage water usage better in our homes. Regulations may prohibit water from a local municipal provider from being used to water gardens even with efficient sprinkler systems. Old rainwater harvesting technology will find updated applications in tomorrow's houses usage linked through your AI which will monitor availability.

> Raindrops falling on the average size custom home, in most of the Midwest and Eastern United States, add up to approximately 120,000 gallons of

water per year. Every drop is an asset of the homeowner in most states. You own it, it has value and with ever-increasing water costs, the value builds. Rainwater harvesting provides a way for every homeowner to take control of your water.

(Rochat, 2020)

> Sustainable Development Goal 13: Take urgent action to combat climate change and its impacts.

Climate change (SDG13) will increasingly impact on the US, particularly, though not exclusively, in the West and Southwest, though other regions are also feeling its effects. In the US and around the world we are using up historical groundwater aquifers by taking more than their annual natural replenishment can support.

An example of this phenomenon is the Ogallala Aquifer, from which seven US States (South Dakota, Nebraska, Wyoming, Colorado, Kansas, Oklahoma, New Mexico, and Texas) extract their water. According to the census, that aquifer supplies drinking water for over 2.5 million people and around 30 per cent of all irrigation for agriculture. It is responsible for the water for one-fifth of the wheat, corn, cotton, and cattle produced throughout the US. Unless policy changes, it will have used up to 70 per cent of all the water, in the seven-state region, by 2060 (Buchanan, 2018).

Dual flush toilets (that use two buttons or a handle mechanism to flush different amounts of water depending on need) are not new and are already in many homes in 2021. Future homes may have this as a requirement. There are already moves towards bathrooms that have showers and no baths.

That development started in many new hotels and flats. The showers of tomorrow will learn what your ideal temperature is and have the water ready for you to enjoy – if you live in an arid climate, this might also be linked to the rain harvesting system you have built into the house. Gone will be the days of unbearably hot or freezing showers. Used shower water – even bathwater, if you have one – will be captured as 'grey water' and recycled for your garden or your toilet (as is already done in Australia, Cyprus, Jordan, and is being considered in parts of the US).

Water metres will become commonplace everywhere, and the misuse of water in large amounts will come with a heavy price. IoT will help us identify water/gas leakages or other issues and it will enable us to control substance presences in the water like lead.

Waterproof TVs will allow someone to watch their favourite programme while showering (Seura, 2020). Perhaps you prefer to sing? If someone wants to sing along with their favourite song while taking a shower, then the showerhead with a Bluetooth in it, linked to a smartphone or laptop will access favourite music tracks for you (Kohler, 2020).

Smart bathroom mirrors will enable you to catch up on news or link to your other smart devices in the house. Mirrors may also be able to analyse your best make-up options and might go as far as to order make-up if you do not seem to have it on hand after your mirror and your vanity drawer 'talk' to each other. Perhaps mirrors would also have the diagnostic capacity for early alerts on skin cancer and other diseases of the skin. You might also use your mirror when you go to bed to put your security system on as you brush your teeth.

Frightening for many, NeuraLink, another Elon Musk company set up in 2016 is exploring ways so that the human brain can be connected to a computer interface. In 2019 it applied to the US regulators to start tailing with humans. Musk has called these implants the 'Fitbit in your skull' and could have really important benefits such as curing blindness, deafness, and possibly paralysis. It is fair to say that the reception has been mixed.

> Using the brain as an interface could mean the end of keyboards, mouses, game controllers, and ultimately user interfaces for any digital device. The user needs only to think the commands, and they will happen. Smartphones could even function without touch screens.
>
> *(Ericsson's, 2019)*

Kitchens of tomorrow

> Ask 'What's in my fridge?' and your fridge will tell you. Running low on milk? Your fridge will automatically order more and get a fresh pint or gallon of milk delivered to your door. Future houses may need an outside place for a drone to drop food that needs to be in a refrigerator, which will recognise the temperature the food needs to be at.
>
> And not just the fridge, but the oven, the microwave, dishwasher, washing machine and loads of your smaller appliances, too. So, while you won't exactly be able to walk into your kitchen and say, 'Make me a Full English', you'll love the time you get back from a speedier, smarter, less laborious cook and clean.
>
> *(Currys, 2019)*

For many people, the kitchen/breakfast room is not only a place where meals are cooked but where people in the house meet and talk. They do this as they cook, eat their meals, make their coffees, and wash up.

The future kitchen will work on voice control and learn what you like. Your fridge can check the night before if you have the ingredients for a recipe you want to use the following day and if not, order them overnight. Based on your previous selection, it may also suggest the meals you would like, saving you significant energy trying to figure out what to do. While it may be problematic if your refrigerator communicates automatically with your neighbourhood grocery store and your bank (to check you have enough money there), the fridge of the future can keep an eye on what food is coming to its end date and therefore help reduce food waste if you take its 'advice'.

Projections for 2030 suggest that agriculture (SDG2) will need to produce 30–50 per cent more food to meet growing demand (Water Institute, 2018), so any reduction in food waste will be helping to address this. The US is the global leader in food waste (just as in food production). In 2019 Americans discarded 80 billion pounds of food waste – 219 pounds of waste per person, which also amounts to 30–40 per cent of the US food supply (RTS, 2020).

Future homes may feature BioWalls (as alluded to previously) for growing food while also cleaning the air by allowing plants linked through the HVAC system to remove carbon dioxide. The plants would also add to the reduction of stress within the house, and if you want to, you can talk to the plants. Many people do.

Our diets will change for many reasons, one being that it's increasingly obvious that the traditional meat industry is unsustainable. The alternatives to meat have not yet, for many people, passed the taste test, but this will be conquered by 2030. As we write this, a new start-up Hoxton Farms suggests that the missing ingredient is fat. Present meat alternatives are based on plant oils such as coconut and palm oil which have large environmental drawbacks with deforestation and destroying biodiversity and contributing to climate change. As Ed Steele explains their approach of growing animal fat without the animals is:

> What sets us apart is the fundamental philosophy that the only way to grow cells cost-effectively at scale is to combine the power of mathematical modelling with synthetic biology.
>
> *(O'Hear, 2021)*

You may have a zero-waste food recycler which converts household waste to fertiliser for your BioWall where you grow some food and spices.

Will we have robots or robotic arms cooking your meals by 2030? Sony has developed an AI kitchen helper arm that helps you cook – but it is unlikely to be in many home kitchens but by 2050 it may feature in some restaurants as an aid to chefs (Sony, 2019).

There are lots of science fiction films or TV series in which the food is produced by a replicator which is basically a 3-D printer. Already some companies produce chocolate and pasta made from sugar paste. Nearly everything can be printed if we have a paste of that food. But much of what is on offer now has a sugar base, so it is not too good for you; over time this will get better. Meanwhile, the first lab-grown meat, launched in 2013, took over two years and US$300,000 to produce (Ireland, 2019). Over the next ten years that may become a food you can print, even if only as a protest against the longstanding hegemony of cows, pigs, chickens, buffalo, deer, and fish. Will this mean less pressure on land for farming?

A future oven will be able to set the temperature for cooking to the right pre-heat, then bake food as you like it, and turn itself off afterwards. Not too far in the future this might see the end of burned or undercooked meals.

The oven and cooktop burners will link to your smartphone, so you do not even have to be in the kitchen watching and waiting for the meal to be ready, although your local fire marshal might prefer that you were. The oven might even link to your VR headset if you are wearing it, so even if you have lost your-self in a VR programme you will know the food is ready.

During the pandemic we have seen online courses by famous chefs, but a future kitchen might have a famous chef via AR or VR or even a 3-D hologram come into your kitchen to help you cook. How amazing would that be?

As mentioned before, water shortages will be a critical issue by 2030. In water-stressed areas, homes will integrate an atmosphere water generator (AWG) that will extract water vapour from the air and generate freshwater to use in our kitchens and to drink. An AWG requires a lot of energy, so it will need a house that can generate excess energy. Those *Star Wars* buffs reading will remember that Luke Skywalker's uncle and aunt were moisture farmers on the planet Tatooine. This may become a job on planet Earth too.

There are two major water-using devices in the kitchen. The first is the dish-washer. In 2017, Electrolux launched a new dishwasher that only uses 0.4 litres of water compared with an Energy Star-rated dishwasher that uses 4 gallons of water. Water with energy savings will be a critical issue for all the dishwasher manufacturers as they compete to market their contributions to a greener kitchen. Henrik Sundstrom, head of Electrolux Sustainability, waxes enthusiastic:

> The green & clean Rack Type is an exciting new product. Not only is the heat-pump using carbon dioxide as the refrigerant but consuming only 0.4 liters of water a wash makes it quite literally the greenest and cleanest dishwasher on the market. It will have a significant positive impact on the environment while allowing professional users to save costs.
>
> *(Sundstrom, 2017)*

The other major water-using appliance – not always in the kitchen – is a washing machine. The two main requirements for a washing machine to work are energy and water, both of which the industry is trying to reduce. In commercial dry cleaners, the company Hydrofinity has already developed a washing system that uses 80 per cent less water. This advance should be reflected in home appliances by 2030 (Hydrofinity, 2020).

There is a new Samsung robot 'Bot Handy' that will take your dishes from the sink, put them into the dishwasher, will pick your clothes up, and put them in the clothes basket for cleaning. It is a cross between the smart vacuum and a kind of security camera and a robotic assistant and arm (Tangermann, 2021).

Clothes are also being developed by new start-ups that require less washing. One of their brands Pangaia (Gaia is the Greek god who represents the Earth) has developed a seaweed fibre T-shirt that requires less washing and, according to them, saves about 3,000 litres of water over its lifetime compared to a normal cotton T-shirt.

Intelligent clothes are another development. By 2030, clothes could be tagged, possibly even with a GPS. They could tell you how the product was made and where it came from and also contribute to a circular economy by saying how to dispose of it (Gill, 20220).

The Defense Advanced Research Projects Agency (DARPA) has been pushing the envelope in looking for new diagnostic tools for early detection of pathogens (including SARS-CoV-2) by using advanced fabrics. These bio-based agents are applied directly to the body where they can neutralise injurious chemical and biological agents before they can do damage (DARPA, 2020).

A washing machine would be able to tell if you have been playing a sport or been to the gym and therefore work out what type of stain your clothes have and use a predicted washing powder and washing cycle to determine the amount of water needed to clean the stains.

> The extent of intelligence can be divided into three subgroups: a) Passive smart textiles can only sense the environment, b) active smart textiles can sense the stimuli from the environment and also react to them, c) very smart textiles take a step further, having the gift to adapt their behaviour to the circumstances.
>
> *(Abeliotis et al., 2015)*

Living rooms in 2030

> Half the world's smartphone users predict that by 2025 we will all be wearing lightweight, fashionable AR glasses. Consumers also predict wearables that can instantly translate languages, allow us to control our sound environment and experience smell, taste, textures, and temperature digitally.
>
> *(Ericsson's, 2019)*

Ultimately the house of the future would be designed to improve your quality of life. The lighting for particular rooms would learn what you like best and at what point in the day. AI and the IoT at the centre of your house would be easily accessed and used.

Traditionally since the invention of the TV (some would say the radio) living rooms have been places for families and individuals to congregate in the evening. The living room is the main room for relaxing, even in households where that means together catching up on the news or favourite TV programmes.

It is hard to imagine that in the 1960s in the US there were only three TV channels (ABC, CBS, and NBC). This would change in 1972 when the nation's first pay-TV network was set up: Home Box Office (HBO), supported by a national satellite system. The second company to use the satellites was a local TV station in Atlanta, owned by Ted Turner, perhaps most famous for launching the Cable News Network (CNN) in 1980.

By 2021 our options of TV entertainment seem infinite, with more channels than we could have ever imagined. The TV also has been adapted to be used by the gaming world where:

> Over 164 million adults in the United States play video games and three-quarters of all Americans have at least one gamer in their household.
>
> *(Entertainment Software Association, 2020)*

The living room which used to have a TV is now also a home theatre and games room. By 2030 it will be a place to immerse yourself in AR and VR. House walls of the future will likely double for cinema or gaming screens. It can help make smaller and more variable houses or flats.

With the COVID-19 pandemic of 2020/21, many people not displaced from service jobs entirely were required to work from home. This also accelerated the use of the living room as a home office.

If the home office was not the living room, it was a dining room or a spare bedroom. What is clear is the house of 2030 would need to not only accommodate entertainment, and leisure but also somewhere to work from. Twitter announced during the COVID-19 pandemic that:

> 'If our employees are in a role and situation that enables them to work from home and they want to continue to do so forever, we will make that happen', but 'If not, our offices will be their warm and welcoming selves, with some additional precautions, when we feel it's safe to return'.
>
> *(Frier and Bloomberg, 2020)*

By 2030 some houses will benefit from being able to reconfigure or repurpose a room for different times in the day and different roles. Our beds can already be repurposed to give us a massage after a hard day working in the lounge (office).

> Our homes will become our haven, workspace, and entertainment spaces too – since [they] will be in use 24/7. So future homes will need to be able to easily adapt to changing needs throughout the day. Flexible floor plans, movable walls, ceilings that rise – completely transformable [houses] to let us be ready for whatever we need.
>
> *(Miller, 2017)*

Home office of the future

> VR enables you to transport your consciousness from one place to another. Most importantly, you can be in that place with someone else from anywhere in the world. There are a few different kinds of VR meeting

environments, depending on what you need. From 3D data visualisation to collaborative VR animation and creating experiences or just for the fun of it.

(Steamed Egg, 2020)

The home office of 2030 will rely even more on the need for the best Wi-Fi signal. The introduction of 5G in the early 2020s will see speeds up to 20 times faster than the present 4G. Estimates are it will be around 2030 that 6G will start to be introduced with even better bandwidth and speed (Fisher, 2020).

Several companies such as Microsoft and Google are working on Holoportation, which is a 3-D representation of a person which the systems compress and transmit to anywhere in real real-time. This uses augmented reality to display information or people. The technology will be used for education and health, but you may also be able to have a coffee with a convincing simulacrum (likeness) of your coworker or boss. As the Twitter quote above suggests, the COVID-19 pandemic has seen many companies reassess whether workers must be in office blocks or if they might be more productive working from home. The 2020 COVID-19-induced lockdown also made remote learning part of many children's lives, and Holoportation might well add to the remote learning experience by 2030.

Facebook CEO Mark Zuckerberg said on 21 May 2020 that he expected half of Facebook workers to remotely work by 2030 (Byers, 2020).

Are you ready for your boss to come to your house by hologram through a VR set to have a virtual coffee with you, or does that prospect seem deeply unsettling?

Holoportation had one of its most prominent outings in the 2008 US election where CNN used it during the night to transport Jessica Yellin from the Obama celebration in Grant Park in Chicago to the studio:

> 'CNN's Jessica Yellin appears live as a hologram before anchor Wolf Blitzer Tuesday night in New York' [the promotional caption read]. 'I want you to watch what we're about to do', CNN anchor Wolf Blitzer told viewers early in the evening's coverage, 'because you've never seen anything like this on television'.

And he was right. Cue CNN political correspondent Jessica Yellin.

> 'Hi Wolf!' said Yellin, waving to Blitzer as she stood a few feet in front of him in the network's New York City studios. Or at least, that is the way it appeared at first glance.
>   Yellin – a correspondent who had been covering Sen. Barack Obama's campaign – was at the now president-elect's mega-rally along the lakefront in Chicago, Illinois, more than 700 miles away from CNN's Election Center in New York.

> It looked like a scene straight out of *Star Wars*.
>
> *(Welch, 2008)*

Whether it is a hologram into your house or an avatar of you into a meeting of the firm from your home, technology will reduce the need for travel and by doing so reduce the impact on climate change. Whether it will dull or sharpen the quest for authentic unmediated experience remains to be seen.

Robots in the home

> Our robots are well-known for their ability to bond with humans, and therefore make excellent platforms for studying eldercare and other medical applications.
>
> *(Hanson Robotics, 2020)*

Sophia the Robot, initially activated on 14 February 2016, is one of the most well-known robots, and the first robot to receive citizenship from a country, Saudi Arabia (2017). A product of Hanson Robotics, Sophia is designed to look humanoid. According to its inventor, David Hanson, it was modelled on Queen Nefertiti, Audrey Hepburn, and the inventor's wife. Sophia was designed to assist with home help and education.

The initial promotion of the Sophia robot focused on it being a 'social robot', or possible companion for older people living alone or in nursing homes and able to complete certain tasks. With an ageing population in developed countries adding around an extra 20 per cent of over 65s to the population, social and health robots may be an important part of someone's quality of life.

A smaller, cheaper robot aimed at the education market is called 'Little Sophie'. Hanson Robotics hopes it will help with teaching STEM (science, technology, engineering, and maths) subjects for children eight years and older.

> Sustainable Development Goal 16: Promote peaceful and inclusive societies for sustainable development, provide access to justice for all and build effective, accountable, and inclusive institutions at all levels.

Hanson is by no means the only company working on robots and not even in the top ten to watch according to 'The Robot Report', which identified some others that may soon find their way into the home or supporting our homes:

1. Amazon: Looking to create Alexa on wheels (Hickman, 2018).
2. Boston Dynamics: SpotMini was used in the COVID-19 pandemic in some countries to ask people to disperse in parks. Its portfolio, though focused on the military use, also has plans to move into home help for the elderly – particularly with telemedicine (Boston Dynamics, 2020).
3. Cruise Automation: Focuses on robot delivery of food.

4. Facebook: They have a patent for a 'telepresence' robot.
5. Harvard's Wyss Institute Bioinspired Soft Robotics Labs: Has developed a RoboBee – a flying microbot half the size of a paper clip.
6. NVIDIA: Developing the go-to brain for the next generation of robots.
7. UBTech: A robot to work in any home or business.

We already have single purpose 'soft robots' in many houses in 2021 such as the Roomba cleaning and mopping robots. It is unlikely that the robots of 2030 will be developed as far as a moving robot able to prepare, cook, and clean … but maybe by 2040:

> There will be robot chefs than can follow recipes precisely and make any dish, using smart, connected ovens and cookers that can be turned on remotely and which know themselves which temperature to use and which sense when cooking is complete.
>
> After you have eaten, robot arms will scrape, rinse and load dishes into a dishwasher (essentially the dishwasher will load itself, wash the plates, cutlery and glasses and then will empty itself and re-stack the cupboard shelves).
>
> *(Hammond, 2019)*

For those who are worried about security, the 'robot dog' may replace the friendly mutt. In 2019, Boston Dynamics has been working with Massachusetts State Police with their robot dog Spot.

By 2030 these may be available in some form for home security (SDG16), although they are usually not cuddly. They do raise issues of potential liability if a person goes on to a property and is attacked by one.

References

Abeliotis, K., Amberg, C., Candan, C., Rainer, S. Ferri, A., Osset, M., & Owens, J. (2015) Trends in Laundry by 2030. Detergents. Available online at: https://www.research gate.net/publication/283211740_Trends_in_laundry_by_2030#fullTextFileContent

Alexa, A. (2019) Will Transparent Wood Become a Viable Construction Material? Quoting éline Montanari. *Core* 77. Available online at: https://www.core77.com/po sts/88157/Will-Transparent-Wood-Become-a-Viable-Construction-Material

Allen, S. (2019) Social Media's Growing Impact on Our Lives. American Psychological Association. Available online at: https://www.apa.org/members/content/social-me dia-research

Andoni, M., Robu, M., Flynn, D., Abram, S., Geach, D., Jenkins, D., McCallum, P., & Peacock, A. (2019) Blockchain Technology in the Energy Sector: A Systematic Review of Challenges and Opportunities. *Renewable and Sustainable Energy Reviews*, 10, 143–174, Elsevier. Available online at: https://www.sciencedirect.com/science/ar ticle/pii/S1364032118307184

Boston Dynamics. (2020) Telemedicine. *Boston Dynamics*. Available online at: https://www.bostondynamics.com/spot/applications

Buchanan, C.R., Wilson, B., Buddemeier, R.R., & Butler, Jr. R.R., (2018) The High Plains Aquifer, Kansas Geological Survey Public Information Circular (PIC) 18. Available online at: http://www.kgs.ku.edu/Publications/pic18/index.html

Bulger, A. (2017) What Life is Going to be Like for Your Kids in 2030, According to a Leading Futurist. *Fatherly.* Available online at: https://www.fatherly.com/parenting/kids-life-2030-futurist/ https://www.weforum.org/agenda/2016/11/5-predictions-for-energy-in-2030/

Burston, J. (2016) 5 Predictions for Energy in 2030. *World Economic Forum.* Available online at: 5 predictions for energy in 2030 | World Economic Forum (weforum.org)

Byers, D. (2020) Mark Zuckerberg: Half of Facebook May Work Remotely by 2030. *CNBC News.* Available online at: https://www.nbcnews.com/tech/tech-news/mark-zuckerberg-half-facebook-may-work-remotely-2030-n1212081

CB Insights. (2019) How Blockchain Technology Could Disrupt Real Estate. *CB Insights.* Available online at: https://www.cbinsights.com/research/blockchain-real-estate-disruption/

Chen, F. (2019) Imagining Our Future Through Tech. *a16z.* Available online at: https://a16z.com/2019/12/30/life-in-2030/

Chicago Department of Public Health, Lurie Children's. (2019) *Chicago Parents Identify the Top 10 Social Issues Affecting Youth in the City.* Chicago Department of Public Health. Available online at: https://www.luriechildrens.org/en/voices-of-child-health-in-chicago/Top10SocialIssues/

Curry's. (2019) What to Expect in the Kitchen of 2030. *Currys.* Available online at: https://techtalk.currys.co.uk/kitchen-home/what-to-expect-in-the-kitchen-of-2030/

Defense Advanced Research Projects Agency. (2020) Voices from DARPA #26 - The Eclectic Biotechnician. DARPA. Available online at: https://www.darpa.mil/news-events/2020-05-14

Del Valle, G. (2018) Millennials prioritize Owning a Home Over Getting Married or having Kids. *DeVox.* Available online at: https://www.vox.com/the-goods/2018/10/10/17959808/millennial-homeownership-student-loans-rent-burden

DeMarco, P. (2019) Housing in 2030 According to Futurists. *The News Herald.* Available online at: https://www.morganton.com/mnh/housing-in-2030-according-to-futurists/article_a306ffbc-9496-535a-89dd-b2b502c6edf0.html

Entertainment Software Association. (2020) 2019 Essential Facts About the Computer and Video Game Industry. Entertainment Software Association. Available online at: https://www.theesa.com/esa-research/2019-essential-facts-about-the-computer-and-video-game-industry/

Ericsson Consumer Lab. (2019) *10 Hot Consumer Trends 2030.* Ericsson Consumer Lab. Available online at: https://www.ericsson.com/4ae13b/assets/local/reports-papers/consumerlab/reports/2019/10hctreport2030.pdf

Euromonitor International (2018) *The Future Consumer Households in 2030.* Euromonitor International. Available online at: http://go.euromonitor.com/rs/805-KOK-719/images/sbFutureConsumerHouseholds2030.pdf

Fisher, T. (2020) 6G: What It is & When to Expect It. *Lifewire.* Available online at: https://www.lifewire.com/6g-wireless-4685524

Frier, S., & Bloomberg (2020) Twitter CEO Gives Employees The Choice To Work From Wherever They Want—Indefinitely. *Fortune.* Available online at: https://fortune.com/2020/05/13/twitter-work-from-home-covid-19/

Fuller, B. (2012) Buckminster Fuller's Synergy Solutions for Today. Available online at: http://www.buckyfullernow.com/blog---a-fuller-view---wwbs-what-would-bucky-say/the-best-way-to-predict-the-future-is-to-invent-it-buckminster-fuller

Gill, A. (2020) comments in peer reviewing the chapter

Google. (2020) Help Your Family Create Healthy Digital Habits. Google. Available online at: https://families.google.com/familylink/

Hanson Robotics. (2020) Sophia 2020 – A Vision for Robots Who Can Help People. *Hanson Robotics*. Available online at: https://www.hansonrobotics.com/sophia-2020-a-vision-for-robots-who-can-help-people/

Hanson Robotics. (2020) What can Little Sophia do? *Hanson Robotics*. Available online at: https://www.hansonrobotics.com/little-sophia-2/

Hammond, R. (2019) *The World in 2040 The Future of Healthcare, Mobility, Travel and the Home*. Allianz Partners. Available online at: https://www.allianz-partners.com/content/dam/onemarketing/awp/azpartnerscom/reports/futorology/Allianz-Partners-The-World-in-2040-Health-Care-Wellbeing-Report.pdf

Hickman, R. (2018) Amazon Consumer Robot: Why A Mobile Echo Show Makes Sense. *The Robot Report*. Available online at: https://www.therobotreport.com/amazon-consumer-robot-mobile-echo-show/

Holder, M. (2019) 2030 Goals: Mattel Aims for 100% Recycled and Recyclable Toys. *Greenbiz*. Available online at: https://www.greenbiz.com/article/2030-goals-mattel-aims-100-recycled-and-recyclable-toys

Hydrofinity. (2020) Hydrofinity Washing System: 1 Billion Litres of Water Saved and Counting… *Hydrofinity*. Available online at: http://www.hydrofinity.com/blog/1-billion-litres-of-water-saved

Ireland, T. (2019) The Artificial Meat Factory – The Science of your Synthetic Supper. *Science Focus*. Available online at: https://www.sciencefocus.com/future-technology/the-artificial-meat-factory-the-science-of-your-synthetic-supper/

Jones, J., & Zdanowicz, C. (2019) A Massachusetts Police Department Just Became the First in the Nation to Test a Robot Dog Named Spot. *CNN*. Available online at: https://www.cnn.com/2019/11/26/us/police-test-robot-dog-spot-trnd/index.html

Julian, K. (2020) What Happened to American Childhood? *The Atlantic*. Available online at: https://www.theatlantic.com/magazine/archive/2020/05/childhood-in-an-anxious-age/609079/

Katanich, D. (2020) The Three Largest Toy Manufacturers are Phasing Out Plastic Bit by Bit. *Euronews*. Available online at: https://www.euronews.com/living/2020/04/13/toymakers-appeal-to-eco-conscious-generation-with-sustainable-changes

Kohler. (2020) Moxie Shower Head. *Kohler*. Available online at: https://www.us.kohler.com/us/moxie-2.0-gpm-single-function-showerhead-with-wireless-speaker/productDetail/showerheads/867508.htm

Labbadi, A. (2019) The Combination of Blockchain and Smarthomes by Gerald Fenech. *Forbes*. Available online at: https://www.forbes.com/sites/geraldfenech/2019/01/21/the-combination-of-blockchain-and-smarthomes/#471c07fba2c4

LaRosa, J. (2018) Top 6 Things to Know About the $28 Billion Sleep Market. *Market Research.com*. Available online at: https://blog.marketresearch.com/top-6-things-to-know-about-the-28-billion-sleep-market

Lawrence, G. (2020) peer reviewer of this chapter

Marsh, J.A. (2020) Solar Panel Windows. *Energsage*. Available online at: https://news.energysage.com/solar-panel-windows-solar-blinds/

Martinez, P. (2017) Bitcoin Mining Consumes More Energy than 159 Countries. *CBS News*. Available online at: https://www.cbsnews.com/news/bitcoin-mining-energy-consumption/

Miller, A. (2017) What Homes in 2030 Will Look Like … You Ready? *VERUX*. Available online at: https://blog.veluxusa.com/professional/future-what-homes-in-2030-will-look-like...you-ready

Miller, M. (2018) Here's How Much Cities Contribute to the World's Carbon Footprint. *Scientific American*. Available online at: https://www.scientificamerican.com/article/heres-how-much-cities-contribute-to-the-worlds-carbon-footprint/#:~:text=The %20bulk%20of%20a%20country%E2%80%99s%20consumption-related%20carbon %20emissions,nearly%2010%20percent%20of%20the%20country%E2%80%99s%2 0overall%20footprint

Murphy, M. (2015) Google Could Turn Your Home's Walls into Screens. *Quartz Daily Brief*. Available online at: https://qz.com/388002/google-could-to-turn-your-ho mes-walls-into-screens/

O'Hear, S. (2021) Quote Ed Steele in Hoxton Farms Raises Gbp2.7 Million Seed to Produce Animal Fat Without Animals. *Techcrunch*. Available online at: https://techcru nch.com/2021/02/09/hoxton-farms/?mc_cid=a5f617daf7&mc_eid=36b1542376 &guccounter=1

Ortutay, B. (2020) Working from Home post-COVID-19? Facebook, Apple, Twitter and Microsoft Embracing Remote Work. Associated Press. Available online at: https:// www.usatoday.com/story/tech/2020/05/22/coronavirus-remote-work-post-pand emic/5242420002/

Perry. (2019) What's the Average Age Kids See Internet Pornography? (Quite Young). *We Stand Guard*. Available online at: https://www.westandguard.com/what-s-the-average-age-kids-see-internet-pornography-quite-young

Rizvi, S. (2021) How Artificial Intelligence Can Support Food Security. *ITP.net*. Available online at: https://www.itp.net/security/95059-how-artificial-intelligence-can-support-food-security

Robitzeki, D. (2020) Mind-Melting AI Makes Frank Sinatra Sing "Toxic" by Britney Spears. *Futurism*. Available online at: https://futurism.com/mind-melting-ai-frank-si natra-toxic-britney-spears

Rochat, E. (2020) An Overview of Residential Rainwater Harvesting, PerfectWater. Available online at: https://4perfectwater.com/blog/overview-of-residential-rainw ater-harvesting/

Rowlatt, J. (2021) How Bitcoin's Vast Energy Use Could Burst Its Bubble. *BBC News*. Available online at: https://www-bbc-co-uk.cdn.ampproject.org/c/s/www.bbc.co. uk/news/amp/science-environment-56215787

RTS. (2020) Food Waste in America in 2020. RTS Partners. Available on line at: https:// www.rts.com/resources/guides/food-waste-america/

Seura. (2020) Hydra Indoor Waterproof TV. Seura. Available online at: https://www.seu ra.com/products/indoor-waterproof-tvs/

Shier, L (2018) Shared Housing Startups are on the rise. *Elegran*. Available online at: https:// www.elegran.com/blog/2018/06/shared-housing-startups-are-on-the-rise

Sony. (2019) Sony Launches New AI Unit for Creation of Robotic Kitchen. *Al Jazeera*. Available online at: https://www.aljazeera.com/news/2019/11/sony-launches-ai-unit-creation-robotic-kitchen-191120141006908.html

SQ4D. (2021) First 3D Printed Home: SQ4D Builds the World's Largest 3D Printed Home. *SQ4D*. Available online at: https://www.sq4d.com/portfolio-items/first-3d-printed-home/

Statista. (2020) *Average Number of Own Children Under 18 in Families with Children in the United States from 1960 to 2019*. Statista. Available online at: https://www.statista.com/statistics/718084/average-number-of-own-children-per-family/

Steamed Egg. (2020) 5 Exciting Virtual Reality Business Opportunities – How to Use VR in Your Business. *Steamed Egg*. Available online at: https://steamedegg.co.uk/5-exciting-virtual-reality-business-opportunities-how-to-use-vr-in-your-business/

Stephens-Borg, R. (2019) 5 High-Tech Contact Lens that Could Change The World. *Lenstore*. Available online at: https://www.lenstore.co.uk/eyecare/5-high-tech-contact-lenses-could-change-world

Steven, E., Saleh, R.W., Lebedev, v., Acquah, F.A.S., Laukhin, C., Alamo, G.R., & Brooks, S.J. (2013) Carbon Nanotubes on a Spider Silk Scaffold. *Nature Communications*. Available online at: https://www.nature.com/articles/ncomms3435

Stripe, M. (2018) How Our Clothing Choices Impact Our Environment and Physical Health. *Women's Voices for the Earth*. Available online at: https://www.womensvoices.org/2018/03/21/how-our-clothing-choices-impact-our-environment-and-physical-health/

Sundstrom, H. (2017) Electrolux New Dishwasher Runs on a Glass of Water. Electrolux. Available online at: https://www.electroluxgroup.com/en/electrolux-new-dishwasher-runs-on-a-glass-of-water-23817/

Tangermann, V. (2021) Watch a Samsung Robot Load Dirty Dishes into the Dishwasher. *The Byte*. Available online at: https://futurism.com/the-byte/samsung-bot-handy-dishwasher

The Tiny Life. (2020) What is the Tiny House Movement? *The Tiny Life*. Available online at: https://thetinylife.com/what-is-the-tiny-house-movement/

The Verge. (2020) Walmart Will Use Fully Driverless Trucks to Make Deliveries in 2021. *The Verge*. Available online at: https://www.theverge.com/2020/12/15/22176179/walmart-fully-driverless-box-truck-delivery-gatik

Thornton, A. (2019) 10 Cities are Predicted to Gain Megacity Status by 2030. World Economic Forum. Available online at: https://www.weforum.org/agenda/2019/02/10-cities-are-predicted-to-gain-megacity-status-by-2030

UNEP. (2019) *2019 Global Status Report for Buildings and Construction: Towards a Zero-Emissions, Efficient and Resilient Buildings and Construction Sector*. Nairobi: UNEP/IEA/Global Alliance for Buildings and Construction. Available online at: https://wedocs.unep.org/bitstream/handle/20.500.11822/30950/2019GSR.pdf?sequence=1&isAllowed=y

UNEP. (2016) *Policy Options for Decoupling Economic Growth from Water Use and Water Pollution*. Environment International Natural Resources Panel. Available online at: https://www.resourcepanel.org/reports/options-decoupling-economic-growth-water-use-and-water-pollution

UNFCCC. (2020) *The Paris Agreement*. Bonn: UNFCCC. Available online at: https://unfccc.int/process-and-meetings/the-paris-agreement/the-paris-agreement

UN Water. (2018) *Executive Summary – SDG 6 Synthesis Report 2018 on Water and Sanitation*. New York: UN Water. Available online at: https://www.unwater.org/publications/executive-summary-sdg-6-synthesis-report-2018-on-water-and-sanitation/

Water Institute. (2018) Water-Energy-Food and Climate Conference. Water Institute, University of North Carolina, Chapel Hill. Available online at: https://waterinstitute.unc.edu/conferences/nexus-2018/nexus-2018-materials/

Welch, C. (2008) Beam Me Up, Wolf! CNN Debuts Election-Night Hologram. *CNN*, Atlanta. Available online at: https://www.cnn.com/2008/TECH/11/06/hologram.yellin/

Williams, G. (2019) How to Estimate Utility Costs. *U.S.News*. Available online at: https://money.usnews.com/money/personal-finance/spending/articles/how-to-estimate-utility-costs

Zilbert, M. (2018) The Blockchain For Real Estate, Explained. *Forbes*, New York. Available online at: https://www.forbes.com/sites/forbesrealestatecouncil/2018/04/23/the-blockchain-for-real-estate-explained/#79f474c4781e

4

TRAVELLING AROUND

Introduction

> Travel is fatal to prejudice, bigotry, and narrow-mindedness, and many of our people need it sorely on these accounts. Broad, wholesome, charitable views of men and things cannot be acquired by vegetating in one little corner of the earth all one's lifetime.
>
> (Twain, 1874)

Travelling from our home to our work or to wherever we want to will change by 2030.

We have progressed through three industrial revolutions (now in our fourth) since the days of horse-drawn carriages. It was French inventor Nicolas-Joseph Cugnot (1769) who first invented a steam-powered carriage that could move four seated people and travel just over two miles per hour (a slow walk). Throughout the 19th century, there were further developments in the use of steam. In 1801, British inventor Richard Trevithick built what he called the Puffing Devil, which was the first roadworthy steam-driven vehicle. The Puffing Devil was limited by the unstable nature of its engine and by it having to be operated near water sources.

In 1807 Nicéphore Niépce developed the world's first internal combustion engine, which he called a Pyréolophore. Fascinatingly, the patent for it was granted by none other than Napoleon Bonaparte.

First-generation steam locomotives were criticised because they could damage roads weighed as much as 14 tons each. Another criticism was that they could go so fast, around 10 mph, surely a danger to everyone!

The Locomotion Act (1861) in the Parliament of the United Kingdom started the regulation of roadways. This Act passed in part because of the damage that

DOI: 10.4324/9781003045496-4

heavy steam-driven vehicles were doing to roadways. A subsequent Red Flag Act (1865) limited the number of passengers and required that someone with a 'red flag' walk at least 55 metres in front of the vehicle. This was possible because, at the time, speeds were limited to 2 mph in towns and 4 mph outside towns. There was no risk of being run over at those speeds. The Act also forbade vehicles from releasing steam while underway.

We mention this potted history of the early development of the automobile in the 19th-century technology to give us an understanding of where we have come from.

The car as we know it was first proposed by the German inventor Karl Benz in 1886, though automobile manufacturing only took off with the mass production of the Model T manufactured by the Ford Motor Company in 1908.

Travelling to work

> Powerful, global forces are fundamentally changing the way we live, work and travel at a rate we have never witnessed before.
>
> *(Guevara, 2019)*

The COVID-19 pandemic has forced several companies to rethink the way they do business. Do they need such large offices? Would employees be more efficient and benefit if they did not have to spend time travelling to work? Is travel to other cities or within cities for meetings with clients really necessary?

Sustainable Development Goal 8: Promote sustained, inclusive, and sustainable economic growth, full and productive employment, and decent work for all.

Writing this book in the middle of the pandemic undoubtedly means that our perception is coloured by that experience. What we have seen, as we explain in more detail in Chapter 5: Education, working life, and health is that a yet unknown proportion of the workforce (SDG8) will be able to work from home in the long term. These decisions will impact commercial real estate, as office space lies vacant or is reconfigured. A potentially emerging byproduct is the expansion of local 'hubs' where employees can gather to work outside of the home and have some social interaction. As many of us are coffee drinkers, we can imagine the further development of more cafés with space for people to work where you are charged not only for the coffee you drink but also for the time you spend there.

Sustainable Development Goal 3: Ensure healthy lives and promote well-being for all, at all ages.

The rigidity of the workday may also yield to more flextime, which is already being explored in return-to-work policies necessitated by the COVID-19 pandemic (SDG3) and 'social distancing'. By 2030, office meetings that would formerly have required a journey will more likely be conducted remotely using online meeting software.

> Sustainable Development Goal 11: Make cities and human settlements inclusive, safe, resilient, and sustainable.

If people are less tethered to offices to work, more people may move outside the cities (SDG11) as they seek a better quality of life for themselves and their family.

Travelling in cities

> What makes a city smart? One factor will be its transport system. This will be more of an integrated network of transport options requiring intelligent IoT solutions that optimize infrastructure and government to better engage citizens in the management of services. Sensors, networks, and applications collect data on energy usage, traffic volume and patterns, pollution levels, and other topics which are then analyzed and used to correct and predict usage and patterns. Making that data available to everyone through open-access systems allow citizens and businesses to leverage that information for their own purposes.
>
> *(Kosowatz, 2020)*

For many, the automobile has played a critical role in our lives as a means of taking us to work, to the supermarket, and out for entertainment, or visiting distant family members or friends. It is also for many people a status symbol – though that is changing with younger people.

> Sustainable Development Goal 13: Take urgent action to combat climate change and its impacts.

The cars of 2030 will increasingly or perhaps entirely be electric, with our impact on the climate (SDG13) being one of the large drivers to the acceleration of first hybrid and then electric cars. In February 2021 Ford announced for the European market that they would stop selling petrol and pure diesel cars in 2026 and work to then phase out hybrids (Krisher and Mchugh, 2021).

Another less talked about result will be the positive impact on pollution in our cities and a reduction in respiratory problems and deaths associated with them. The combination of more self-driving cars will reduce the number of road accidents and deaths of both passengers and pedestrians. The National Highway

CARTOON 4.1 The mom and the dad are in a self-driving car, probably working while commuting. They get stopped by a police officer and they pull down their window to speak to him

Safety Administration found that 94 per cent of car accidents are caused by driver mistakes (Burns, 2020).

Sustainable Development Goal 7: Ensure access to affordable, reliable, sustainable, and modern energy for all.

As we write this book (2021), we are about to go through a huge increase in the choice of electric cars. Virtually all the car manufactures are planning the release of 'affordable' electric cars (SDG7) in 2021 or 2022. In addition to moving to electric cars we are also seeing the development of fully automatic self-drive cars expanding in the next ten years. It is estimated that 1 in 10 cars will be self-driving by 2030. These cars utilise AI and big data and analytics and are linked through your personal IoT to ensure they are safe – though it is worth mentioning there are no grade 5 (fully automatic cars) on the market – yet (Reese, 2020).

In the US, estimates are that at least 20 per cent (by 2030) of new car sales will be electric (Lambert, 2018). Given the relationship between electric car production and taxpayer-funded subsidy, this percentage may increase substantially depending on who is US president in the period 2025 to 2030 (EEI, 2018).

Sustainable Development Goal 6: Ensure availability and sustainable management of water and sanitation for all.

Toyota, Honda, and Hyundai have been exploring this as an alternative way to power cars. An advantage for hydrogen at present could be that the existing petrol or gasoline stations could be converted into hydrogen cell replacement centres. However, the transition period for petrol/gasoline stations would also have to provide the hydrogen cell replacements which would be challenging. Perhaps the most important advantage is that the fuel cell uses hydrogen and water (SDG6) to generate the electrical current, with the byproduct being water vapour. The car itself is also potentially more efficient and reliable than cars we currently drive.

On the other hand, disadvantages of a hydrogen car have to do with its safety – the need to deep cool the hydrogen and compress it coupled with the limited infrastructure range, as implied by the fact that in the US there were only 61 private hydrogen stations by the end of 2019 (Siddigui, 2020). In the UK, there are 17 stations (Nicoll, 2019). Exploring the disadvantage of hydrogen-powered cars and the public worry about their safety, Nicoll observed in 2019:

> Hydrogen is an explosive gas.
>
> *(Nicoll, 2019)*

Due to the Hindenburg disaster of 1937, a hydrogen Zeppelin has a long historical shadow. Nevertheless, it is worth noting that many survived the mid-air fire at a 100 m altitude – unlike present-day aircraft crashes.

Sustainable Development Goal 9: Build resilient infrastructure, promote inclusive and sustainable industrialisation, and foster innovation.

The European Union Directorate-General (DG) for Internal Market, Industry, Entrepreneurship and SMES (DG-GROW) worked with Hydrogen Europe to organise a conference in October 2019. One of the key strategic value chains for the conference was:

> EU Strategy: Develop a joint European wide vision and (integrated, concerted) masterplan/roadmap for a future European Hydrogen Economy and ensure a coordinated approach of the EU, national and regional support to the H2 technologies. To do so, also create and agree on a joint decision base.
>
> *(Hydrogen4climate action, 2019)*

The conference saw investment pledges from European countries of US$56 billion for research into hydrogen and its infrastructure (Nicoll, 2019).

Elon Musk has called hydrogen-fuel cell technology 'fool cells' (Garret, 2020). Is this a reasonable scientific assessment, or simply a worry that his Tesla company might face a competing technology?

Could this be a similar argument to the old one between VHS and Betamax over which video player system was best? Betamax had better picture quality but did not record for more than an hour in the beginning, while VHS could record for two and then up to six hours. The deciding factor was that JVC, which produced the first VHS recorder, built a relationship with the motion picture houses that then produced movies to buy or rent on VHS.

Back in 2009 electric and hydrogen cars technologies were competing neck and neck. The difference in the years since then has been the development of battery technology – something Tesla has utilised very effectively in their disruption of the electric automobile market by producing cars that could go over 300 miles (and counting) before recharging. They also helped build a recharging infrastructure in each US State. Solid state batteries are coming on the market soon which can improve the range to up to 1000 Km, and recharge in less than ten minutes. Finally, there is the ability, by 2030, to power your battery from solar panels on your roof, which would make it virtually free. It is difficult to see how hydrogen cars could catch up.

Setting up a good recycling system for the batteries of electric cars will help reuse the critical earth elements cobalt and lithium which are available through most of the reserves of cobalt which are found in the at times unstable Democratic Republic of Congo. Electric vehicles also use two precious earth metals gold and silver but in small minute amounts on circuit boards – both fully recyclable.

Augmented reality (AR) technology will be integrated into the windscreens (Americans call them 'windshields'), allowing the driver instant real-time information not only about the journey but any nearby stores or restaurants they might eat at.

The idea of driverless cars will not appeal to everyone – at least not by 2030. If we don't have to drive our cars, then we will have time to do other things while we journey. That could be entertainment with videos or even a workspace to start the workday before you arrive at the office. Those on lengthy commutes today are often seen working in cramped space on a train or the metro. That may become a more pleasant experience in a self-drive car with a designed workspace. It could also enable you to have the opportunity to have some time to read that great book (like this one) you have been wanting to read or even start writing your own book as you improve your quality of life, regain time previously lost travelling.

Hacking of autopilots is a serious concern as witnessed in 2019 when Chinese hackers modified Tesla's self-driving software and caused the cars to swerve into the oncoming traffic lane. In that case the hack was undertaken by 'white hackers' – these are those that were from Keen Security Labs who were researching security faults. In 2020 autopilot software is not fully autonomous, but that should change by 2030. The security of the autopilot will need to be very robust against the threat of potential hackers (Huddleston, 2019).

Taxis and Air Taxis: As mentioned before, it is estimated that 1 in 10 vehicles will be autonomous (that is, self-driving) by 2030 (Friedrich, 2020). By the time the last of Generation Z (born 1995–2012) will have started working (2030), will they even own a car? As autonomous taxis become more available, the estimate of the cost of a taxi ride is 80 per cent less than the same trip with one person driving. According to AAA, owning a car in 2017 costs on average US$8,469, assuming 15,000 mileage. A taxi ride in North Carolina from Apex to Raleigh (a journey of 21 miles) now costs US$50. For a robotaxi, that would be approximately US$10 on today's costings. Using a 'robotaxi' for a roundtrip every weekday would cost nearly half of what owning a car would at US$4800. In that case, why have a car? This would enable a generation to become free with no responsibility for a vehicle and its maintenance.

In 2018 Waymo started its self-driving taxi service called 'Waymo One' in one neighbourhood in Phoenix, Arizona. The cars are completely driverless and can be requested on an app as you would a normal taxi. Waymo, by the way, is owned by Google. Big tech companies like Amazon, Tesla, Uber, Google are investing and buying start-ups (for example, Amazon has recently acquired Zoox, a company developing self-driving cars). There has developed a kind of 'arms race' around self-driving cars by these companies.

Air taxis have been the dream of children and science fiction-focused adults since the 1950s. On 28 July 2020 New Hampshire became the first US State to allow you to register your 'flying car'. The bill NH HB1517 was nicknamed the 'Jetsons Bill' after the 1960's Hanna-Barbera animated production futuristic sitcom – a space-age equivalent to *The Flintstones*. Uber Air is aiming initially for a set of Skyports in cities to board these air taxis. In December 2020 it unveiled its air taxi at the GITEX Technology Week in Dubai. The air taxi can fly up to 100 Km on a five-minute charge and go up to speeds of 290 kph. It is expected to be available in the commercial market by 2028.

An Indian competitor company, Skai plans to land on rooftops or parking lots by the mid-2020s. The electric vertical take-off and landing (eVTOL) pickup taxi will take you from the suburbs to the centre of a city.

The FAA has given approval for another flying car, the Terrafugia Transition, which can fly at 100 mph and at 10,000 feet. The prototype can achieve 35 mpg on the road and flies at a cruising speed of 100 mph with a range of 400 miles (Verdon, 2021).

By 2030 these air taxis are likely to be available in certain major cities with pilots taking four people above the traffic jams to transport hubs enabling them to get to other places in the city (Uber, 2020).

Buses and metro: In the US in 2018 there were 9.9 billion trips on public transport. In addition to buses and metro, this included: Commuter trains, water taxis and ferries, tramways and trolleys. In the US each week around 34 million people travel using one or more of these modes of public transport every day. Nearly half the US population doesn't have access to public transport. There is no question that mass transport reduces the carbon footprint. In 2018 it was estimated that 37 million metric tons of carbon emissions were saved through the utilising of public transport (American Public Transport Association, 2019).

AI/ICT and other new technology utilising big data and the IoT will help management, maintenance, planning, disruption-handling, passenger communication, and automation of urban rail systems. Driverless metros started in London in 1987 with the Docklands line which has been followed by other cities such as Paris.

In 2019 a Center for American Progress report argued that a future infrastructure bill could reduce CO_2 emissions by an additional 44 million metric tonnes by upgrading existing present public transport to low or zero emission vehicles (Costa et al., 2019).

Many buses and metro trains are already adding GPS technology to make wait times for buses more accurate and adding Wi-Fi to bus stops to help. The role of 5G will help this a lot.

In a report by Kantar (2020), the world's leading data, insights, and consulting company studied 31 of the world's largest cities to look at how mobility was changing and what it might look like by 2030. In these cities around 39 per cent of urban commuters travel by car to work. The research estimates that this will decrease by 10 per cent by 2030 as public transport increases. The survey suggested the following were best to deliver sustainability and convenience:

- Mobility-as-a-Service (MaaS) – this concept integrates multiple transport modes, such as buses, trams, bikes, and car sharing, into a single app and ticket to streamline multi-modal travel into a user experience that matches the convenience of a personal car.
- Bikes haven't escaped the link to the IoT and access to big data. In Copenhagen, cyclists can link to an app that tells them when the traffic lights will turn red or green and whether to slow down or increase their speed. The app also helps them to monitor their calories burnt, and links to their friends' health league tables – hopefully optional – as they bike to work too.
- Smart mobility hubs – connected to smart city development and located on the outskirts of cities, these hubs enable commuters to switch from polluting cars to zero-emission vehicles like electric buses, e-bikes, and e-scooters, to help decrease urban congestion and pollution. Dubai in 2020 already has

an AI monitoring system used by its bus drivers which has reduced traffic accidents.

- Autonomous parcel delivery – 'Self-driving delivery vehicles function as mobile parcel stations to reduce unsuccessful delivery journeys that significantly increase traffic congestion' (Kantar, 2020).

- 'By 2030 the battery electric bus fleet is expected to increase by at least 817,000. Another report, this time by IDTechEx, suggests that most of the buses will be electric as opposed to fuel cell. BloombergNEF estimate the figure to be much higher and in October 2020 the first electric intercity bus was launched. In 2020 also the first large electric school bus order was made with Thomas Built Buses and Proterra in the U.S' (Sustainable bus, 2021).

Major US cities and regional governments have set zero carbon targets for their buses by 2030 (Los Angeles) or 2040 (New York).

New York and 14 other US States, as well as the District of Columbia, are ramping up their electrification of buses. States involved are California, Connecticut, Colorado, Hawaii, Maine, Maryland, Massachusetts, New Jersey, North Carolina, Oregon, Pennsylvania, Rhode Island, Vermont, and Washington.

This is likely to spread to other major cities and regional government under the Biden Presidency and its green recovery plan.

New York governor Andrew Cuomo said:

> With a lack of federal leadership and an outright failure to follow science, it has fallen to the states to address the climate crisis by working together to eliminate greenhouse gas emissions from all sources.
>
> Reducing pollution from medium- and heavy-duty vehicles will result in cleaner air for New Yorkers, particularly low-income neighborhoods and communities of color that have historically and disproportionately borne the brunt of the worst environmental consequences. As New York continues to implement nation-leading climate initiatives, this multi-state agreement furthers the critical leadership roles of the states in combating climate change and establishes an example for other states to follow.
>
> *(Smart Energy International, 2020)*

In 2016 Amsterdam introduced, as an experiment, their first 'Future Bus', which is a fully semi-autonomous transport vehicle that runs along a Bus Rapid Transit route in Amsterdam. It does have a driver present to deal with any problems but basically is driverless. By 2030 many major cities globally will have these buses in use but probably still with a driver there in case of problems (*The Times of India*, 2019).

Travelling between cities

Travelling between cities is evolving and by 2030 will be using big data and analytics to help. Based on your previous travel history, algorithms will be able to offer the best options for your travel. For business travel, automatic review of proposed trips and comparison with your company's travel policies can ensure that the trip is in line with your preferences, your company's preferences, or both. This might include reducing the time of a business trip to its minimum and/or looking for the best travel option for the sake of limiting CO_2 emissions.

Airplanes: Applying big data in 2030 to air travel would include looking at the age of the planes that are on offer – though interestingly an old two-engine turboprop may be more fuel efficient than a newer twinjet regional jet – as well as the projected volume of CO_2 emissions per seat based on the percentage of seats sold or whether the flight is using synthetic fuels. Other factors include the use of alternative fuel and importantly, operational parameters such as availability of the most direct flight routing may have a much bigger impact.

Your whole journey might be processed through a blockchain. The use of blockchain – safely protecting your expenditure – in the travel industry is developing as a more secure payment for the services that are part of your travel, linking together any reward system you have for flights, taxis, or hotels into the blockchain, and enabling a travel plan secured into one place, therefore, saving time, money, and lessening the impact on the environment.

Travelling to the airport, in a driverless electric car or a driverless electric minibus, you might be thankful that your trip was shorter than expected, in part because your car or minibus would be totally aware of the traffic flows and be able to accurately predict its arrival time at the airport. The travel in 2030 with more driverless cars would see fewer accidents and therefore fewer traffic jams and probably fewer cars on the roads.

> Sustainable Development Goal 2: End hunger, achieve food security and improved nutrition, and promote sustainable agriculture.

As the issue of climate change moved up the international agenda, so did the issue of travelling and its contribution to CO_2 emissions. Earlier use of biofuels (2011) as a fuel for transport was recognised as a problem as it created a food v fuel (SDG2) debate with land being used for producing fuel instead of feeding people.

The airline industry has been working on synthetic or lower carbon fuels for a while – United Airlines started doing it using a mix of such fuels on a regular basis for flights between LA and San Francisco back in 2016.

On World Environment Day, 5 June 2019 United Airlines made history by flying the most eco-friendly commercial flight in aviation history.

> United became the first known airline to demonstrate all of the following key actions on a single commercial flight: utilization of sustainable aviation biofuel; zero cabin waste efforts; carbon offsetting; and operational efficiencies.

(United, 2019)

The flight used a 30/70 per cent blend of sustainable aviation fuel to traditional jet fuel.

Several pilot schemes are moving to scale on household waste to air fuel which reduces CO_2 emissions by up to 70 per cent and reducing landfill at the same time – a win–win. The latest venture by Essar and Fulcrum Bioenergy will be operational by 2025 in the North East of England and in addition to the carbon reduction it will reduce 90 per cent of particulates – improving air quality around airports as well (Money Control, 2021).

> Sustainable Development Goal 15: Protect, restore, and promote sustainable use of terrestrial ecosystems, sustainably manage forests, combat desertification, and halt and reverse land degradation and halt biodiversity loss.

Biofuels have a range of disadvantages, including potential damaging competition for land with nature (SDG15) and food production, a very high water consumption, high energy consumption, and lifecycle reductions of CO_2 ranging from 50 to 80 per cent. With aviation growing to ten times its current volume, and fuel consumption becoming at least five times current consumption, even 80 per cent reduction would mean constant CO2 emissions. To do better, it was the German government that looked deeper into synthetic fuels, also called electro- or e-fuels – which use CO_2, a little bit of water and renewable energy to produce kerosene (Schmidt et al., 2016).

When the CO_2 used in the Power-to-Liquids (PtL) process is directly captured from the atmosphere the carbon cycle can be fully closed and aviation being made literally climate neutral. The only real drawback is the high energy consumption for the process and – less energy consumption – for Direct Air Capture (German Environment Agency, 2016). Then the higher cost of the fuel would, by 2030, lead to about 10–20 per cent higher ticket prices as compared to a situation without e-fuels mixed in (Peeters, 2020).

Synthetic fuels, the next development, is where biotechnology takes the CO_2 out of the atmosphere and adds back to water to create short molecule fuels. Steve Oldham, CEO of Carbon Engineering, said in a 2019 Ted Talk and to the Senate Environment and Public Works Committee that:

> To understand where our technology fits, imagine that the atmosphere is simply a bathtub that holds all gases including carbon dioxide (CO_2). The world is measuring a higher and higher fill level on the amount of CO_2 in the bathtub, so in our attempts to decarbonize, we are trying to turn down the CO_2 tap.
>
> But the other way to deal with too much CO_2 in the atmospheric bathtub is to open up the drain. While there are natural carbon removal techniques like afforestation, never before have we been able to open up the bathtub drain at large scale through technical means.

(Oldham, 2019)

In June 2020, the first electric plane was certified by regulators in the European Union. It was a two-seater Pipistrel Velis Electro which has a range of up to 80 minutes and takes up to 70 minutes to recharge. Later in June 2020, the French government announced a €1.5 billion funding for R&D into developing engines that can run completely on biofuels or on hydrogen. These may not be able to do more than 100 miles range so it may be that other forms of transport are better. ZeroAvia, which is developing a hydrogen fuel cell aircraft that has already the potential of providing big medium-range and even long-range aircraft based on proven existing technology.

The funding is to develop ultra-efficient hybrid-electric or hydrogen planes for short-haul domestic or European flights. By 2030, short-haul planes will be on their way to be more carbon neutral or low carbon through waste to energy and on the way to all planes becoming carbon neutral by 2040. A major factor here will be battery weight and technology (Morgan, 2020).

Hydrogen is a promising potential source for Power-to-Liquids (PtL) for air transport; however, for propulsion it would require significant aircraft R&D, further development of fuel cell technology and liquid hydrogen tanks, modifications in aircraft design, and investment in fleet and hydrogen infrastructure. At this point it is unclear if there is a plan to address the issue of having the infrastructure and supply available in a range of origins and destinations. At the same time commercial aircraft have a long life and most of the current fleet has been grounded due to the pandemic – if and when these aircraft return to the skies, they will either require fossil fuels or, hopefully, PtL, which has the distinct advantage of being drop-in capable. One clear advantage of hydrogen propulsion is that it would reduce all GHGs almost to zero, while PtL would do that essentially for carbon dioxide (CO_2) (Lyle, 2020).

Airports: Travelling through airports became for many people an unpleasant experience in 2021. It was made even more unbearable by the pandemic. This accelerated the move towards automatic biometric checking and boarding authentication systems. AI applications will improve airport security by scanning some biometrics characteristics such as fingerprints, iris pattern, facial structure, your travel health certificate, and voice tonality. If your biometrics do not correspond to the information on your ticket, then a robot security guard will whisk you away to be vetted by a human being.

IATA's One ID programme is seeking to link one-time biometric data, your ticket, hotel reservation, car hire booking, etc., all in one record. Once you leave home, all the necessary partners on your trip – immigration, customs, airline, airport, hotel, car hire, etc. will know you have embarked on your trip and all the elements of your travel will be hopefully seamlessly linked. It will also be linked to blockchain for data management (Steele, 2020).

LaGuardia airport introduced their first robot security guard in 2018 with a mixed response from evaluators, including at least one who said:

It's upsetting to have that thing creep up on you.

(Sheehan, 2018)

When robots are not there to prompt obedience, they may be working at the airport information desk. British Airways introduced this functionality in Heathrow Terminal 5 in 2020.

More of the airport shops and restaurants will have moved to automatic service by 2030. Robots can already take your order and bring food to your table. They may also be booking your table while you're in the driverless car to the airport. As you go through security, your action of going through could let the restaurant know if you will be on time, and then the kitchen will be able to prepare food accordingly.

Gatwick Airport was one of the first airports to use AR-enabled apps to help the traveller navigate the airport, have up to date information on their flight and personalise offers available in the airport.

As the use of AI in airports and travel increases and improves the delivery of services, your flight times will also be more exact. AI will be able to identify any problems and help troubleshoot disruptions. You will be able to monitor real-time weather changes which might impact your flight and also monitor wait times at security or taxi ranks.

Hotels and Airbnb:

> As artificial intelligence becomes the forefront of the future, hotel rooms will no longer need so many amenities; they would be brought to you through voice command. China's Alibaba hotel group has been demonstrating how AI robots soon could be used to greet guests and provide in-room service. While this won't be the 'norm' just yet, it does pave the way for what other technological amenities we can expect to see.
>
> *(Canaterio, 2019)*

Travelling between cities and checking into a hotel or Airbnb in 2030 will be financially more secure and easier with blockchain, but what will the hotel experience be like?

Before you book, you may have used your virtual reality glasses to walk around the hotel or house/flat you are renting. In 2030 VR will be an important part of your booking process. No longer will there be well-taken photos of rooms that turn out to be converted broom closets. Travellers will expect to be able to do a quick VR walk around the facilities that are promoted for the hotel. They will be able to walk into the different bedrooms and get a feel for the size and what is on offer in the rooms. They can look out the window and see if it's a good view or just a brick wall. They may also be able to walk around the neighbourhood close by and see what shops or parks are available. According to a survey conducted in 2020 by Oracle, 66 per cent of consumers said that a VR tour of a property before they go there would improve their experience and 70 per cent of those surveyed:

> believe that ordering room or hotel services by voice recognition software will be widespread by 2025.
>
> *(Oracle, 2020)*

Virtual reality (VR) footage will be more readily available during the decision-making process, and guests can opt to see the VR footage with integrated guest reviews. More in-depth profiling on those leaving reviews will help deter fake or misleading reviews, and potential guests will be better able to determine the value of the reviewer's preferences based on advanced visibility of the reviewer's social footprint.

Just as in the airport example, hotels may scan guest biometrics as part of the check-in process. A hotel of 2030 may offer an opt-in to its own equivalent of 'Nextdoor' (a neighbourhood online hub), in this case a 'community' of people staying at the hotel at the time you are there. It will optionally or automatically link to your Facebook, Instagram, YouTube, and LinkedIn profiles. As the digital equivalent of a concierge, it would also have information about local restaurants, and sights, as well as activities in the hotel.

> Sustainable Development Goal 16: Promote peaceful and inclusive societies for sustainable development, provide access to justice for all and build effective, accountable, and inclusive institutions at all levels.

Similar to the Nextdoor business model, privacy settings would enable you to choose how much information you wanted to share, if any at all. If their own data share settings permitted it, you could ping someone you knew for a coffee or to meet someone who has similar interests in the hotel. If you have allowed access to your social media platforms (SDG16), the hotel might make recommendations of what you might enjoy doing in the city while you are there.

How would hotel bedrooms be different? As discussed in Chapter 3: Home life, the television will become part of a wall or a drop-down large glass screen where programmes would be projected. It could be linked to your own laptop to access any of your preferred platforms, so you can enjoy those in addition to what the hotel has to offer.

The room may be able to reconfigure itself to enable you to work and/or the hotel will provide flexible space for working and for building a community. If you are a regular traveller your travel profile would include what room temperature and what lighting you prefer in the room.

Hotels and other forms of commercial accommodation account for around 1–2 per cent of the global CO_2 emissions, so addressing their energy use is a critical part of moving towards carbon neutrality. For hotels this can be done by using renewable energy, jointly with energy efficiency measures. A smart hotel in 2030 will be able to monitor energy and water use throughout its property. Sensors in every room will enable the hotel to reduce or increase heat when needed. Rainwater harvesting – an old technology – would in many locales enable water captured to be used for toilets or watering vegetation and reduce the need to pull from clean water sources. Data and analytics will play a critical role in monitoring the use of water and energy in a hotel in 2030.

As mentioned in Chapter 3 on home life, future freezers and refrigerators will link through IoT to suppliers and reduce food waste as they will identify and even order items that need to be used.

Super Trains: In 2020, the average speed for Amtrak's flagship Acela Express in the US is 68 mph. The train can reach 150 mph on a small part of the line, but that is hardly fast by bullet train standards. Fast trains in other countries put the Acela Express to shame: France (198.8 mph), Japan (198.8 mph), Spain (217.4 mph), Italy (223.6 mph), and China (267.8 mph) all top the Amtrak number, not least because they run on dedicated tracks rather than on lines shared by passenger rail and freight rail (TMW, 2021). Scientists have even developed Maglev systems that have been designed to allow travel up to 1,800 kmh (New Atlas, 2014).

> Automation and artificial intelligence: real time management of the operation, along with new concepts such as virtual coupling and platooning, will support the increase of flexibility in operations. Autonomous trains and automated freight operation will bring additional predictability and versatility. All these elements together will support an increase of the capacity and resiliency of the system without major infrastructure investments, [they] will also lead to more end-user/citizen satisfaction from improved traffic management enabling better punctuality and comfort and more flexibility for real-time demand fulfilment.
>
> *(European Rail Research Advisory Council, 2019)*

The US has been behind other developed countries in upgrading their rail system. There were plans before President Trump was elected to develop a high-speed network. This may be revisited now under the President Biden recovery plan. In the US, railroad decisions are usually taken at the state level with federal support, as in the case of the California High-Speed Rail envisioned to run between Los Angeles and San Francisco with the help of a federal grant which the Trump administration cancelled. The US has 11 mega regions that rail activists want to link with a fast train system, but so far this has not been possible. If this changes by 2030, then it will reduce short-haul flights and carbon dioxide emissions. The success story of China introducing HSTs and the incredible growth rates of use is an example of this.

It is not just fast trains that are part of the equation for mass transit. The move in cars, trucks, and taxis is also being developed for autonomous trains systems.

In 2020, the longest automated metro system (124 miles) is the Singapore Mass Rapid Transit (MRT) system.

Another fascinating development has been the Hyperloop, for which two leading companies – Virgin and Space X – are competing. In November 2020, the Virgin Hyper Loop took out for a spin for its first 500 metres of a test strip in Las Vegas. The transport system is built around the vehicle in which the travellers are held in in a vacuum tube which can travel at speeds as high as 600 mph. Elon Musk's Boring Company has had verbal government approval that would see a Hyperloop between New York and Washington, hence bringing the journey time down to 29 minutes. The first longer distance Hyperloop may be built in a developing country first. This would be the Virgin Hyperloop between Mumbai and Pune – a distance of 75 miles apart is the furthest along the procurement of a service between two cities.

Because mobility generates a significant proportion of total carbon dioxide emissions, encouraging large numbers of people to use green mass transit will help reduce emissions. Already there are many examples of almost zero-emissions railways in Europe in Switzerland, Sweden, Norway, Netherlands, France, Austria, and parts of Germany. Who wants to be able to travel without emissions from the south of France to the north of Sweden at just a few kg of CO_2?

Returning to the fuel cell hydrogen tech that is now entering service in railways, it would enable refuelling stations at the central train depot, taking the place of refuelling with diesel. Hydrogen trains are a clean, sustainable, and flexible alternative (Ruf et al., 2019).

Travelling abroad

Before the COVID-19 pandemic, there were a number of assumptions about the growth of travel in general. After a 3 per cent increase in 2018, the Carlson Wagonlit Travel (CWT) Global Travel Forecast predicted in 2020 that travel would only increase by 2 per cent and in 2021 by only 2.1 per cent. The reason for that slower growth was attributed to an increased perception of insecurity in the world. To put this in context, in 1950 only 25 million people travelled internationally. In 2019 that figure was 37.79 million for US citizens alone, while the worldwide total was 1.4 billion (Our World in Data, 2020).

Mobile passports, facial recognition technology, automated check-in and checkout for hotels, just like with domestic travel, will be part of our daily experience with big data and analytics playing an increasing role. As with domestic travel, the international traveller of 2030 will be using VR to look at their hotel and places they want to visit. It will enable them to get the most [out] of any trip. They may be wearing AR glasses which will give them additional information on historical sites they visit. The IoT will give them access to the information they need. Machine learning will converge with the use of AR to create a more 'hands-free experience' (Dajee, 2017).

Travelling for pleasure

As expressed above, big data and AI will play an important role in the travel that people undertake. When planning a holiday, you may be using an AI virtual travel agent to help you plan. You may be greeted by an AI when you register at the hotel.

The World Economic Forum in 2020 identified changes in the type of traveller we are becoming. Its report speculated about what future travel personalities might look like:

Simplicity searchers: prioritize ease as they plan and experience their travels. They are happy to have a trusted third party make decisions to avoid hassle.
Cultural [searchers]: are travellers who want to disconnect from their day-to-day lives, and immerse themselves completely in the local culture.
Social capital seekers: are digitally connected individuals who will make decisions to maximize social reward. They realize the value of travel to those around them. They want to be seen and will share their experiences on social media.
Reward hunters: will use travel to 'treat' themselves to what they don't have in their day-to-day lives. They might focus on a mix of luxury, self-improvement and health.
Obligation meeters: make their travel decision based on a duty. They may have to go to a wedding, on a family trip, a religious holiday or a business trip, for instance.
Ethical travellers: will allow their beliefs and conscience guide their travel decisions. This could be linked to environmental, political or even social issues. (Misrahi, 2016)

An interesting dichotomy is that ethical travellers might care more about the income they bring to poor regions than the carbon footprint that would be connected to their long-haul flight (Peeters, 2020).

Let us explore these in the context of how our disruptive industries might help these new travellers for pleasure. Much of Generation Z (born 1996–2010) is environmentally conscious and will be looking to holiday or vacation in ways that protect the environment. Ecological footprint, the measure of our activities and their impact on the planet, will be part of the decision-making process for many as they plan holidays. Such planning includes asking questions about the carbon or water footprint of the holiday, and how is it helping the local economy or local people's income. To address this, the traveller will need data and analytics linked through the IoT to their phones, laptops, or AR glasses.

Those AR glasses would have details of the local history, and guidance about which shops are selling local products or which taxi company is using electric cars or for that matter which entertainment venue or bar was environmentally engaged.

By 2030 the carbon content of what we do, and what we eat will be available on products we use and so we will be able to have a personal carbon tracker and also look to offset our carbon where we can be increasing support for biodiversity and particular tree planting that encourages that.

By 2030 we shall see hyper-customised holidays based on your preferences and interests, particularly for the much-travelled person. Those going on holiday will share personal data where they see there is a clear advantage. Then through big data and analytics and the IoT your preferences will inform the options that you are seeing. The advantage of this person: customisation, more than what could be found in a guidebook. The guidebooks of tomorrow will be virtual ones tailored to your previous choices. Blockchain will enable a linked and secure experience of booking your holiday.

Habitas, set up by Travis Kalanick and Justin Mateen, built the first 3-D-printed hotels. Kalanick is one of the co-founders of Uber, and Mateen is a cofounder of Tinder. Their first 3-D printing of a hotel was in 2019 for Tulum, Mexico, a municipality on the Caribbean coastline of that country's Yucatán Peninsula. The Habitas Tulem Hotel was flat-packed in a shipment to the location and then customised to fit the local environment – positioning itself as 'the hotel of the future'. The focus for the hotel is 'people, community and experiences'. It puts environment and sustainability into its core with procurement, and has a 'manifesto' in line with our times:

> We believe that beauty, love & sharing,
> Combined with elevated, mind-blowing experiences ….
> Are needed now more than ever.
> We believe that the world needs new spaces, places, homes and temples,
> Where like-minded souls can connect and grow,
> And dance until 4 am.
> Our mission is to create an extraordinary world,
> Where strangers become best friends,
> And friends become family.
> A world where the only luxury we need,
> Is the kind that feeds our souls and expands our minds,
> Over a candle-lit dinner with friends.
> We live to inspire more authentic moments,
> Rather than sharing photos on Instagram,
> And in making lifelong friends Instead of collecting followers and Likes.
> We believe that there's more to life than working, sleeping, eating, repeating,
> Because life can be taken away from us in an instant,
> And because we never know when we'll see our last sunset.
> Most of all, we believe giving is more rewarding than receiving,
> Because the more we give, the more we can change the world.
>
> *(Habitas, 2020)*

3-D printing will also offer hotels the chance to replace items broken very quickly and those printed tend to last comparatively longer. If you have left something behind the hotel may be able to print you a replacement or a 3-D print shop could make something overnight and have it at the reception desk when you wake up.

Travelling on the ocean

Sustainable Development Goal 14: Conserve and sustainably use the oceans, seas, and marine resources for sustainable development.

Before the pandemic, the cruise industry (SDG14) was coming under increasing focus for its carbon footprint. In 2017 there were 26 million people who went on a cruise. Cruise ships have often been compared to a 'floating city' with the amenities that they have on them. Those enjoying the services do not often consider the impact of a cruise ship. The pandemic has focused on the ability to spread a contagious disease which future potential passengers will have to factor in if they are planning a cruise holiday. One of the other factors that a more environmentally conscious population will consider is the pollution a cruise ship produces, whether it is discarding its trash, its fuel, its sewage, or its exhaust fumes, and what its carbon footprint is.

> It is estimated that over 50,000 Europeans die prematurely every year as a result of shipping-based pollution.
>
> *(Ellsmoor, 2019)*

The Cruise Lines International Association – a leading voice for the industry produced a report in September 2020 which looked at the use of advanced technology and its potential impact on CO_2 emissions to 2030. The members have committed to reducing their carbon emissions by 40 per cent by 2030 on 2008 figures. This is based on using Liquefied Natural Gas (LNG) as a fuel and exhaust gas cleaning systems. Like airplanes and cars there is also work being undertaken to use alternative fuels and battery/hybrid power.

The cruise experience by the individual will be enhanced using AR to help augment the experience not just on the cruise ship but the ports of call the ship visits. It will enable the passenger to understand what is on offer on the ship and available at any time. This will enable a much easier booking system. If you have linked your social media platforms (IoT) to the AI of the ship, then it can make suggestions on what you might like and book those experiences for you. As you disembark on one of the ports the ship is visiting it will enable you to see the history as you walk through the town or city – it will show you were the best shops or restaurants are for you to fully appreciate the experience. It may also tell you where the other passengers are so you can experience a less hectic time.

Not only for cruise ships but also for shipping generally, firefighting robots have been developed by the Naval Research Laboratory working with Virginia Tech and other US universities. The robots can resist temperatures of up to 500 degrees Celsius and so can help in finding survivors.

Hull robots or the 'Robotic Hull Bio-inspired Underwater Grooming tool' (Hull BUG) as it likes to be called may be used for cleaning up the hull of a ship – particularly cleaning off marine organisms – known as biofouling, which can create drag for a ship requiring it to use up to 40 per cent more fuel (Kumar, 2020).

Rolls Royce is developing robotic vessels that would be unmanned remote controlled cargo ships. According to research by Chambers University of Technology in Sweden, 84–88 per cent of taker accidents are due to human error, as are 75 per cent of fires and 79 per cent of towing vessel groundings and 89–96 per cent of collisions. Unmanned ships like unmanned cars, lorries, and trains are in our future and if not without a human to watch them by 2030 then not too far beyond that date.

Finally, in February 2021 one of the largest commercial shipping companies Maersk announced that they would have their first carbon-neutral vessel in 2023 – that is, seven years earlier than it had originally planned for. The Danish company is working with other partners such as SAS on building a new sustainability fuels facility which they hope will be operational sometime in 2023 (George, 2021).

Travelling to space

> Space: the final frontier. These are the voyages of the starship Enterprise. Its continuing mission: to explore strange new worlds, to seek out new life and new civilizations, to boldly go where no one has gone before.
>
> *(Kirk, 1966)*

Space tourism may be the last thing we should be focusing on in a book on the future and the impact of our lives on the planet's sustainability, but it is going to happen. Maybe not by 2030 but definitely by 2050 space tourism will be normal, as even people of relatively modest means take holidays in the theme parks on Mars or the water pools on the moon.

By 2030, though, we might have space tourism using VR, but not likely in person. Space tourism isn't part of a sustainable future in the short or medium term. This may change in the long term as the use of fuels might change. Martin Ross, a senior project engineer at the Aerospace Corporation, and others have raised concerns that we do not know enough about the impact on the atmosphere (Ross and Vedda, 2019).

The first space tourist was the American engineer and entrepreneur Denis Tito in 2001. Tito, a multi-millionaire, spent eight days as a crew member of ISS EP-1 visiting the International Space Station on a controversial trip arranged by

MirCorp (now defunct) and the Russian Federal Space Agency. This lark cost Tito a reported US$20 million.

Virgin Galactic in 2020 offered a regular suborbital flight up into space and back for around US$250,000, not for days but only for 2.5 hours, of which only six minutes would be weightless. Space hotels will be available by 2030, but most people will be unable to afford them. The going price quoted in 2020 for the first 12-day trip to a space hotel is US$9.5 million. Tim Alatorre, the architect of the Von Braun Space Station, a wheel-shaped rotating space hotel, expressed the dream this way:

> Eventually, going to space will just be another option people will pick for their vacation, just like going on a cruise, or going to Disney World. ... There is potential for playing fictional games such as Quidditch from the Harry Potter series and the battle games from the Ender's Game series.
>
> *(McFall-Johnson, 2019)*

With funding from the Japanese billionaire Yusaku Maezawa, Space X is aiming to have the first lunar tourism with a single circumference around the moon before 2030. Yusaku has bought the whole first trip with his passengers – six to eight artists – flying for free. He is a former rock-band drummer for Switch Style, and became the founder of the online retailer Zozotown. Yusaku wanted a painter, a musician, and a film director aboard so that they could 'inspire the dreamer within each of us' (Mosher, 2019).

Space exploration has created a number of advancements such as artificial limbs, solar cells, scratch-resistant lenses, wireless headphones, portable computers, 3-D food printing, and ice-resistant airplanes. The future will bring its own set of amazing new developments.

Elon Musk has a company working on a human-computer brain interface called Neuralink. This would link the human brain to artificial intelligence. Musk explains this as follows:

> You're already digitally superhuman. The thing that would change is the interface having a high-bandwidth interface to your digital enhancements …The thing is that today, the interface all necks down to this tiny straw, which is, particularly in terms of output, it's like poking things with your meat sticks, or using words – either speaking or tapping things with fingers. And in fact, output has gone backward. It used to be, in your most frequent form, output would be 10-finger typing. Now, it's like, two-thumb typing. That's crazy slow communication. We should be able to improve that by many orders of magnitude with a direct neural interface.
>
> *(Burlacu, 2019)*

For trips in space and their attendant complexities, would an implanted Neuralink help? Probably, but it may be a slippery slope – are people ready for chips in their brains? This kind of merging of computers and human brains poses an ethical dilemma that we will face before 2030. The Neuralink has potentially very positive applications for addressing brain injuries from a stroke or Parkinson's disease, for example. It may also be able to give people with robotic limbs better control and the feeling of touch in them. Trials with humans were planned for 2020/2021, so by 2030 we will probably see its use in limited cases.

Biotechnology will also be critical to our space travelling and our colonisation of the moon, Mars, and other planets. This will include the need to make food and nutrients in space.

> Because space travel takes a toll on the human body, we're also researching how biotechnology can be used to advance the field of regenerative medicine.
>
> Related cells that are joined together are collectively referred to as tissue, and these cells work together as organs to accomplish specific functions in the human body. Blood vessels around the cells vascularize, providing nutrients to the tissue to keep it healthy.
>
> *(NASA, 2020)*

Humans have long relied on the medicinal and nutritional qualities of plants. Researchers are looking at growing plants that can produce medicines in a small space and on demand. The living space that interplanetary colonists would live in by 2030 might resemble early versions of attempts by NASA's California-based Ames Research Center to grow our habitats. To colonise the moon or Mars, we'll also have to recycle waste by turning urine into drinking water, for example. Again, the NASA report:

> Biology can serve as an effective recycling factory. Microorganisms such as yeast and algae feed on all kinds of things classified as 'mission waste'. Processing their preferred form of nourishment generates products that can serve as raw materials used to make essential supplies like nutrients, medicines, plastic and fuel.
>
> *(NASA, 2020)*

The 2016 Ridley Scott film *The Martian*, with Matt Damon playing astronaut Mark Watney stranded on Mars provided good insight into what it might be like to live there autonomously … which is frightening:

> If the oxygenator breaks down, I'll suffocate. If the water reclaimer breaks down, I'll die of thirst. If the Habitat breaches, I'll just kind of implode. If none of those things happen. I'll eventually run out of food and starve to death. So yeah. I'm fucked.
>
> *(The Martian, 2016)*

Ridley Scott's film was based on a 2011 novel of the same name by Andy Weir.

We opened this chapter with a quote from Mark Twain about how travel reduces prejudice, bigotry, and narrow mindedness. Those who have had the chance to travel in space have often returned from their trip with a greater appreciation for the planet we live on, for its fragility, and for the imperative not to destroy it. Yuri Gagarin, the pioneering Russian cosmonaut, put the experience well and contributed to the ecological debate:

> When I orbited the Earth in a spaceship, I saw for the first time how beautiful our planet is. Mankind, let us preserve and increase this beauty, and not destroy it!
>
> *(Davenport and Vitkovskaya, 2019)*

But we should remember that if we need all 7 billion people to visit space to have this impact, then we have lost the ability to create a sustainable planet for humankind.

References

American Public Transport Association (2019) Public Transportation Facts, APTA. Available online at: https://www.apta.com/news-publications/public-transportation-facts/

Burlacu, A. (2019) Elon Musk Wants to Link Human Brains to AI with Neuralink to Help with Brain Injuries And Improve Communication, Tech Times. Available online at: https://www.techtimes.com/articles/205556/20170421/elon-musk-wants-to-link-human-brains-to-ai-with-neuralink-to-help-with-brain-injuries-and-improve-communication.htm

What Percentage of Car Accidents are Caused by Human Error?, Burns, Cunningham & Mackey, P.C. Available online at: https://www.bcmlawyers.com/what-percentage-of-car-accidents-are-caused-by-human-error/

Canaterio, S (2019) 2034 and the Hotel of the Future: What Will It Look Like?, Guestline Available online at: https://www.guestline.com/hotels-of-the-future/

Costa, K., Goldfuss, C. and DeGood, K. (2019) Reducing Carbon Pollution Through Infrastructure, Center for American Progress. Available online at: https://www.americanprogress.org/issues/green/reports/2019/09/03/473980/reducing-carbon-pollution-infrastructure/

Dajee, E. (2017) Why the Potential of Augmented Reality is Greater Than you Think, Singularity Hub. Available online at: https://singularityhub.com/2017/02/24/why-the-potential-of-augmented-reality-is-greater-than-you-think/

Damon, M. (2016) The Martian (film), 20th Century Fox.

Davenport, C. & Vitkovskaya, J. (2019) 40 Astronauts in their Own Words, The Washington Post. Available online at: https://www.washingtonpost.com/graphics/2019/national/50-astronauts-life-in-space/

Edison Electric Institute (2018) EEI Celebrates 1 Million Electric Vehicles on U.S. Roads, EEI. Available online at: https://www.eei.org/resourcesandmedia/newsroom/Pages/Press%20Releases/EEI%20Celebrates%201%20Million%20Electric%20V ehicles%20on%20U-S-%20Roads.aspx#:~:text=Annual%20sales%20of%20EVs%20will,in%202025%20versus%201.2%20million

Ellsmoor, J. (2019) Cruise Ship Pollution is Causing Serious Health and Environmental Problems, Forbes. Available online at: https://www.forbes.com/sites/jamesellsmoor/ 2019/04/26/cruise-ship-pollution-is-causing-serious-health-and-environmental-problems/?sh=5ce898b237db

European Rail Research Advisory Council (2019) Rail 2030: Research Innovation Priorities, European Rail Research Advisory Council. Available online at: https://errac.org/wp-content/uploads/2019/09/errac_rail_2030_research_and_innovation_priorities.pdf

Friedrich, S.A. (2020) By 2030, One in 10 Vehicles Will be Self-driving Globally, Statista. Available online at: https://www.statista.com/press/p/autonomous_cars_2020/

Garret, O. (2020) Elon Musk Mocks Nikola Motors' Hydrogen Fuel Cells As 'Dumb.' Is He Right? Forbes. Available online at: https://www.forbes.com/sites/oliviergarret/2020/06/17/elon-musk-mocks-nikola-motors-fuel-cells-as-dumb-is-he-right/#36f4ea2b78d8

George, S. (2021) Maersk Accelerates Plans for Carbon-neutral Shipping, Industry News. Available online at: https://industrialnews.co.uk/maersk-accelerates-plans-for-carbon-neutral-shipping/

German Environment Agency (2016) Power-to-Liquids. Potentials and Perspectives for the Future Supply of Renewable Aviation Fuel, German Environment Agency. Available online at: https://www.lbst.de/news/2016_docs/161005_uba_hintergrund_ptl_barrierrefrei.pdf

Guevara, G. (2019) World, Transformed: Megatrends and their Implications for Travel & Tourism, WTTC. Available online at: https://wttc.org/Research/Insights/moduleId/1038/itemId/19/controller/DownloadRequest/action/QuickDownload

Habitas (2020) Our Mission and Manifesto, Habitas. Available online at: https://ourhabitas.com/manifesto

Huddleston, Jnr. T. (2019) These Chinese Hackers Tricked Tesla's Autopilot into Suddenly Switching Lanes, CNBC. Available online at: https://www.cnbc.com/2019/04/03/chinese-hackers-tricked-teslas-autopilot-into-switching-lanes.html

Hydrogen4climate action (2019) Strategic Value Chains, Hydrogen for Climate Action. Available online at: https://www.hydrogen4climateaction.eu/strategic-value-chains

Kantar (2020) Mobility Futures: The Next Normal, Kantar. Available online at: Mobility Futures 2021: The Next Normal (kantar.com)

Kirk, T.J. (1966) Opening of Star Trek TV series, NBC. Available online at: https://en.wikipedia.org/wiki/Where_no_man_has_gone_before#:~:text=by%20Patrick%20Stewart%3A-,Space%3A%20the%20final%20frontier.,the%20end%20of%20each%20film

Kosowatz, J. (2020) Top 10 Growing Smart Cities, The American Society of Mechanical Engineers. Available online at: https://www.asme.org/topics-resources/content/top-10-growing-smart-cities

Krisher, T. & McHugh, D. (2021) Ford to Go All Electric in Europe by 2030, U.S. News. Available online at: https://www.usnews.com/news/business/articles/2021-02-17/ford-to-spend-1b-to-switch-german-factory-to-electric-cars#:~:text=Ford%20announced%20a%20major%20push%20into%20electric%20vehicles,maker%20restarts%20the%20production%20after%20the%20coronavirus%20lockdown

Kumar, S. (2020) 5 Innovative Robotic Technologies for the Maritime Industry, Marine Insights. Available online at: https://www.marineinsight.com/future-shipping/5-innovative-robotic-technologies-for-the-maritime-industry/

Lambert, F. (2018) Survey Shows that 20% of Americans Will Go Electric for their Next Car, Great Progress but Could Improve, Electrek. Available online at: https://electrek.co/2018/05/08/survey-americans-electric-car-adoption/

Lyle, C. (2020) Peer Reviewing Comments for the Chapter.

McFall-Johnson, M. (2019) At least 3 Companies Plan to Launch Space Hotels Into Orbit, Offering Inflatable Rooms, 16 Sunsets per day, and Even Space Quidditch, Business Insider. Available online at: https://www.businessinsider.com/space-hotels-could-launch-in-2021-photos-2019-10

Misrahi, T. (2016) What Would Travel Look Like in 2030? World Economic Forum. Available online at: https://www.weforum.org/agenda/2016/09/what-will-travel-look-like-in-2030/

Money Control (2021) Essar, Fulcrum BioEnergy Announce 600 Million Waste-to-Fuel Plant in England, <Money Control. Available online at: https://www.moneycontrol.com/news/business/essar-fulcrum-bioenergy-announce-600-million-waste-to-fuel-plant-in-england-6512571.html

Morgan, S. (2020) France Unveils €15bn in Aerospace Aid, EURAACTIV. Available online at: https://www.euractiv.com/section/aerospace/news/france-unveils-e15bn-in-aerospace-aid-sets-green-goals/

Mosher, D. (2019) Ahead of SpaceX Moon Mission, Billionaire Yusaku Maezawa Sells a $2.3 Billion Stake in his Fashion Company to Yahoo Japan, Business Insider. Available online at: https://www.businessinsider.com/yusaku-maezawa-zozo-ceo-resigns-sells-yahoo-spacex-starship-flight-2019-9

NASA (2020) How is Biotechnology Preparing us to Live on the Moon and Mars? NASA. Available online at: https://gameon.nasa.gov/2020/01/30/how-is-biotechnology-preparing-us-to-live-on-the-moon-and-mars/

New Atlas (2014) Scientists Build Super-Maglev Train that Could Hit 1,800 mph, New Atlas. Available online at: https://newatlas.com/1800mph-maglev/32213/

Nicoll, F. (2019) Behind the Wheel of a Hydrogen-Powered Car, BBC. Available online at: https://www.bbc.com/news/business-50212037

Oldham, S. (2019) Written Testimony of Steve Oldham CEO, Carbon Engineering Before the Senate Environment and Public Works Committee, Carnon Engineering Available online at: https://www.epw.senate.gov/public/_cache/files/f/b/fb79ee86-07ab-43a8-8b13-82d9dff4226a/10A3FA273885B9FC0C3578A4FE8B635E.02.27.2019-oldham-testimony.pdf

Oracle (2020) Hotel 2025, Oracle. Available online at: https://go.oracle.com/LP=48739/?elqCampaignId=90838&nm=1

Our World in Data (2020) International Arrivals by World Region, Our World in Data. Available online at: https://ourworldindata.org/tourism

Peeters, P. (2020) Peer Reviewed Comments on the Chapter.

Reese, H. (2020) 1 in 10 Vehicles Will be Autonomous by 2030, Tech Republic. Available online at: https://www.techrepublic.com/article/1-in-10-vehicles-will-be-autonomous-by-2030/#:~:text=Over%20the%20next%20decade%2C%20the,a%20new%20report%20from%20Statista.

Ross, M. and Vedda, A.J. (2019) The Policy and Science of Rocket Emissions, Center for Space Policy and Strategy. Available online at: http://aerospace.wpengine.netdna-cdn.com/wp-content/uploads/2018/04/RocketEmissions.pdf

Ruf, Y., Zorn, T., De Neve, P.A., Andrae, P., Erofeeva, S., Garrison, F., & Schwilling, A. (2019). Study on the Use of Fuel Cells and Hydrogen in the Railway Environment, Science Direct. Available online at: https://www.sciencedirect.com/science/article/abs/pii/S0360319920338106

Schmidt, P., Weindorf, W., Zittel, W., Rakasha, T. and Goericke, D. (2016) Renewables in transport 2050 – Empowering a sustainable mobility future with zero emission fuels. Available online at: Renewables in transport 2050 – Empowering a sustainable mobility future with zero emission fuels | SpringerLink

Sheehan, K. (2018) LaGuardia Airport's Security Robot is Giving Women the Creeps, New York Post. Available online at: https://nypost.com/2018/05/03/laguardia-airports-security-robot-is-giving-women-the-creeps

Siddigui, F. (2020) The Plug-in Electric Car is having Its Moment. But Despite False Starts, Toyota is Still Trying to Make the Fuel Cell Happen, Washington Post. Available online at: https://www.washingtonpost.com/technology/2020/02/26/hydrogen-fuel-cell-cars/

Smart Energy International (2020) New York and 14 US States to Ramp Up Electrification of Buses and Trucks, Smart Energy International. Available online at: https://www.smart-energy.com/industry-sectors/electric-vehicles/new-york-and-14-us-states-to-ramp-up-electrification-of-buses-and-trucks/

Steele, P. (2020) Peer Reviewing Chapter.

Sustainable bus (2021) Around the World, Sustainable Bus. Available online at: https://www.sustainable-bus.com/electric-bus/electric-bus-public-transport-main-fleets-projects-around-world/

The Times of India (2019) Techtonic: Futuristic Vehicles Currently in Development, The Times of India. Available online at: https://timesofindia.indiatimes.com/business/india-business/techtonic-futuristic-vehicles-currently-in-development/articleshow/72580722.cms

TMW (2021) Top 10 Fastest Trains in the World 2021, TMW. Available online at: https://themysteriousworld.com/10-fastest-trains-in-the-world/

Twain, M. (1874) The Innocents Abroad, The American Publishing Company

Verdon, M. (2021) The FAA has Cleared the World's First Flying Car for Takeoff, Robb Report. Available online at: https://robbreport.com/motors/aviation/faa-cleared-jetsons-flying-car-1234595921/

5

EDUCATION, WORKING LIFE, AND HEALTH

Introduction

An economy in the 2030s will be built on a different kind of education, one which is more flexible, and less place-based as you get older. The present generation, known as Generation Alpha (2013–2025) are yet to be educated for the workplace of 2030.

By 2030 we will benefit from a healthier population with the acceleration of non-polluting electric-based mobility and through the move to providing clean renewable energy. These developments will reduce the number of illnesses and deaths from air pollution and car accidents. Health services will be much more preventative-based and focused on individual health care as they will have more information in real time about the health of a person.

Work itself, for many, will be vastly different than today and far from what your parents experienced. Gone will be the staff that stayed with a company, if not for life, then for decades. Few people will have stable long-term employment. The work force of 2030 will be much more entrepreneurial, flexible, temporary, part-time, and freelance-based. They will require constant re-education to be able to be employed in an ever-changing job market. Lifelong learning will become the norm.

Education

Sustainable Development Goal 4: Ensure inclusive and equitable quality education and promote lifelong learning opportunities for all.

DOI: 10.4324/9781003045496-5

CARTOON 5.1 The family wakes up in the morning and are in the living room/eating area having breakfast

> Education is the most powerful weapon which you can use to change the world.
>
> *(Mandela, 1990)*

For a moment let us just reflect on what education (SDG4) is about: It is about the sharing of a body of knowledge, building a set of skills, values, beliefs, and habits. This will include skills such as digital literacy, life skills, problem-solving, adaptability, social awareness, communication, and collaboration. Both students and teachers will need to be data literate and could collect, manage, and employ data in their learning, teaching, and living. AI can predict a person's skill gap and help focus their education to address this – it can bring together teams of students and help them build better cooperative approaches to problem-solving (Horan, 2021).

The way learning is delivered in 2021 is different than what it was in 2010 or 2000 or 1990, and so it will be different in 2030.

Generation Z (1995–2012) have grown up through high levels of technological change and have emerged as the first generation that have both an online and a real-life persona and existence.

Together with Generation Alpha, born after 2012, they will be at the centre of the huge changes in education that will be experienced over the coming decade.

> Sustainable Development Goal 13: Take urgent action to combat climate change and its impacts.

Generation Z have led the pressure on addressing climate change, with Greta Thunberg's climate strikes (SDG13) bringing millions of school and college students onto the streets in 2019 and 2020.

This book will be out before the Glasgow (UNFCCC) Climate Conference (November 2021), and so we will not know the outcome of the conference. This generation is one of the most socially active ones. Many see social activism as part of their education. Will the impact of the climate strikes result in higher national commitments on reducing greenhouse gas emissions? What we are seeing is a highly educated generation putting pressure not only on politicians, their families, and the institutions they are educated at but also industry as a whole. Generation Z will want to work for a company or institution that takes care of the world we live in.

> For way too long, the politicians and the people in power have gotten away with not doing anything to fight the climate crisis, but we will make sure that they will not get away with it any longer. We are striking because we have done our homework and they have not.
>
> *(Thunberg, 2019)*

With the pandemic experienced over the past year (2020–2021) Gen Z and Alpha elementary or preschool children have already experienced a disruptive schooling. They have gone through a massive learning curve as far as online education is concerned – as have their teachers. It is important to underline that this was not experienced the same way by all of them.

In the past year, the digital divide between rural and urban areas became much clearer. A report by BroadbandNow in February 2020 estimated that something like 42 million (US) people do not have high-speed Internet access (Busby et al., 2020). This will need urgent action in the coming years and government investment to make personal access to the Internet a reality. Has access to the Internet become a right that everyone should have? But with all rights there are responsibilities, and this includes teaching the ability for critical thinking and to think logically and apply that to life in 2030.

> Sustainable Development Goal 3: Ensure healthy lives and promote well-being for all at all ages.

The pandemic (SDG3) saw 850 million children worldwide shut out of schools (Beard, 2020), requiring educators to rethink what is needed. America and many developed countries – not to mention developing countries – were poorly prepared for online schooling.

The large-scale move to online schooling has had both positive and negative impacts, but as a whole, these generations are 'comfortable' as far as using the Internet as a source of knowledge and learning.

So how might this develop in the future? What will be the elements of education in 2030?

The World Economic Forum in their Future of Jobs Report 2018 goes as far as to say that 65 per cent of children entering primary school now will find jobs that do not yet exist (World Economic Forum, 2018).

The schools and colleges of 2030

> Any curriculum worth its salt would focus not on content but on developing critical survival skills, such as leading by influence, agility and adaptability, initiative and entrepreneurship, effective communication, analyzing information, and curiosity and imagination. In an age of fake news and alternative facts, we ought to focus on teaching our youth to distinguish between information, misinformation, disinformation, and propaganda.
>
> *(Roberts, 2018)*

Will schools and colleges even exist in 2030? The answer is of course 'yes'. They and the teachers play a critical role in a child's development, particularly in the younger years, and in strengthening the community 'as a whole'.

Just for a moment, let us look at the school or college as a physical place.

> Sustainable Development Goal 11: Make cities and human settlements inclusive, safe, resilient, and sustainable.

How would students get to school? By 2030 the school buses may be electric, and the driver may be doubling as a teaching assistant because the bus drives itself to school. Maybe 'bus work' will become part of 'homework' time or contribute to flipped learning – where work that is normally done in class is now done out of school. Others will arrive at school and college using electric self-driving cars or the new electric bikes that Uber has been exploring since 2019 (SDG11).

> Exciting announcement from @UberATG at today's @DIYRobocars event. 'Micromobility' = autonomous scooters & bikes that can drive themselves to charging or better locations.
>
> *(Anderson, 2019)*

You might say to a scooter, 'take me to school but by via the best doughnut shop that still gets me to school on time'. You would be able to access through big data what the best doughnut shop of the day is.

Sustainable Development Goal 6: Ensure availability and sustainable management of water and sanitation for all.

As mentioned in previous chapters, the worldwide projection of demand over availability of water in 2030 will be around 40 per cent. Schools and colleges will be designed around low water use where possible or retrofitted with rainwater harvesting systems (SDG6). The aim would be to capture water from roofs and parking lots to use for athletic fields or with filters as grey water for toilets utilising AI to ensure their effective use.

For a new building at Virginia Tech (2020), it was estimated that such a scheme would reduce its water consumption by 750,000 gallons per year (Mesenbrink, 2020). According to the water industry, the average person in the US in 2020 uses around 3,000 gallons of water a month.

Sustainable Development Goal 7: Ensure access to affordable, reliable, sustainable, and modern energy for all.

As far as energy (SDG7) use, a school or college will need to become more energy independent while using less energy. By 2030, many will have been retrofitted with solar panels or roofs and linked into local smart grids with renewable energy sources for additional energy needs. Those institutions that produce more energy than they need will be able to make money through a feed-in tariff. It may be that the local energy provider rents space on their roofs, thereby giving them another income.

There are already examples of this one in a rural school district in Arkansas. In 2017 they, with five other education centres, converted an unused field into a solar farm (1,500 panels). This converted an annual 'US$250,000 annual budget deficit into a US$1.8 million surplus' (Tagermann, 2021). They then invested those savings in giving teachers up to a US$15,000 increase in salary.

The Internet of Things (IoT) in a school or college will monitor and conserve water and energy, as well as securing the buildings, identifying any person who should not be there and perhaps dispatching a robot security guard to apprehend the person.

IoT could also enable a teacher to know where a student is at any particular time, which is very useful in an emergency situation and might save lives. Of course, many students dream of taking something like a *Ferris Bueller's Day Off*.

Many of us sympathise with Ferris (played by Matthew Broderick in that 1986 movie), especially because – as he told his friends –

> Life moves pretty fast. If you don't stop and look around once in a while, you could miss it.
>
> *(Brodderick, 1986)*

The ability to skip school may be a thing of the past in 2030 if your temperature and other vital signs can be monitored through a watch or health band that you wear and which the school may have access to for school days and times. Even school restrooms may be equipped with technology such as an:

> Internet-connected toilet that safeguards health by using discreetly placed sensors and artificial intelligence to analyze waste. Such a toilet could detect early signs of disease and help people manage chronic conditions such as diabetes.
>
> *(Baggaley, 2019)*

Students will be immersed in a whole IoT education ecosystem. AI using big data analytics will enable teachers to monitor a student's abilities across different lessons and see incredibly early where there are problems. It will help identify vulnerable students and help guide them through their education in a more positive way (Horan, 2021).

For parents, AI will facilitate a near real-time ability to see how their daughter or son is doing. Gone will be the forging of school reports or the student saying the 'dog ate my homework' because the work will be on personal devices in files which can be linked to the school.

Gone too will be physical out of date books, which will be replaced by online up to date books, articles, teaching videos, and related material. Schools have embraced the use of content such as TED talks that are available and introduce students to emerging issues in an extremely attractive way.

What about teaching? Many people can remember the great teacher they had for this subject or that and how they impacted our lives, but by on and large not all teachers are great. Using AI and big data and analytics will enable the student to have many more perfect lesson experiences with perhaps the best recorded lecture or lesson – from around the world. The teacher will become more of a coach, a guide, a mentor, a counsellor, rather than a subject expert.

When the teacher/coach/AI asks you to read a book, they will know if you did since the book could be linked to the school IoT. It could record if you read the book, how long you spent on different pages, and how long it took for you to write your assignment and any pages you had problems with. It might also show the pages you researched to develop your final product.

In fact, with not having to teach the class the same material at the same time, AI opens each child to a limitless learning experience. It creates a kind of education adventure in which the student is engaged in finding the answers to problems. With the AI collecting data and analytics on the learning experience of the individual children, teachers and coaches can focus on the individual needs of each student so much more. Techno-evangelists for AI:

Believe its powers will shed new light on the working of the human brain – how repetitive practice grows expertise, for instance, or how interleaving (leaving gaps between learning different bits of material) can help us achieve mastery. As a result, we will be able to design adaptive algorithms to optimise the learning process.

(Beard, 2020)

The less positive view of AI suggests that teachers of 2030 will become the Uber drivers of education (Beard, 2020).

The use of Virtual Reality and Augmented Reality for studying was mentioned in Chapter 3: Home life. By 2030, it will be an integral part of teaching.

Lessons will be taught where through VR you can actually be a character in a historical event or be in the event watching what is happening. This will enormously improve understanding of the occasion and therefore the ability of the student to learn from it and write about it. VR may play an important role in addressing issues such as racism if students experience more of what has happened to different ethnic groups in different circumstances.

One of the positive aspects of all this is the cost of education will come down and another will be that lifelong learning will become part of our everyday lives. The old bricks and mortar universities of 2021 may not disappear by 2030, but they will need to drastically change.

> Sustainable Development Goal 10: Reduce inequality within and among countries.

Imagine, using VR, being one of the four freshmen (Ezell Blair Jr., David Richmond, Franklin McCain, and Joseph McNeil) at North Carolina Agriculture and Technical College who went into the Woolworth's in Greensboro on 1 February 1960 and sat at the lunch counter which was only for whites. Experience the racial abuse they did, and you might better understand racism, civil rights, and white privilege which would spearhead the civil rights movement of the 1960s. This is something that is still being addressed in 2021 as it created a greater inequality between different ethnic groups (SDG10).

History from around the world will be more understandable when you spend a day in the cell, using VR, that Nelson Mandela lived in for 27 years and think how he could then come out of that to help build a multi-racial society in South Africa. Or you could walk on the moon with Neil Armstrong and Buzz Aldrin from Apollo 11.

We do not know how 'real' these experiences will be by 2030. VR does offer a huge opportunity for rebuilding a conversation for the next generation that is more likely to be positive than what it is in 2021. Education plays such an important role in building our communities and society.

As far as AR is concerned, we have seen with 'Pokémon GO', where the AR added digital images onto the physical environment. AR will become a kind of 'private teacher' where you move around the world having access to the history of a place, a person you meet, the environment you are experiencing. It will be able to tell you when you buy food at the supermarket if it has been block-chained, where it was grown, and by whom on its journey to the supermarket. Like VR it will enrich the learning and educational experience.

The use of VR and AR in the classroom offers a huge opportunity for making lessons much more interesting and personalised than just sitting and listening to lectures. AR can add animated figures or objects to enhance an interactive learning process. You might, for primary school or kindergarten, choose your companion AR character, perhaps your favourite Muppet, to help you work through problems on your device.

Perhaps the slowest changes in education will be at the university level. These are huge institutions with traditions and tenured professors that take time to change their teaching and teaching methods.

The COVID-19 pandemic has not yet played through the education system, but many universities are having serious financial difficulties, and some will have to close.

The impact of this may ultimately be positive and enable a refocusing of the higher education system to the needs of 2030 and not the last century. Due to the pandemic, to teach virtually, professors have had to develop new ways to engage with their students and learn different teaching methods.

The next ten years will see a rapidly changing job market with the gig economy and automation and will require new skills to be learned throughout someone's working life. The idea of a lifelong learning approach, not a new concept, will now be at the centre of higher education.

The traditional approach to education was that you went through from a high school to university (first undergraduate and then graduate school). In 2030 that will be much less true, and the traditional degrees of 2020 may also need to include more what we would have called 'trade schools' in the past and move towards more of a 'skills' model by 2030.

> Fast-growing innovators in educational technologies and education industry outsiders are already challenging the status quo by structurally undermining the long-established business models of higher education. These new actors use technology and data to introduce new, alternative approaches that deliver better on the evolving expectations of learners. Imagine tech giants such as Google, Microsoft, or Amazon offering inexpensive, personalized, AI-driven education, maybe on a flexible 'Netflix for education' style scheme.
>
> *(Ostergaard and Nordlund, 2019)*

Those entering higher education by 2030 will find a much more fragmented higher education landscape. The student will be immersed in the digital world, looking for courses that enable them to build on the skills they have already mastered. It may be more, as Ostergaard suggests above, a 'Netflix for education' system. Another way to think of it would be the old sweet shop 'mix and match', meaning that for a similar price you take different courses, perhaps at different institutions, and the combination gives you what you want.

It may mean that you will not be spending three to seven years at a physical higher education institution but much shorter periods at several of them or utilising IoT to do some of the courses online. There has been a growth of bootcamps and online certification which are much shorter courses (three to six months) where they are focusing on software development, data analytics, and digital marketing to mention a few. These are enabling young people and those older ones wanting to retain for the employment market of tomorrow to have the right skills. And just like schools adapt, a teacher in the near future can focus on more individual learning for her or his 'student consumers'.

It is also important to recognise the role that education plays, where we learn from our peers, build networks for life through shared experiences, and gain exposure to other values, ideas, beliefs, and cultures. The play aspect of school or higher education – whether it's the playground, or the playing of sports, or even hanging out with friends going to social events – all play a role in our personal development (Horan, 2021).

Blockchain use for your academic credentials can secure student transcripts. It also will be critical for a 'mix and match' approach to education. As the student, you would have direct access to your own transcripts. Why is this important? An example: A friend of one of the authors' had been an immigrant to Spain and had been taught in a school set up for immigrants. Twenty years after leaving the school, she needed her transcripts to prove she had had the education. The school no longer existed, and no one seemed to know where the records had gone.

This is perhaps an extreme case, but blockchain also protects against falsifying an academic record. A blockchain that follows a student in 2030 would enable a full disclosure of their education history from primary through to applying for higher education or completing additional courses or training. The 'mix and match' approach of taking courses at different higher education institutions would require validation and blockchain offers that; it would enable a future employer to see all the success and any challenges they had faced in education. A final comment from the *Financial Times*:

> The risk is that the education system will be churning out humans who are no more than second-rate computers, so if the focus of education continues to be on transferring explicit knowledge across the generations, we will be in trouble.

The AI challenge is not just about educating more AI and computer experts, although that is important. It is also about building skills that AI cannot emulate. These are essential human skills such as teamwork, leadership, listening, staying positive, dealing with people and managing crises and conflict.

(Financial Times, 2017)

Working life

> Sustainable Development Goal 8: Promote sustained, inclusive, and sustainable economic growth, full and productive employment, and decent work for all.

New technology will drive the world economy of 2030 (SDG8). The world economy will likely be dominated by Asian economies, with China having the largest projected GDP of around US$62.2 trillion (T), followed by India at around US$46.3 T, the US at US$31.01 T, and Indonesia at US$10.1 T. Rounding out the top five will be Turkey at US$9.1 T. (Desjardins, 2019). India will also have the largest population in the world by 2030 (Curran, 2019).

While gross domestic product (GDP) is not the best way to measure a country's development, it is commonly used to track economic performance because it measures the market value of goods and services in an economy over a particular interval. Bobby Kennedy's speech at the University of Kansas on 18 March 1968 expresses some of the deficiencies that we still have in relying too much on GDP:

> It (GDP) counts special locks for our doors and the jails for the people who break them. It counts the destruction of the redwood and the loss of our natural wonder in chaotic sprawl.
>
> It counts napalm and counts nuclear warheads and armored cars for the police to fight the riots in our cities. It counts Whitman's rifle and Speck's knife, and the television programs which glorify violence in order to sell toys to our children.
>
> Yet the gross national product does not allow for the health of our children, the quality of their education or the joy of their play. It does not include the beauty of our poetry or the strength of our marriages, the intelligence of our public debate or the integrity of our public officials.
>
> It measures neither our wit nor our courage, neither our wisdom nor our learning, neither our compassion nor our devotion to our country, it measures everything in short, except that which makes life worthwhile.
>
> *(Kennedy, 1968)*

According to the US Federal Reserve, climate change presents one of the key threats and opportunities for the global economy. A lot of new technology is driven by efforts to reduce climate impact. Extreme weather events are, of course, a disaster for homeowners, but they can also force farms, utilities, and other companies to declare bankruptcy.

During the UN General Assembly on 22 September 2020 China announced that it aimed for 'carbon neutrality by 2060'. China and other countries that have projected carbon neutrality by the earlier date of 2050 will also be an additional engine of change in the kind of industries and the associated jobs that will be part of the workforce by 2030. It is estimated by the World Economic Forum that 'fighting climate change could add US$26 trillion to the global economy by 2030'.

Freelancing: In 2019, about 57 million Americans were freelancers, earning US$1T. It has been estimated that by 2030 that something close to 80 per cent of the global workforce may be freelancers (Petrov, 2020). This change is being fuelled by the new technology, and 5G will make it even easier to link freelance clients and the work needed to be undertaken together through an IOT platform.

In 2030, few will have jobs for life as was often the situation for previous generations. The emerging gig economy will see freelancing or short-term contracts becoming the 'new normal' compared to permanent jobs of previous decades or even centuries.

The gig economy is increasingly a greener economy because many of the new technologies of 2030 will be less polluting. The gig economy will enable certain workers a more flexible lifestyle. Some might even find it possible to do their work from a café on a beach or overlooking the Blue Ridge Mountains. Where you work will come down to connectability, what software you have, and what disposable income you have.

In 2021 the PricewaterhouseCoopers (PwC) UK Economic Outlook Report said that:

> Covid-19 has fundamentally changed the way we view cities.

It went on to say:

> City-dwellers are now rethinking their living situations in light of the pandemic, and re-evaluating the importance of larger homes, green spaces and connections with the local community.
>
> *(McKeever, 2019)*

The growth of freelancing will be complemented by growth in matchmaking websites that link freelancers with possible clients.

Most of us already experience people freelancing at the community level through sites such as Nextdoor or Home Advisor, which link services for your home to tradesmen who are available in your local area. We probably did not think that was going to become something that might also apply to us and the work we do.

The closer we get to 2030, the more we should expect the use of freelancers by companies that will be able to utilise people wherever they are in the world. We have already seen a considerable growth of sites like Upload, Toptal, and Freelancer dot com, which are places for people searching for work and clients searching for those willing to do the work, often at the lowest possible price.

Not surprisingly, niche sites that are focused on a particular skill base (such as Designhill if you are a designer) are growing. Already in 2020, interior designers are offering you the chance to take photos of your house so that they can remotely give you a 3-D view of their suggested changes to it. As the use of VR/AR becomes more normal, you will be able to co-design in a virtual space.

These virtual platforms enable a free market of skills which brings prices down because the freelancer is no longer just competing in their locality, state, or even nation, but globally. By 2075, the competition might even be planetary!

We are moving from a physical workplace to one that will be increasingly digital. This may have a positive impact on immigration. Most of those that become refugees due to economic reasons say that they are happier to stay where their families are and to help build the economy in their own country.

> Office buildings, cubicles, meeting rooms – even water-cooler gossip – are being reshaped by virtual and augmented reality, artificial intelligence, machine learning and other emerging software capabilities.
>
> *(Loten, 2020)*

Interviews for work may be conducted by a neutral avatar which will base hiring decisions on the capabilities of the freelancer or worker more generally. An AI-driven video interview will include facial and voice analysis as well as an assessment of the personalities of those being interviewed. HR departments will shrink as their role is taken over by AI.

Freelancing to complete proposed work does not usually come with any health or retirement plan, which saves companies additional costs. An employer will be able to check your health record through blockchain and may require you to have a wear a health monitor if your health causes them concern. It raises issues of civil liberties on issues which may be worked out as we move out of the COVID-19 pandemic over the issue of where and when we will need 'vaccine passports'.

If a new employee needs additional training, this training is likely to become something the freelancer would need to already have to compete in the marketplace, and training costs in most cases will fall on individuals and not the companies they freelance for.

If the freelancer needs to travel, that will be much easier (See Chapter 4: Travelling around), particularly if it is in the US or other developed countries. Business travel may be done via self-driving cars that enable people to work while they travel.

In addition to health records, blockchain can protect payment information, education certificates, and references.

The rights of a gig economy worker are emerging as an important area. The first recorded strike by workers was in 1768 when tailors in New York protested at a wage reduction. The first trade union was the Federal Society of Journeymen Cordwainers (shoemakers), formed in 1794. The 19th and 20th centuries saw trade unions play a critical role in the improvement of working conditions for their members as wages increased and working hours were reduced. For gig economy workers around the world, union-inspired perks of this kind are much more difficult to offer support for.

In the 2020 election in the US in California, Proposition 22 asked the people whether companies like Uber, Lyft, and DoorDash should treat drivers as employees. Proposition 22 passed, so app-based companies can continue to treat their employees as independent contractors and do not have to provide them with minimum wage, overtime, paid sick leave, or unemployment insurance. As Robert Reich, former Secretary of Labor, said of the proposition before it was passed:

> Labor unions recognize its importance as well. If Uber and Lyft win this, more employers around the country will classify more of their employees as contract workers. That would mean big savings to employers, since contract workers don't get Social Security or worker's compensation, minimum wage, or other labor protections. By the same token, workers would be disadvantaged.
>
> *(O'Brien, 2020)*

The Prop 22 fight represents the beginning of a long war over the gig economy to stop a rush to lower labour and pay standards and rights. This proposition dealt with the issue of the gig economy in a particular geographical area, but the gig economy will not be geographically limited, and how can you protect workers in different countries, or prevent companies from hiring gig workers from countries where the pay is much lower than that of the country they are based in?

Workplace: As mentioned in Chapter 3: Home life, where we do our work is changing, and the pandemic of 2020/21 accelerated this development. For some people, it has become evident that they do not need to work in an office in a city and have their family live in the suburbs. The possibility of an increased quality of life for families will become an increasingly important driver which will accelerate an exodus of people from the cities to more rural areas.

If your workplace can be your home, the lost hours of travelling from your house to work can be used to spend more time with your family or take up pursuits that you had always wanted to do. Statista asked the question in 2020: Would you like to continue to work at home or in the office? They found that 43 per cent of survey respondents wanted to continue working remotely and 35 per cent wanted to go back to as it was before (Bajarin, 2020).

CARTOON 5.2 The room retrofits slightly to accommodate remote working, with the eating table being split into 4 smaller desks, that can be moved and put in different corners

Already some companies are exploring virtual offices where you can still chat with colleagues through your avatar. Others are exploring having a robot represent you in meetings with your face on the screen. This has allowed some advancement in meetings where everything is unidirectional, something experienced through Zoom and Skype. By controlling robot movement, you can potentially have bilateral interaction with others in the group as if you are there. Thus, making the meetings more like being there in person.

Meetings in 2030 will see more advanced AI robots attending meetings either with people or with other AI robots that represent people. It may be that for key people, a particular robot is assigned to them to operate whenever they are needed.

As a result of changes like these, office blocks will need to be repurposed. Some of them may become urban agriculture hubs to produce food for their cities and reduce the need for food to be transported so much. Other office blocks may become residential options.

This great exodus is not for everyone, and there will still need to be a strong service industry supporting those still in the urban areas. As economic activity changes, communities have found themselves becoming ghost towns. Urban planners designing our new smart cities and towns will need to be careful not to fail and create new 'ghost towns' of the 21st century. One of the most famous is Bodie in California, which had grown quickly in gold rush times (1876). Once the gold ran out, however, so did the reason for the people to live there.

With the accelerated transport opportunities in 2030 discussed in Chapter 4: Travelling around, those who do need to come into the city will be able to do that more quickly and in a more environmentally friendly way.

Migration to the rural or suburban areas will also result in a need for an increased service industry to support the new population in those areas. Some large companies may set up smaller satellite offices to support their staff relocating. It might be an attractive offer to a potential freelancer for a company to have hubs in areas where the landscape is beautiful, and the cost of living is reasonable. Work hubs will have rooms that enable home workers to go to more secure locations for key meetings or just to get out of the home and be able to work around other people even if they aren't employed by the same company.

Areas that were finding it difficult to retain their populations because of the reduced need for people in mining, farming, or the mills and factories that once kept rural towns vibrant may find that the future yields growth opportunities even for small towns.

Lost jobs: Over the past 20 years, we have seen a massive change in the job market. Key jobs in 2000 no longer exist in 2020, and jobs with large footprints in 2020 may no longer loom as large by 2030.

As an example, let us look back at some of the key employers in 2000 and where they are now. For the young reader who is used to watching films or TV programmes livestreamed to their phone, iPad, or laptop, things were different in 2000.

At the turn of the millennium and the tail end of the Third Industrial Revolution, we would all rent our films and TV series on VHS tapes, usually from a local Blockbuster store.

At one time, Blockbuster had over 9,000 stores, but their last store (in Bend, Oregon) closed in August 2020.

Taking note of the nostalgia for Blockbuster felt by several generations, the last store converted into a Blockbuster Airbnb (Airbnb, 2020).

You can now stay in a bedroom designed around the themes of the store, while in the reception area you can rent out an old VHS tape to insert into an old video player in your bedroom and watch as you did in 2000. Of course, you are always hoping the tape is not going to be eaten by the video player before the end of the film. DVDs would replace VHS tapes in the early 2000s.

Music stores suffered a similar fate over the last 20 years. HMV or Virgin music stores that used to be part of the mainstream shopping centres where you would buy your CDs/DVDs have nearly disappeared as people download song tracks onto their phones, computers, or TVs. Interestingly, there has been a huge increase in people buying vinyl long playing (LP) records, which were the main source through which to play recorded music before CDs. As mentioned before, LPs outsold CDs in 2020 for the first time in 34 years (Corcoran, 2020).

Typewriters became obsolete as personal computers became mainstream, and digital technology-enabled still cameras produce video as well. By 2020, all of this became a function of our phones.

The expansion of the IoT linking our movies, music, photos, and work files to all our devices enables us to listen, watch, or work wherever we want to and on whatever device we want to. You could take your laptop linked through 5G on to the African Queen boat moored in Key Largo and watch the film *The African Queen* (1951) with Humphrey Bogart and Katherine Hepburn. At the same time, through a watch party, you could have friends on the Ulanga River in Tanzania where the film is situated, watching and commenting on it with you in real time.

By 2030, several jobs that we are doing today may not exist, or at least will not exist in the numbers that they did because of changes in the nature of the services they are delivering.

Travel agents may soon become extinct. Many readers of this book likely recall visiting a travel agent in local shopping centres. Remember looking through travel brochures produced by companies trying to persuade us to take our holidays with them? Most of us now just look online and use services such as Booking.com, Expedia, Trivago, or Priceline to get a hotel at a reduced rate that a local travel agent could not get. Added to that, one should not underestimate the convenience of booking at home and not having to go into a shopping centre and lose half a day. The same goes for booking your flight. By 2030, you will be able to ask your equivalent to Alexa to get together your options and order them based on a set of criteria you have given it.

There is a group of jobs related to the delivery of goods to our houses that may be replaced by drones by 2030; these include our fast-food delivery and mail carriers.

Supermarkets and fast-food restaurants already have self-service tills (registers). Petrol (gas) stations are experimenting with self-service pumps and kiosks that do not need cashiers. Coming into a store your phone will be able to produce a list of what you are missing from your fridge because it is linked up to it. It will also be able to recognise where the products are in the store, and whether the supermarket is offering any deals at the time.

By 2030, cashiers will mostly be found in more nostalgic or local convenience stories. Payment will be 'contactless', meaning that it will not involve a face-to-face or hand-to-hand interaction with another human. Some shops already take only electronic payments. We are also starting to see a small number of places where you can purchase goods using a cryptocurrency. This is increasingly attractive because it reduces fees associated with credit cards and banks. In an increasingly digital world, it also creates a strong security for your money because the encryption through blockchain is a safeguard against fraud and anyone trying to tamper with your account.

One of the other major areas that will be hit will be the transportation of people and goods. Taxi, bus, and lorry (truck) drivers all could be replaced by self-driving electric vehicles. The magnitude of change like this in the US alone is huge, because at present, there are 5 million Uber drivers in the US, as well as something like 200,000 taxi drivers, 650,000 bus drivers, and approximately 3.5 million truck drivers. It is not just the jobs as drivers, but all the ancillary repair workers will be impacted because there will be less need for maintenance. Another impact will be fewer accidents with self-driving vehicles and potentially less need for roadside emergency service workers or doctors and nurses.

Top jobs in 2030: Some of the key jobs for 2030 might include being an Alternative Energy Consultant who helps advise households and business on how they can move to renewable energy use and monitors it as a small energy provider.

In health care, there will be job opportunities for people who can 3-D print new organs. Ageing populations will drive a continuing need for registered nurses, but skilled nursing done by humans will be supplemented by robots to help with home care, and more accurate diagnosis through the medical IOT. The ranks of nurse practitioners are also expected to grow as they help diagnose and treat illness. Physical therapists will also be in greater demand, because of the ageing population, helping people recover from disease, injury, or the toll taken by old age.

Jobs in biotechnology will grow over the next ten years, particularly those in medical and clinical laboratory settings, such as technologists and technicians, medical scientists, biochemists, and biophysicists.

You may have a digital currency advisor – these may at the beginning be humans who help you with your cryptocurrencies and your investments, but over time, further still in the future, by 2050 currency advising will probably be done by AI.

The increased use of drones to deliver to our houses will require some form of drone traffic control to ensure that there is not complete chaos and crashes. Again, drone traffic control is likely to be done with human oversight initially but will over time be performed by AI.

There will be a reduced need for car mechanics because electric cars need less and different maintenance but a growth in specialised electric car and self-driving car mechanics. These mechanics will need to understand the technology in the car and how to work out what is wrong and how to replace it. The car's onboard computer will help, but the mechanics will need to sort out problems. If they are not sure of a diagnosis, they will be linked to the car company mechanics, who can remotely help them address problems. A remote mechanic will through VR be able to see a version of the same car linked together through IOT and AI in the car. She or he will be able to help the actual onsite mechanic finds problems and sort them out.

Cyber security jobs will be in high demand as each year more and more attacks are made on our data. People working at home as opposed to in a secure office environment create the need for a larger security net for companies and the freelancers who might be working for them.

Sustainable Development Goal 9: Build resilient infrastructure, promote inclusive and sustainable industrialisation, and foster innovation.

COVID-19 recovery packages: The changes in the coming ten years are enormous, but there is also an opportunity to ease these changes in for the generation most impacted and need of retaining.

In many developed countries and in the US, crumbling infrastructure (SDG9) needs urgent attention. Many of the skills of the blue-collar workers that might be most exposed to the impact of the Fourth Industrial Revolution can be turned to help remake the infrastructure of the US and other developed countries through COVID-19 recovery packages. 'Build Back Better' was one of the slogans of the successful Biden Presidential campaign in 2020 and also the European Union, and the UN Secretary General.

This gives up to a ten-year buffer offering a chance to retrain a group of workers as they more gradually learn new skills to join a different workforce that will be needed in 2030.

Bizarre jobs of 2030: A few projected jobs for 2030 may seem bizarre compared to what is available now – although they are simply extensions of what is already happening. As society moves towards a more electronic-based energy and transport system, there will be an increase in e-waste. E-waste from tablets, laptops, smartphones, batteries, solar panels, car chargers amount to a record of 2.7 million tonnes in 2020 but will grow by 2030 to an estimated 81 million tonnes.

> Garbage designers will be key players in a future economy built on environmentally friendly practices.
>
> *(CST, 2020)*

The move towards a circular economy for goods will increase the need for garbage collectors and designers, particularly with the growth of solar power and battery technology. The waste stream will need to take critical elements out (heavy metals such as cadmium and lead) which also harm the natural environment. Much of the new technology uses rare elements such as gallium and indium in photovoltaic (PV) cells. We can also find rare earth elements in computer memory, rechargeable batteries, mobile phones, catalytic converters, and hydrogen storage.

A study by the International Renewable Energy Agency (IRENA) estimated that by 2050, the market for recycling solar modules could be as large as $US15 billion (IRENA, 2016).

Our garbage designers of the future will also be looking to 'upcycle' – where waste is converted into other products – which is different from recycling. Upcycling is a new way of expressing what in the past was often the activity of many of the poorest in society who lived around landfills or collected certain rubbish around a town or city which they could sell or reuse. Upcycling and recycling will become more possible as many goods will be tagged so that they can be found in the waste stream through an IoT of garbage.

A subcategory of interior designers called 'nostalgists' will help recreate memories for older people using AR and VR to enable them to go back in time to important parts of their lives and mix home videos and photos with actual events (Smith, 2014).

Other unusual jobs of 2030 can be found in Table 5.1.

Skills for jobs in 2030: As the labour market will change dramatically in the next ten years, so the focus of education and training needs to evolve as well. 'Future proofing' the education will mean having a good qualification in science, technology, engineering, and mathematics (STEM). We are used to STEM, but not so many of us have heard of or are aware of an increasing term in education and training that workers will also need SMAC (social, mobile, analytics, and cloud) skills.

Entering the job market in 2030 a person would need to be digitally literate and have computational thinking prowess – being able to express problems and solutions so that the computer can execute them.

Companies will be looking for employees who show emotional and social intelligence. They will be able to measure that when job candidates are interviewed by an AI. An inventive mindset which can create something that cannot be replaced by a robot will prosper. People who can see the interlinkages between sectors and offer good judgement and decision-making while developing hybrid solutions will be in high demand.

OECD in their report *Skills for 2030* also identified three different types of skills as part of a conceptual learning framework:

• Cognitive and meta-cognitive skills, which include critical thinking, creative thinking, learning-to-learn, and self-regulation.
• Social and emotional skills, which include empathy, self-efficacy, responsibility, and collaboration.
• Practical and physical skills, which include using new information and communication technology devices. (OECD, 2018)

Underlining these skills will be the ability of those in 2030 and beyond to be able to continually learn and develop their skills to engage in the job market.

TABLE 5.1 Top future jobs in 2030 (Duggal, 2020)

1. **Virtual Store Sherpa:** Will focus on customer satisfaction through virtually advising customers using knowledge of the product line.
2. **Personal Data Broker:** Will ensure consumers receive revenue from their data. The broker will establish prices and execute trades.
3. **Personal Memory Curator:** Will consult with patients and stakeholders to generate specifications for virtual reality experiences.
4. **Augmented Reality Journey Builder:** Will collaborate with talented engineers and technical artists to develop vital elements for clients.
5. **Highway Controller:** Will monitor automated road and air space management systems to ensure no errors occur.
6. **Body part maker:** Will create living body parts for athletes and soldiers.
7. **Nano-medic:** Will transform healthcare.
8. **GM or recombinant farmer:** Will transform farming and livestock.
9. **Elderly wellness consultant:** Will cater to the physical and mental needs of the elderly.
10. **Memory augmentation surgeon:** Will boost patients' memory when it hits capacity.
11. **'New science' ethicist:** Will ford the river of progress.
12. **Space pilots, tour guides, and architects:** Will allow pilots, tour guides, and architects to live in lunar outposts.
13. **Vertical farmers:** The future of farming is straight up. Vertical farms in urban areas could significantly increase food supply.
14. **Climate change reversal specialist:** Regardless of what you think about human-induced climate change, it's clear we'll need scientists who specialise in altering it.
15. **Quarantine enforcer:** When a deadly virus spreads rapidly, quarantine enforcers will 'guard the gates'.
16. **Weather modification police:** If weather patterns can be altered and adversely affect other parts of the world, law enforcement will be needed to keep things legal.
17. **Virtual lawyer:** As international law grows to supersede national law, lawyers will be needed to handle cases that involve people living in several nations with different laws.
18. **Classroom avatar manager:** Intelligent avatars will replace classroom teachers, but the human touch will be needed to properly match teacher to student.
19. **Alternative vehicle developers:** Goodbye, internal combustion engine. Zero-emission cars will need smart people to design and manufacture them.
20. **Narrowcasters:** As in, the opposite of 'broadcaster'. Media will grow increasingly personalised, and we'll need people to handle all those streams.
21. **Waste data handler:** Think of it as an 'IT axe man' ... for information. Waste data handlers will destroy data for security purposes.
22. **Virtual clutter organiser:** Now that your electronic life is more cluttered than your physical one, you'll need someone to clean things up – including your e-mail, desktop, and user accounts.
23. **Time broker/Time bank trader:** What's more valuable than precious metals, stones, or cold, hard cash? Your time.
24. **Social 'networking' worker:** A social worker for the Web generation.
25. **Branding managers:** These already exist for celebrities, but now everyone needs a 'personal brand' so others can easily digest who you are and what you stand for.

Shopping Malls: What will the shopping malls of 2030 look like, or will they even exist?

The pandemic accelerated the move towards online shopping for much of what you needed, including your food. Because restaurants were not able to open for long periods of time other than for outside seating or delivery, many people became used to ordering their food to be delivered from restaurants that had never done this before.

The increasing move to healthier foods saw meal kit deliveries in 2019, accounting for US$7.6 billion. The projected market by mid-2020 for the service for 2020 was US$12.10 billion and it is expected to grow in the next five years to nearly US$28 billion.

The pandemic-induced spike in the popularity of food delivery created jobs for many people who were out of work or under-employed, but by 2030 food delivery will likely be done by drones or autonomous vehicles. The cost of this will be less because people are taken out of the equation and of course the end of tips. Tasha Keeney, an ARK analyst, estimates that:

> Drones will deliver food orders for only US$0.25 per order at scale, boosting food delivery as a percent of food-away-from-home from 2 percent today to nearly 40 percent by 2030.
>
> *(Keeney, T. 2020)*

The shopping mall itself will look a little different in 2030 than it does today. For a start, most of the electricity will come from solar-powered roofs. Target, one of the largest retail brands, expects to have 500 of their 1,855 stores decked with solar panels before this book comes out. This reflects the position of being number one in onsite solar capacity that Target has held for three years. Walmart Inc., its main competitor, is also moving towards providing electricity for its stores and warehouses by solar or other renewable sources. Just like energy, water will be critical.

Many shopping malls are already losing their anchor stores, and this was accelerated by the pandemic in 2020 because more retail companies reduced their stores while investing in their online presence. The end result was a huge reduction in the number of shopping malls. According to Michael Gale (Gale, 2020), shopping mall properties in the US alone dropped from 1,000 to 600.

The malls of 2030 will be more of a life experience housing gyms as well as movies/VR experiences, food halls, and medical drop-in locations possibly run by AI robots. They may also have education/gaming activities featuring holodecks and nostalgia shops – although nostalgia may fare better in promenades along small-town main streets. Malls might host mini-Amazon fulfilment centres and even some urban farms.

The shopping mall of 2030 will be a hybrid of what we have today, integrating new technology with traditional shops. If we are looking for clothes – and we want to try them on – 3-D printing them and having them delivered may be OK for some clothes, but for others we want the experience of a real person advising us or of just trying them on before we buy them, even if there is an additional cost for that.

In the UK, John Lewis and Partners, a high-end department store chain, has been converting its large stores into apartments in the centre of the cities and towns where it owns property.

Shopping, and shopping at malls, are more than a consumer experience. People shop to feel happier, to be creative, and even to get some exercise. We also appreciate the traditional advantage of being where we can be entertained or socialise with friends. Some of us treat a trip to the mall as a reward for our hard work. This attitude was immortalised by Audrey Hepburn (playing Holly Golightly) in *Breakfast at Tiffany's*:

> Well, when I get it, the only thing that does any good is to jump in a cab and go to Tiffany's. Calms me down right away. The quietness and the proud look of it; nothing very bad could happen to you there. If I could find a real-life place that would make me feel like Tiffany's, then – then I'd buy some furniture and give the cat a name!
>
> *(Capote, 1958)*

Health

> Sustainable Development Goal 3: Ensure healthy lives and promote well-being for all, at all ages.

> Perhaps the greatest opportunities for IoT in health care lie in helping clinicians make faster, more accurate diagnoses and more precise, personalized treatment plans. This can improve outcomes, reduce costs, and ultimately provide greater access to high-quality care for more people across the globe.
>
> [The] Internet of things – sensors in things like phones and wearable medical devices – will help your doctor know your health in real time.
>
> *(Wolf, 2020)*

The developments in the next ten years will be supported by predictive analytics perhaps enabling the doctors of tomorrow to help you address diseases before they even happen.

The pandemic (SDG3) in 2020–21 opened up the use of online health consultations in a way that might otherwise have taken a decade or more to happen. In 2020 virtual health visits by patients at least once increased by 57 per cent, and for chronic illness by 77 per cent (Doximity, 2020).

By 2030, a virtual health consultation via video conference technology linking through smartphones, tablets, or PCs will be the norm, and in many cases the first healthcare option for someone feeling unwell.

Virtual health consultations offer huge advantages for those feeling unwell. Many, perhaps most, will no longer need to take half a day off work or school or arrange childcare to go to a doctor's office. Patients will be logged in on their preferred device and a doctor can potentially be available 24/7 depending on their provider. Patients might even have an avatar as their interface with the doctor or nurse in a 'second life' type of consultation. Similarly, a virtual doctor may be chatting to you in your house.

Big data and the Internet of Medical Things (IoMT) will enable your doctor to have real-time information on your health, whether it's through your toilet, your mobile phone, your Fitbit, or equivalent self-monitoring wearable devices. We already have smartphones and gadgets that check our pulse, blood pressure and blood glucose, or kidney functions. These technologies enable a doctor to see potential health problems as they arise rather than waiting to see patients at annual checkups and will play an important part in saving lives in the future. Doctors will also be able to keep track of whether medicines have been taken, particularly important for older people. Twenty per cent of American citizens are expected to be age 65 or over soon (US Census Bureau, 2020). When the baby boomer generation reaches retirement age in 2030, all developed countries will see a huge increase in older people. By 2034, the older population will likely outnumber children in the developed world.

The development and application of nanotechnology in medicine offers some very interesting possibilities. Nano robots could be used to make repairs at the cellular level in our bodies.

> Nanotechnology in medicine currently being developed involves employing nanoparticles to deliver drugs, heat, light or other substances to specific types of cells (such as cancer cells). Particles are engineered so that they are attracted to diseased cells, which allows direct treatment of those cells. This technique reduces damage to healthy cells in the body and allows for earlier detection of disease.
>
> *(UnderstandingNano.com, 2021)*

Home robots and AI are already starting to be used to help older people. They can play several roles, acting not only as helpers but also as companions. At its simplest, an AI-powered chatbot is an extension of Apple's Siri or IBM's Watson, but in a moveable physical form.

A survey in the US by Cigna/Ipsos found that something like 25 million over the age of 60 suffer chronic loneliness, and this is expected to rise to 35 million by 2030 (Shlagman, 2020).

Hanson Robotics has through 'Sophia' created the most human-like robot. Sophia can recognise human faces and emotional expressions and react accordingly. By 2030 such robots will be available in different forms, and the ones that are most humanoid will probably be the most expensive. If your partner dies and you want a robot that looks like him or her to help address your loneliness, that may well be possible by then.

It could also be that celebrities licence their image for your robot help. How cool would it be to be chatting, if you are from the UK, with James Bond or Doctor Who, as played by whichever actor you most like? In the US, robots may borrow an actor's image from popular TV shows like *Magnum P.I.* or *Friends.* The options are nearly limitless. Whatever face the robot would have, it would be collecting your health data for your doctor or nurse and alerting them if there is a problem. They will become your first respondent. This is not a replacement for good old-fashioned human interaction and touch but may be all that is available for some.

The air pollution in our cities and towns is a critical health issue. Around 200,000 Americans die from air pollution every year (McCall, 2019), and worldwide in 2019 it was estimated that 4.5 million deaths were linked to outdoor pollution exposures (Limaye, 2020). According to research from Harvard, one in five premature deaths worldwide can be attributed to the burning of fossil fuels which is twice as much as previously thought (Carpenter, 2021).

If the move to driverless cars accelerates in the next ten years, the number of deaths and accidents on the roads will reduce substantively, if not by 2030, then certainly within ten years of that. The move towards smaller community-based hospitals where most diagnosis and treatment will be dealt with without the need to stay will also accelerate. This will not replace large urban trauma centres or teaching hospitals, but for most people it will become the place for much of their health care.

Associated with the move towards electric cars and renewable energy the impacts of particle pollution will reduce and make the air more breathable, particularly for those who suffer from asthma. Particle pollution is linked to lung cancer, type 2 diabetes, chronic kidney disease, dementia, and pneumonia. It can affect breathing and cause problems for those with heart disease. There is additionally a great link between particle pollution and economic inequality. Many of those most affected by air pollution come from low-income groups such as African Americans, Hispanics and Latinos, and Native Americans. In addition to the diseases mentioned, there is also a link between pollution and our intelligence (McCall, 2019).

Over 110 countries (November 2020) have set carbon neutral plans for 2050 and so it is not inconceivable that by then air pollution from fossil fuel burning will be reduced substantially if not eliminated. China set theirs for 2060 (September 2020), which, if kept to, will reduce the temperature rise by 2100 by between 0.2 and 0.3 degrees Celsius (Climate Action Tracker, 2020).

With so much of people's health data being shared, a secure system will be needed, and this is where a health blockchain between you and your health provider will be critical. The collection of big data in health will not only help the individual patient but help health in general as far as recognising trends or dealing with pandemics.

Trace and track will be extremely easy by 2030, which will enable containment of future pandemics to be much easier. It will also help to flag issues such as air pollution incidents where there is a cluster of health problems. In the past, a doctor or a group of doctor surgeries might not have the information or be able to link patients living or working together near a locale with bad air quality. In the future, this will be easy to pinpoint and deal with. Medical professionals will be able to contact the company or government authority to rectify the problem at its source, or at least attempt to.

The healthcare/service is in the process of moving to a real patient-focused approach over the next ten years. They will have an ability to not only offer real-time healthcare but also to know at any one time where – compared to where the patient is – the critical diagnostic and therapeutic equipment is, and if or when it might be available. Big data will also know where medical staff are and where doctors who have the skills for addressing your diagnoses might conveniently be found.

Hospitals are already starting to incorporate 3-D printing to print some surgical instruments. This manufacturing at the point of use enables the hospital or doctor to not only create a more patient-focused object or drug but also not require so much stock or be worried about running out of a particular item.

During the pandemic in 2020, there was a shortage of personal protective equipment (PPE). The 3-D community through the National Institutes of Health published nearly 600 designs, of which 30 were approved and produced. In 2030, there would not be any shortages because the 3-D printers in hospitals or doctors' surgeries would produce what was required when it was required. Also introduced during the Covid pandemic was the robot nurse Tommy, first used in the Circolo hospital in Italy. 'Tommy' acted as a way for patients to communicate with the doctors remotely. It was able to measure blood pressure and oxygen saturation for ICU patients hooked up to ventilators (Romero, 2020).

3-D printing is offering a more personalised product for the individual with knee or other joint replacements. The porous nature of the 3-D structure helps enable tissue growth, and the integration of the replacement knee or other joint. Dentists likewise have increasingly turned to onsite 3-D printing for help with the implements and artefacts of oral surgery.

By 2030, it may be that the manufacturing of pharmaceuticals is also undertaken at the hospital when needed, with drug companies issuing licences to manufacture drugs to health providers. 3-D printing could enable a combined pill for someone taking many different medications, and therefore making it easier on the patient. The US Food and Drug Administration approved the first 3-D-printed pill in 2015.

One of the most exciting developments in 3-D printing is that of printing skin and organs. Bioengineers are taking samples of a patient's cells and trying to recreate them so that they can print replacement skin for burn victims.

> 3-D bio printing has actually played a starring role in advancing the field of skin engineering. Karande et al. (2013) published one of the first papers in the field showing that researchers could make a bio-ink from two types of living human cells and use a 3-D printer to produce a skin-like structure. The traditional procedure for making skin was to take cells, mix them up with collagen, and spread them in thin layers.
>
> *(Giggs, 2020)*

Bioprinting may seem like science fiction, but it is, like many of the applications of the disruptive industries in this book, already being rolled out. There are over 100,000 patients waiting for organ donors, so the idea of printing organs is incredibly attractive to those waiting for an organ that is suitable for a patient. There are several factors to find a match between a donated organ and a patient expecting an organ; this includes blood type, body type, and how severe the patient's medical state is.

Over the next ten years, the question is how far medicine will have come in designing the correct vasculature needed for successfully transporting nutrients, oxygen, and waste to keep an organ alive.

Like schools and universities, hospitals in 2030 will be different. The move to more preventative medicine and real-time information on your health will mean that time in hospitals will be reduced.

Surgeons will have less need to wield a scalpel. In 2020, Microbot Medical released the world's first:

> fully disposable endovascular surgical robot … for use in a variety of cardiovascular, neurovascular, and peripheral vascular procedures, manipulating catheters in a fly-by-wire way.
>
> *(Medgadget, 2020)*

The next generation of surgical robots will focus on autonomous miniaturisation and telesurgery technologies.

Already doctors are using 3-D visualisation with precise robotic movements. It's hard to believe that the first robotic surgery was in 1985, when a robot was guided as it inserted a needle into a brain for a biopsy (Williamson 2020).

The health section of this chapter ends with an enthusiastic reflection on the enormous advancement that was made in 2020 with Moderna and Pfizer developing RNA-/mRNA-based vaccines.

These are the first of a completely new approach to addressing viruses, and when the research started, many people did not believe it would work. The approach will enable the development of vaccines for emerging or re-emerging infectious diseases such as Zika, pandemic influenza, Nipah, and Ebola. They are:

> Tiny snippets of genetic code are essential in telling cells to build proteins, a basic part of human physiology – and key to unleashing the immune

system … to trigger the immune system to produce protective antibodies without using actual bits of the virus.

(Chow, 2020)

We live in a world where you can access your entire genetic makeup for around US$300, and that price is continuing to drop. Twenty years ago, it was US$2.7 billion. Many people are aware of a more simplified version in 23andMe or Ancestry that assists with searching for your ethnic ancestry and the 10–12 health conditions that simplified genetic profiles can pick up. Knowing the genetic and molecular makeup of a person will enable targeted treatment of diseases like cancer.

> This might also mean that with further understanding of the sequence of events leading to antigen expression, innate activation, and adaptive responses could guide the development of a portfolio of mRNA molecules and delivery systems with differential attributes. This will create a tool-box to tackle different applications, such as prophylactic versus therapeutic vaccines, infectious disease versus host disease (e.g., cancer) targets, or delivery of vaccine antigen versus therapeutic molecules (e.g., molecular antibodies).
>
> *(Maruggi et al., 2019)*

In his final State of the Union address (January 2016), President Barack Obama endorsed then-Vice President Joe Biden's call for 'a moonshot in this country to cure cancer'. That is increasingly becoming a possibility, perhaps even by 2030.

References

Airbnb (2020) Store Manager Lists World's Last BLOCKBUSTER® on Airbnb for Local Residents, Airbnb. Available online at: https://news.airbnb.com/store-manager-lists-worlds-last-blockbuster-on-airbnb-for-local-residents/

Anderson, C. (2019) Tweethttps://twitter.com/chr1sa. Available online at: https://twitter.com/chr1sa/status/1086793568767729665?ref_src=twsrc%5Etfw%7Ctwcamp%5Etweetembed%7Ctwterm%5E1086793568767729665%7Ctwgr%5Eshare_3%2Ccontainerclick_1&ref_url=https%3A%2F%2Fwww.bicycling.com%2Fnews%2Fa26038997%2Fuber-self-driving-bikes%2F

Baggaley, K. (2019) Here's How Smart Toilets of the Future Could Protect your Health, Mach. Available online at: https://www.nbcnews.com/mach/science/here-s-how-smart-toilets-future-could-protect-your-health-ncna961656

Bajarin, T. (2020) Statista in the Future of the Office – Hubs and Dedicated Meeting Centers, Forbes. Available online https://www.forbes.com/sites/timbajarin/2020/05/19/the-future-of-the-officehubs-and-dedicated-meeting-centers/?sh=789e1bbf3ec3

Beard, A. (2020) Can Computers Ever Replace the Classroom, The Guardian. Available online at: https://www.theguardian.com/technology/2020/mar/19/can-computers-ever-replace-the-classroom

Brodderick, M. (1986) in Ferris Bueller's Day Off, written by John Hughes, Paramount Picture.

Busby, J., Tanberk, J. and Broadband Now Team (2020) FCC Reports Broadband Unavailable to 21.3 Million Americans, BroadbandNow Study Indicates 42 Million Do not have Access, BoradbandNow Research. Available online at: https://broadbandnow.com/research/fcc-underestimates-unserved-by-50-percent

Capote, T. (1958) Breakfast at Tiffany's, Random House.

Carpenter, S. (2021) Fossil Fuel Air Pollution Kills Twice As any As Previously Thought, Stidy Finds, Forbes. Available online at: https://www.forbes.com/sites/scottcarpenter/2021/02/10/fossil-fuel-air-pollution-kills-nearly-as-many-as-cancer-study-finds/?sh=324d70df1dba&twclid=11369614012447682560&s=09

Chow, D. (2020) What is mRNA? How Pfizer and Moderna Tapped New Tech to Make Coronavirus Vaccines, NBC News. Available online at: https://www.nbcnews.com/science/science-news/what-mrna-how-pfizer-moderna-tapped-new-tech-make-coronavirus-n1248054

Climate Action Tracker (2020) China Going Carbon Neutral Before 2060 Would Lower Warming Projections by Around 0.2 to 0.3 Degrees C, Climate Action Tracker. Available online at: https://climateactiontracker.org/press/china-carbon-neutral-before-2060-would-lower-warming-projections-by-around-2-to-3-tenths-of-a-degree/

Corcoran, N. (2020) Vinyl Sales Surpass CD Sales for the First Time in 34 Years, Consequence of Sound. Available online at: https://consequenceofsound.net/2020/09/vinyl-sales-surpass-cds-34-years/

CST (2020) Garbage Designer, CST Consulting. Available online at: https://careers2030.cst.org/jobs/garbage-designer/

Curran, E. (2019) These Could Be the World's Biggest Economies by 2030, Bloomberg. Available online at: https://www.bloomberg.com/news/articles/2019-01-08/world-s-biggest-economies-seen-dominated-by-asian-ems-by-2030

Desjardins, J. (2019) Chart: The World's Largest 10 Economies in 2030, Visual Capitalist. Available online at: https://www.visualcapitalist.com/worlds-largest-10-economies-2030/

Doximity (2020) Doximity Study Finds Telemedicine Will Account for $29 Billion in Healthcare Services in 2020, Cision PR Newswire. Available online at: https://www.prnewswire.com/news-releases/doximity-study-finds-telemedicine-will-account-for-29-billion-in-healthcare-services-in-2020-301132131.html

Duggal, N. (2020) Future of Work: What Job Roles Will Look Like In 10 Years, Simplilean. Available online at: https://www.simplilearn.com/future-of-work-article

Financial Times (2017) Education Must Transform to Make People Ready for AI, Financial Times. Available online at: https://www.ft.com/content/ab5daa64-d100-11e7-947e-f1ea5435bcc7

Gale, M. (2020) The Real Future of Retail. An Independent View of 2030 from the Lens of 2020, Forbes. Available online at: https://www.forbes.com/sites/michaelgale/2020/09/29/the-real-future-of-retail-an-independent-view-of-2030-from-the-lens-of-2020/?sh=6a76bb5c1c37

Giggs, N. S. (2020) 3D Printing Living Skin with Blood Vessels, ASME. Available online at: 3D Printing Living Skin with Blood Vessels - ASME

Horan, D. (2021) Comments on the Chapter by David Horan.

IRENA (2016) End-of-life Management: Solar Photovoltaic Panels, IRENA. Available online at: https://www.irena.org/-/media/Files/IRENA/Agency/Publication/2016/IRENA_IEAPVPS_End-of-Life_Solar_PV_Panels_2016.pdf

Karande, P., Lee, V., Singh, V., Trasatti, P., Bjornsson, C., Xu, X., Nga Tran, T., Yoo, S. & Dai, G. (2013) Design and Fabrication of Human Skin by Three-Dimensional Bioprinting, Tissue Engineering Part C: Methods Vol. 20, No. 6. Available online at: https://www.liebertpub.com/doi/abs/10.1089/ten.tec.2013.0335?journalCode=tec

Keeney, T. (2020) in Drones x Food Delivery = An ETF Opportunity for the Ages, Nasdaq. Available online at: https://www.nasdaq.com/articles/drones-x-food-deli very-an-etf-opportunity-for-the-ages-2020-12-10

Kennedy, R. (1968) Bobby Kennedy on GDP: 'Measures Everything Except that Which is Worthwhile' Reprinted in the Guardian (2012). Available online at: https://www.theguardian.com/news/datablog/2012/may/24/robert-kennedy-gdp

Limaye, V. & Davies, E. (2020) Report: Air Pollution a Major Driver of Ill Health Worldwide, NRDC. Available online at: https://www.nrdc.org/experts/vijay-limay e/report-air-pollution-major-driver-ill-health-worldwide#:~:text=According%20 to%20their%20data%2C%204.5%20million%20deaths%20were,million%20de aths%20were%20caused%20by%20indoor%20air%20pollution.

Loten, A. (2020) What Office Life Might Look Like in the Year 2030, Wall Street Journal. Available online at: https://www.wsj.com/articles/what-office-life-might- look-like-in-the-year-2030-11583362501?shareToken=st8ab6e3295d4843ebab973 981e0c05693

Mandela, N. (1990) Education is the Most Powerful Weapon Which you can use to Change the World, The Elders. Available online at: https://www.theelders.org/news/ %E2%80%9Ceducation-most-powerful-weapon-which-you-can-use-change-world %E2%80%9D

Maruggi, G., Zhang, C., Li J., Ulmer, B. J. and Yu, D. (2019) mRNA as a Transformative Technology for Vaccine Development to Control Infectious Diseases, Molecular Therapy. Available online at: https://doi.org/10.1016/j.ymthe.2019.01.020

McCall, R. (2019) Around 200,000 Americans Die Every Year from Air Pollution that Meets EPA Standard, Newsweek. Available online at: https://www.newsweek.com/ 200000-americans-die-every-year-air-pollution-that-meets-epa-standard-1473187

McKeever, V. (2019) London's Population Could Decline in 2021 for the First Time this Century. Here's Why People are Leaving, CNBC Make it. Available online at: https:// www.cnbc.com/2021/01/08/why-uk-workers-are-leaving-london-amid-the-coron avirus-pandemic.html?utm_term=Autofeed&utm_medium=Social&utm_content =Intl&utm_source=Facebook&fbclid=IwAR0reAXsvBc4DiLl8LdkCeYxSB dQCy0_fEW7GKobtvFiUjicSK0Ax3Mr0Us#Echobox=1610277665

Medgadget (2020) Fully Disposable Endovascular Robot Unveiled. Medgadget. Available online at: https://www.medgadget.com/2020/01/fully-disposable-endo vascular-robot-unveiled.html

Mesenbrink, J. (2020) Rainwater Harvesting Education Gaining Momentum Through Steadfast Leadership, Contractor. Available online at: https://www.contractormag. com/green/article/21141155/rainwater-harvesting-education-gaining-moment um-through-steadfast-leadership

O'Brien, A., S. (2020) Prop 22 Passes in California, Exempting Uber and Lyft from Classifying Drivers as Employees, CNN Business. Available online at: https://www. cnn.com/2020/11/04/tech/california-proposition-22/index.html

OECD (2018) OECD Future of Education and Skills 2030, OECD. Available online at: https://www.oecd.org/education/2030-project/teaching-and-learning/learning/ skills/Skills_for_2030_concept_note.pdf

Ostergaard, F.S. and Nordlund, G.A. (2019) The 4 Biggest Challenges to Our Higher Education Model – And What to do About Them, World Economic Forum. Available online at: https://www.weforum.org/agenda/2019/12/fourth-industrial-revolution-higher-education-challenges

Petrov, C. (2020) 21+ Freelance Statistics to Know in May 2020, Spendmenot. Available online at: https://spendmenot.com/blog/freelance-statistics/#:~:text=Some%20experts%20estimate%20that%20freelancers%20will%20represent%20about,2019%2C%20about%2057%20million%20Americans%20worked%20as%20freelancers

Roberts, R. (2018) Reimagining Education in the Exponential Age, SingularityHub. Available online at: https://singularityhub.com/2018/09/20/reimagining-education-in-the-exponential-age/

Romero, D.M. (2020) Tommy the Robot Nurse Helps Italian Doctors Care for COVID-19 Patients, The World. Available online at: https://www.pri.org/stories/2020-04-08/tommy-robot-nurse-helps-italian-doctors-care-covid-19-patients

Shlagman, W. (2020) How Computer Learning Can Make a Difference, HomeCare. Available online at: https://www.homecaremag.com/september-2020/potential-ai-homecare

Smith, J. (2014) 9 Futuristic Jobs we could see by 2030, Business Insider. Available online at: https://www.businessinsider.com/bizarre-jobs-well-see-by-2030-2014-5#:~:text=Here%20are%20nine%20jobs%20that%20will%20likely%20be,formally%20called%20%22farmers.%22%20The%20role%20of%20the%20rewilder%2C

Tagermann V. (2021) A School Bought Solar Panels and Saved Enough to Give All Its Teachers Raises, The Byte. Available online at: https://futurism.com/the-byte/solar-panels-save-teachers-raise

Thunberg, G. (2019) Teen Climate Activist Greta Thunberg Speaks at Four School Strikes in a Week, Video 1:57, Source: Reuters, The Guardian. Available online at: https://www.theguardian.com/world/video/2019/mar/01/teen-climate-activist-greta-thunberg-speaks-at-four-school-strikes-in-a-week-video

UnderstandingNano (2021) Nanotechnology in Medicine – Nanoparticles in Medicine, UnderstandingNano. Available online at: https://www.understandingnano.com/medicine.html

United States Census Bureau (2020) Demographic Turning Points for the United States: Population Projections for 2020 to 2060, US Census Bureau. Available online at: https://www.census.gov/library/publications/2020/demo/p25-1144.html#:~:text=The%20year%202030%20marks%20a,to%20be%20of%20retirement%20age

Williamson J. (2020) The Eyes Behind Surgical Robots, Photonics Media. Available online at: https://www.photonics.com/Articles/The_Eyes_Behind_Surgical_Robots/a65221

Wolf, M. (2020) IoT in Health Care: Unlocking True, Value-based Care, SAS Insights. Available online: https://www.sas.com/id_id/insights/articles/big-data/iot-in-healthcare--unlocking-true--value-based-care.html

World Economic Forum (2018) The Future of Jobs Report 2018, World Economic Forum. Available online at: https://www.weforum.org/reports/the-future-of-jobs-report-2018

6

ENTERTAINMENT

Introduction

> Want Marilyn Monroe to star in a newly created *Fast and Furious* film? No problem! Keen to cast your brother in one of the original *Star Wars* movies? It might soon be as easy as contracting an AI to edit him in, ready for his next Jedi-themed birthday.
>
> *(Diamandis, 2019)*

Films and TV

In 2020, backers for the film *b* cast a robot in a lead role. Kohel Ogawa, one of the two Japanese scientists behind 'Erica' (the robot) had to actually teach her to act:

> 'In other methods of acting, actors involve their own life experiences in the role', Khoze says. 'But Erica has no life experiences. She was created from scratch to play the role. We had to simulate her motions and emotions through one-on-one sessions, such as controlling the speed of her movements, talking through her feelings and coaching character development and body language'.
>
> *(Keegan, 2020)*

AI is also being used to advise on film development: LargoAI has a database of 30,000 movies and the software can identify if the chosen music is likely to fit with the film well or can advise on the release of a film in different countries based on different cultural norms. An AI may also give an idea of if the film is likely to be a success or not – though what makes a good movie can be very subjective. A decent AI system should be able to determine the characteristics of

DOI: 10.4324/9781003045496-6

a film that would appeal to a certain demographic, but would it be successful? How much of that success is down to the writers and the directors? By 2030 we may very well find out.

The use of actors who have died is becoming an increasing issue in the film and TV industry. It has been prompted in part with the Star Wars movies: First, *Rogue One* (2016) recreated Peter Cushing, who had died in 1994. Second, Carrie Fisher (Princess Leia) died in 2016 before the final shooting of *Star Wars: The Last Jedi* (2017). There was some dialogue the filmmakers wanted to use from previous things she had said, but also to finish, so they had to digitally create one scene with her in it using CGI. Finally, the most discussed use of a deceased actor was in the 2019 film, *The Rise of Skywalker*, when AI was used to create a number of scenes for Princess Leia. In the end, they also found footage from *Star Wars: The Force Awakens* (2015), which they could digitally insert into the more recent film.

Deepfake: Deepfake has exploded in the last year and is where a video or audio content has been changed or manipulated using AI to make it seem as if someone is saying or doing something they never did. We are seeing it increasingly used in politics and porn.

On 4 May 2016 *The Tonight Show*, the late-night talk show that is broadcast from the NBC Studies in the Rockefeller Center in New York City, did a skit where host Jimmy Fallon played Donald Trump and Dion Flynn played President Obama talking on the phone to each other. They were made up to look like the people they were playing but of course you could easily see it was Fallon and Flynn.

In 2019 this was altered, appearing on YouTube under the title 'The Presidents', where Fallon and Flynn were replaced by Trump and Obama seemingly saying the exact words that Fallon and Flynn had said (The Presidents, 2019).

BOX 6.1: HOW TO SPOT A DEEPFAKE

A lack of blinking: Many older deepfake methods failed to mimic the rate at which a person blinks – a problem recent programmes have fixed.

Face wobble: Shimmer or distortion is a giveaway. Also, look for abnormal movements from fixed objects in the frame – a microphone stand or a lamp, for example.

Strange behaviour: An individual doing something implausible or out of character should always be a red flag.

But obvious fakes may not be what they seem. It is easy to sow doubt about real footage by adding an inconsistency.

Source: Alexander Adam, data scientist, Faculty (Parkin, 2019)

In August 2020 Babyzone took the original *Avengers* game and replaced the car-toon versions of *The Avengers* with the movie versions for a trailer. BabyZone described what they had done:

> I created this video using AI machine learning DeepFake technology. In particular, I used DeepFaceLab 2.0 by IPerov to create the face models for each actor. I used my own 192 DF model trained over 1M iterations. Face set for each actor was created from marvel's [sic] *Avengers* movies and then trained separately for each cut scene.
>
> *(Tassi, 2020)*

Unsurprisingly deepfake also moved into porn. There you can often find your favourite actor depicted doing things they never did.

> Up to 1,000 deepfake videos have been uploaded to porn sites every month as they became increasingly popular during 2020, figures from deepfake Detection Company Sensity show. The videos continue to break away from dedicated deepfake pornography communities and into the mainstream.
>
> *(Burgess, 2020)*

Already deepfakes are being produced in real time based on just one photo of a person. The use of people's identities and what they say and do should be in their control, and this will be central to the deepfake legislation over the next ten years.

New York State became the second government after California (October 2019) to pass:

> a bill updating the right of publicity and prohibiting the distribution of digitally created sexually explicit performances – known as 'deepfakes' – without the consent of the performer.
>
> *(Robb, 2020)*

'No provider or user of an interactive computer service shall be treated as the publisher or speaker of any information provided by another information content provider' (Congress, 1995).

The bill passed in a rare example of bipartisanship in the New York Senate in July 2020 by 60 to 0. The reality is that it will need both national and interna-tional agreement to ensure that it stops. In the US this would require an amend-ment to the federal Communications Decency Act (Section 230).

Currently, there are even no laws against deepfakes in the European Union which usually has strong protection laws. There is a 'Code of Practice on Disinformation' (2020) for online platforms which doesn't seem to be work-ing; this is being reviewed as we write, and expect legislation in the coming years. There are a number of suggested laws that have passed the House of

CARTOON 6.1 Entire family relaxing in the living room. Everyone is sitting on the couch, maybe looking at their respective screens

Representative in the US, such as the 'Deepfakes Accountability Act' and 'The Identifying Outputs of Generative Adversarial Networks' (IOGAN) Act. The second has progressed to the Senate Committee on Commerce, Science, and Transportation but has not yet been discussed in the Senate as a whole. This misuse of actors and politicians has been a central piece of the present action on deepfakes.

In the 2000s, phone hacking by the media was a preeminent issue, where conversations and photos that people thought were private became frontpage news. Although unpleasant, the issues around phone hacking weren't challenged until the case of Milly Dowler, a 13-year-old schoolgirl who was reported missing and whose remains were eventually found in Yateley Heath Woods on 18 September 2002.

Scotland Yard's subsequent investigation found that Milly's phone had been accessed by journalists from the UK newspaper the *News of the World*. This had given hope to the parents and police that she was still alive. Public outcry was so great that ultimately it contributed to the closing down of the newspaper, whose circulation at the time was over 2.5 million.

It may take more than celebrities and politicians to persuade legislatures of action needed to introduce appropriate laws and punishments to deter deepfakery. As deepfake programmes become more accessible to the 'general public', the potential for misuse is enormous and the impact on people's lives huge.

A sobering thought in the US:

> Use of any US law to regulate deepfakes will come under First Amendment scrutiny, meaning any regulation – existing or in the works – must be tailored to apply only to instances of actual malice or reckless disregard, and where the material is not newsworthy.
>
> *(Lovells et al, 2020)*

The issue of deepfakery has moved up the political agenda and in September 2020 Microsoft announced a tool to detect deepfake. Machine learning enables the detection of deepfake. Ultimately it may be that blockchain will need to be introduced as a digital fingerprint for uploading videos. This would attempt to ensure that anyone trying to post deepfake videos would be identified and any potential prosecution would be possible when legislation catches up. Deepfakes will eventually be able to convince people that someone said or did something that they did not. The video will be disseminated widely among a gullible audience – even when proved wrong, the damage would already have been done.

Finally, to show the danger of deepfake Channel 4 in the UK broadcast a deepfake Christmas Message from the Queen at the same time as the Queen was giving her message on other channels. The AI-generated deepfake message started with:

> On the BBC I haven't always been able to speak plainly and from the heart. So, I grateful to Channel 4 for giving me the opportunity to say what I like.
>
> *(Channel, 4, 2020)*

Sport

In sport AI is already being used to ensure that coaches can improve the techniques of the players. By 2030 – or even earlier – it will be possible that AI could look at the skills a team has, work out its weaknesses, and look at players across the world who could replace those that are not effective in a particular position in the team.

AI would be able to play simulations against other teams and advise the manager and coaches the best way to play the game. Additionally, it will be able to monitor player's diets and correlate them with the amount of exercise players need to be in prime physical condition.

The use of AR/VR is growing in sport and improving the players or individual's ability to perform. By 2030 the fans may be able to put themselves into a game and see how their team would play with them as members. Fans may also be able to watch games through the eyes of different players as they play.

If you are a Formula One (F1) or NASCAR driver, you can already practice the turns of a race using VR. During the race, AR glasses will increasingly give you and the driver real-time information on the race situation and your position. They will be able to increasingly show your health using big data and analytics with up-to-the-second readouts on the state of the tyres or any weak parts in the engine before something happens. This may result in fewer crashes, although statistically most crashes are due to driver error. It also remains to be seen whether advances like these help pit crews or sideline them by abrogating knowledge that in simpler times was shared only by veterans of racing's intuition.

Esports developed a virtual Grand Prix series (2017) initially with no drivers from F1 during the COVID-19 shut down to fill the void of no races in person and the virtual platform expanded. The cancelled races that moved to the platform started with a virtual Bahrain Grand Prix on 22 March 2020. The race ran for half the number of physical laps originally planned but introduced a whole new audience to the platform as it was broadcast from the official F1 website, as well as Facebook and YouTube. Frank Sagnier, Chief Executive Officer, Codemasters, had this to say before the event:

> We're excited to be a part of the new F1 Esports Virtual Grand Prix Series. With sporting events currently on hold around the world, it is great that the official F1® video game can help fill the void by bringing together an exciting line-up of talent to race online during the postponed race weekends. It's going to be competitive, action-packed, and a lot of fun for everyone involved.
>
> *(Codemasters, 2020)*

In 2019 Formula 1 announced a plan to be net zero carbon by 2030, and this was not only on track but also the whole operation behind the teams (Formula 1, 2019).

Regarding another sport, the National Basketball Association (NBA) is investing in VR. Vice President of Global Media Distribution, Jeff Marisio, summarises NBA motivation this way:

> Imagine that a virtual camera is like a bumblebee that can fly anywhere on the court, you could even fly the bumblebee right on the nose of your favorite player, and its video output could be incorporated into the television broadcast or sent straight to a VR headset, so the viewer is looking out of the bumblebee's eyes. We are still a couple of years away, but this science-fiction reality isn't as far off as you might think.
>
> *(Golliver, 2017)*

Sustainable Development Goal 3. Ensure healthy lives and promote well-being for all at all ages.

Biotechnology and sports have mostly focused around helping athletes to return to fitness (SDG3) after an injury. By 2030 athletes will immediately be able to have a clear idea of their injury, what diagnosis is, and how best to address it.

Head injuries in sports like American football (though that seems a strange name for a sport that is seldom about kicking the ball with the foot) and rugby have become recognised since 1906, when a Harvard student athlete died from a head injury. His team doctors released a report titled 'The Physical Aspect of American Football' in the *Boston Medical and Surgical Journal*.

The National Football League did not start to really address its head injury problem until 1994. It took until 2017 for there to be a helmet developed (by Vicis) that would record the appropriate data and have more layers to cushion the impacts of tackles or collisions. In 2018, a blood test was developed that recognises two elevated proteins in the brain in the athlete that has had a concussion. By 2030, these advances will be instantaneous during a game and a player can be brought off the field immediately when there is any danger – as future helmets would be able to monitor any problematic issues. Similar advances are expected for recognising potential spinal cord injuries, which amount to around half a million people a year, with 40 per cent being permanently disabled.

Biotechnology for increasing the performance of athletes through gene doping has also advanced, although it is, of course, illegal because it goes against the 'fairness doctrine' at the centre of sport. Detecting illegal performance enhancements in real time will help to tell whether someone is trying to cheat and enable real-time action to be taken.

> Sustainable Development Goal 7. Ensure access to affordable, reliable, sustainable, and modern energy for all.

Sports clothing, like other fashions, has come under environmental scrutiny due to its demands on material resources, energy (SDG7), and water, not to mention emissions footprint and contribution to the waste stream. Moving to biodegradable material and to a circular economy approach will, by 2030, be standard for most sports uniform makers. AMSilk of Munich worked with Adidas to produce trainers (in the US, they are called athletic shoes) that are made from synthetic spider silk. The move away from acrylic-based clothing will reduce the number of microfibres released into the water system and thereby impact the environment positively.

Personal exercise

In 2020, you can choose an app with your favourite online trainer who, using machine learning, image recognition, and motion tracking, can give you real-time advice during your workout, especially on high-end exercise bikes. If you are looking for a more boot camp approach, then something like 'Effective Focused Fast Exceptional Creative Training' (E.F.F.E.C.T.) exists for you. Online alternatives for supervised exercise have mushroomed, and you can find nearly anything you would wish for. This includes ballet, pilates/yoga, strength work, bodyweight training, boxing … well pretty much everything is available through an app. With the more advanced programmes, your phone camera can check to see whether your form for particular exercises is correct.

Will this replace – in person – personal trainers? It might by 2030, because technology gives you constant feedback for a fraction of the cost. You will be able to use the wall or your VR glasses at home to project onto as you join a pack of bikes going up a hill, simulating the feeling of actually being there.

Companions on your exercise routine may be projected through a 3-D image along with the collection of data on how you are doing against your friends. This service will offer personal training targets you need to take on to improve, while potentially monitoring your diet and other habits (including sleep) 24 hours a day, 7 days a week, and 52 weeks a year. Through IoT, workout services will be able to synchronise with your diary, and find free moments in your busy day to have you do the most relevant exercise for that time.

Robot referees and umpires

With the growth of instant replay across many sports, the use of robot referees calling ball-strike or goal is not far off. By 2030 the use of people to referee games may be left to the amateur world.

> FIFA (Fédération Internationale de Football Association) wants to intro-duce the use of robots as assistant referees and plan to implement the new technology in time for the 2022 World Cup.
> FIFA's director of technology, Johannes Holzmuller, has outlined his plan for the new system which would see assistant referees replaced with computer technology which automatically generates offside lines.
>
> *(Cheesbrough, 2020)*

I'm sure everyone reading this book has a story of a terrible referee decision that they remember and has at one time or another commented negatively about the ability or sight of a referee in a game that they cared about. Perhaps the worst referee decision of the last ten years was the red card for Robin van Persie playing for Arsenal against Barcelona (2011) in the Champions League round of 16 and which Barcelona then won and then went on to win the Cup (should have been Arsenal). TV late-night host Jay Leno put it this way:

> I wanted to have a career in sports when I was young, but I had to give up the idea. I'm only six feet tall, so I couldn't play basketball. I'm only 190 pounds, so I couldn't play football, and I have 20/20 vision, so I couldn't be a referee.
>
> *(Kollen, 2019)*

Many sports are already looking at the use of robots as a complement to the pre-sent referees. By 2030 it is difficult to believe that someone hoping for a career as a professional referee will find there are anywhere near the number of jobs that there are today. Even opportunities to referee professionally at amateur sport levels will likely decrease.

> [Anyone] who follows NFL football knows the rules of the game are ever-changing. Every play, every call, every inch lost or gained on the field is scrutinized to the point where I have to ask, are we ever going to be OK with allowing the human element of officiating be a part of the NFL game? Because if we aren't, let's just start working on removing all human officials now and bring in Skynet to take over our beloved football games.
>
> *(Schlehuber, 2019)*

Tennis has had a hybrid system where they still rely on people being line judges – with each set each player can challenge up to three times a call. All major tournaments have a camera-based system to check if the ball is in or out but are only used if there is a challenge. By 2030 can we expect that the referee will be fully using the system without any line judges?

Music and concerts

Platforms like Spotify and Amazon Prime already use AI, big data, and analytics to help listeners find music they like, based on previous searches.

This has helped many of us encounter artists and genres that we might never have experienced if we were still only listening to the radio or buying CDs or vinyl records. Of course, there is nothing wrong with vinyl once you have found a track you like. It may be that by 2030 your 3-D printer or a 3-D printer locally can print you a vinyl album based on your favourite tracks you like at that moment. Vinyl overtook CD sales in September 2019 – vinyl last being top in 1986. A year later, the sales of vinyl were nearly twice that of CDs. After all vinyl is the best and is a return to quality as well as being an echo of a bygone time returning.

The first recording of computer-generated music was created by Alan Turing, the famous computer scientist, who broke the Enigma code.

> The recording was made 65 years ago by a BBC outside-broadcast unit at the Computing Machine Laboratory in Manchester, England.
>
> The machine, which filled much of the lab's ground floor, was used to generate three melodies; God Save the King, Baa, Baa Black Sheep, and Glenn Miller's swing classic 'In the Mood.'
>
> *(Agence France-Presse, 2016)*

David Bowie started using a digital lyric randomiser to help with his inspiration in the 1990s. In 2018 'Hello, World' became the first album composed by an artist – SKYGGE – with the help of the Magenta Studio from Google, an open source music generating package, which through machine learning has four tools to help musicians compose, record, arrange, mix, and master their music. Magenta Studio is but one of many that are looking to use AI to create original music, IBM Watson Beat and AI Computer are some others. The Internet of Musical Things (IoMusT) is growing with the possibility of smart instruments and (as we go into below) assistance for writing songs and music. As IoMusT develops, the audience can let the band know what they want played and so could help direct the mood of a concert.

François Pachet, the director of Spotify's Creator Technology Research Lab states:

> The amount of music produced by AI is very little compared to the activity on the research side … We are still in the very beginning.
>
> *(Chow, 2020)*

The use of AI in the music world is in its infancy but by 2030 AI, as opposed to Taylor Swift, may be writing the next number one song. AI may also be actually generating the music itself or maybe you are composing or singing from your bedroom because the tools will be available to you to do so.

AI-generated music will increasingly be used for commercials, films, and TV soundtracks. Using big data, a film composer or producer or maybe just an intern will have the music from successful films in the same genres available. AI will then be able to produce similar but copyrightable equivalents, or at least options which can be reviewed before a human makes the final decision.

AI-generated music may have a place in the music landscape, but it will not replace what has been created by people … at least not by 2030. One of the successes of globalisation and the use of the Internet is it has opened up music from around the world to everyone who might be interested. The fragmentation of music into many different genres has opened up a lot of creativity. AI-generated music will find its place there.

YouTube, Facebook, and Instagram have been platforms for new artists to emerge. Someone in their bedroom in a small town in Iowa could be the next star. Some of the most successful artists of today, including Ed Sheeran, Pentatonix, Shawn Mendes, Tori Kelly, and Justin Bieber, started their careers on YouTube. In an earlier age, they might not have succeeded or even been heard.

Bands by 2030 will be projecting 3-D images of themselves around the world for concerts that are broadcast at the same time. It seems that in 2030 you will be able to be in more than one place at the same time … at least virtually!

In 2020, Lund University in Sweden hosted the first concert where all the instruments were 3-D printed. The band members were from the Malmö Academy of Music which is part of the University. As Professor Olaf Diegel explained:

> 3-D printing allows me to make complex shapes that are impossible to do any other way. I can also tailor instruments very precisely for musicians who want their instruments custom made.
>
> *(Lund University, 2020)*

During the COVID-19 lockdown, digital VR platforms were used to create concerts and make them easy to share with the fans. Most of the concerts are via social media platforms, but some are distributed using VR technology. As these develop, they will allow an artist to have different backdrops or virtual stages for different songs. New systems may even enable fans to choose which option (Vuksic, 2020).

Finally, the development of Music: Not Impossible (M:NI) helps deaf music fans through vibrations to enjoy a concert or music from one of the online music platforms through IoT at home.

Sustainable Development Goal 2: End hunger, achieve food security and improved nutrition, and promote sustainable agriculture.

Restaurants and cafés

> If your menu has the words 'sustainably sourced', your ingredients are considered 'clean' and you're prepared to tell the stories behind the food you're serving.
>
> *(National Restaurant Association, 2019)*

The last decade has seen a huge change in what people expect from their food (SDG2) and what they might eat in a restaurant. An example of this is the huge growth of farmers' markets in the US, from 3,000 in 1999 to 5,000 in 2009 to more than 8,800 in 2019 (Civil Eats, 2019). People are looking for more healthy foods, and even fast-food restaurants are offering 'healthy' options.

Skyscraper farms have started to emerge – vertical farms either as part of new skyscraper developments or converting old buildings into a 21st-century farm in the middle of a city or town.

Sustainable Development Goal 6: Ensure availability and sustainable management of water and sanitation for all.

The use of hydroponics and aeroponics recycles the use of 95–99 per cent of the water (SDG6). Food is grown in soil but is water rich with nutrients and sprayed with a mist full of nutrients. The food is harvested in the city and so the food miles – the carbon used for transport – is as close to zero as can be.

The use of blockchain in sourcing food is growing fast with blockchain platforms such as IBM Food Trust or Greenfence or Hungry Coin or ripe.io. These platforms aim to bring transparency and more efficient delivery of food to the food chain. In 2018, Walmart was the first supermarket to use blockchain as a solution to food safety.

> Most supply chains are bogged down in manual processes. This makes it difficult and time consuming to track down an issue should one like the

E. coli romaine lettuce problem from last spring rear its head. By placing a supply chain on the blockchain, it makes the process more traceable, transparent, and fully digital. Each node on the blockchain could represent an entity that has handled the food on the way to the store, making it much easier and faster to see if one of the affected farms sold infected supply to a particular location with much greater precision.

(Miller, 2018)

AI assistants like Siri, Google Assistant, Watson, Alexa or Huawei's Xiao Ai learn their owner's preferences for everyday decisions such as what they like to eat, and they can link this to your healthier diet and recommend restaurants that offer these. Such assistants can also check if restaurants are adopting sustainability policies that fit in with your goals.

Sustainable Development Goal 13: Take urgent action to combat climate change and its impact.

For a restaurant there are several areas that will need to see considerable advancement by 2030 if restaurants are to play their role in helping to deliver the Paris Climate Agreement (SDG13) and the SDGs. An example of how this is starting to impact even in 2020 is Restaurant Brands International (RBI). RBI which accounts for the brands Tim Hortons, Burger King, and Popeyes and a turnover of US$34 billion a year and 27,000 restaurants in over 100 countries have looked at how they can contribute to help deliver the SDGs (RBI, 2020).

By 2030 the energy and water use of restaurants will need to be reduced and be as efficient as possible. This is being helped by the development of more energy- and water-efficient appliances in the kitchens – their use linked through your IoT so you can reduce use at any time.

For restaurants another key area that needs addressing is that of food waste. In the US, restaurants generate around 22 to 33 billion pounds of waste a year.

According to the Cornell University Food and Brand Lab, on average, diners leave 17 percent of their meals uneaten and 55 percent of edible leftovers are left at the restaurant.

(FoodPrint, 2020)

By redirecting unopened and otherwise still good uneaten foods to foodbanks, soup kitchens, and the like, and by repurposing food waste from preparation and that uneaten by diners to composting or energy-recovery facilities, the restaurant industry can make a meaningful contribution to reducing hunger, consumption and production, and climate change.

Sustainable Development Goal 9: Build resilient infrastructure, promote inclusive and sustainable industrialisation, and foster innovation.

For example, cities like New York are seeing the growth of microhauling – the small-scale collection of materials by bikes or low emission vehicles – that serve smaller food waste generators that do not have enough volume to warrant a conventional waste truck to service them (SDG9).

Food waste is transported to nearby neighbourhood composting sites that utilise a variety of technologies to convert organic material into composts and soil amendments for use locally. In addition to reducing road congestion and emissions from transport, the diversion of restaurant food waste from landfill reduces the methane emissions associated with traditional waste disposal methods.

> Sustainable Development Goal 10: Reduce inequality within and among countries.

The salaries of those working in a restaurant are low, with a server getting US\$3.50 to \$US7.50 (plus tips) an hour (Job-applications.com, 2020). Income inequality (SDG10) has grown over the last decade. AI and big data offer the chance for information on what a restaurant is paying someone to be flagged, and that information might then play a role how you choose where you want to eat out. As this book is being written, there is legislation being proposed that the minimum wage in the US will increase to US\$15 per hour.

One of the most enjoyable forms of entertainment is going out with friends for a meal at a favourite restaurant or perhaps a new one that 'pops up' as word on the grapevine is that the food and service there is good. Some restaurants in 2020 are experimenting with the use of blockchain so you know that the fish you are eating is actually from where it says it is.

Blockchain will enable 'ocean to table' tracking to happen. In October 2019 starting in California, TAPS Fish House and Brewery built on the IBM Blockchain Platform. You will find a bar code on the menu with which your smartphone scanner can see the date the scallop (for example) was caught. The plan by Nordic and Raw Seafoods is to have a video so you could also see what you are eating, being caught whatever restaurant you are eating at (IBM, 2019).

As these experiments start to expand, the food producers need to be brought onboard and the infrastructure for this is not yet there in 2020. By 2030, however, you would expect the food you buy and the food you eat at restaurants to be sustainably sourced, and that you could verify that through a bar code (and the blockchain) as opposed to just asking the server.

AI and robots will combine to reduce the number of people employed as restaurant staff. Automating a part or the whole of a restaurant is a high financial outlay initially but reduces ongoing costs. Fully automated restaurants will be part of the landscape by 2030. Even if the restaurant is not fully automated with robots making your food or delivering it to you, more tasks within restaurants will be automated.

Sustainable Development Goal 11: Make cities and human settlements inclusive, safe, resilient, and sustainable.

In the last few years, the idea of co-locating restaurants in food halls has gained traction. The COVID-19 pandemic impact on restaurants will accelerate this approach. Food halls give restaurants a cost-sharing system which could also include a common AI platform to address deliveries, paying bills, staff scheduling and management, marketing, and electronic contact with the customers who bought your food. Moving to smartphone or kiosk ordering will reduce staff but will enable the restaurant to focus on delivering good food. AI kiosks with chatbots also offer instant language translation for visiting tourists and can also give the customer a reliable estimate of the time when ordered food will arrive (SDG11).

Data collected by the restaurant can drive decisions on menus like offering different ones at different times of the day or different days and offering specials based on the weather.

As discussed in the Chapter 3: Home life, the fridges, freezers, and general inventory will be controlled by AI and will enable the restaurant to have the freshest food while automatically dealing with re-ordering. Gone will be the days when you are told that what you want is out of stock.

> An AI with the algorithmic ability to analyze and synthesize inhuman amounts of data and information about foods, beverages, ingredients, chemical compounds, and tastes will result in the creation of recipes, dishes and beverages beyond, and unlike, what humans would produce. Some AIs will become as well-known as human chefs, baristas and bartenders.
>
> *(National Restaurant Association, 2019)*

Although the first 'pop-up' restaurant idea is older than 2007, it was in 2007 that Ludo Lefebvre brought the concept to a wider audience with his 'LudoBites' in Los Angeles. The idea caught on not only in LA but around the planet. Pop-up business will increasingly rely on social media and big data to identify its target clientele, in addition to word of mouth, of course.

Food delivery options were pioneered by the pizza industry but have taken on new heights during the pandemic with the growth of DoorDash, GrubHub, Uber Eats, and other delivery services.

By 2030 your meal may be delivered by self-driving cars or even by drones in urban areas. Online ordering may give restaurants access to data on where else you went before deciding on them to provide your meal. Big data and analytics also provide insights to restaurant owners and chefs about the best places to advertise for a good return. This future is envisioned by Heloise Blause, founder of HomeKitchenLand.com:

> First and foremost, most restaurants are going to see a huge drop-off in the number of customers who dine in. As a customer, being able to have almost anything you want delivered to your door makes you reconsider the purpose of going to restaurants. I mean, why get in the car and fight through traffic if you can stay in, watch a movie, and enjoy your favorite food?
>
> *(Modern Restaurant Management, 2020)*

Restaurants will see new opportunities to apply data analytics to predict and capitalise on consumer demand and optimise supply chain economics.

Dark, cloud, and ghost kitchens have expanded to serve the delivery companies. These kitchens live in underused real estate, therefore saving overhead costs and also offering virtually 24-hour service. They can also have much more already-prepared food backed by big data and AI. With those tools, they can focus throughout a day or a week on being prepared for what customers might order based on previous information and even determine their preferences based on the weather of a particular day.

These innovations in delivery reflect what will be an increasing tension over the next ten years in the industry between mobile ordering and foot traffic into actual restaurants. Successful bricks and mortar restaurants will not only have to compete for the best food but also for the best atmosphere.

If you are thinking of going out or ordering in, then there needs to be a better reason than just the food if you can order it to be delivered and watch a cool film on your wall. Brendan Flanigan of Brendan Flanigan Interiors Inc. points to the need for strong social media profiles:

> Restaurants need to be Instagrammable. Sketch London designed by Parisian designer India Mahdavi is in fact the most Instagrammed room in the world. Note: not just the most Instagrammed restaurant in the world, but the most Instagrammed room. It's a tearoom that transforms nightly into a cocktail lounge, and it shows that restaurants are now designed spaces, not simply for food and drink, but for an aesthetic. Successful restaurateurs will need to be curating design finds as much as they do high quality provisions and talent.
>
> *(Modern Restaurant Management, 2020)*

Cafés: We could not finish this section without talking about cafés. So many books are written at cafés around the world that it is worth just taking a moment to consider what is happening there and what might be the café of 2030. By the way, many of the chapters in this book were written at the Wake Zone café in Apex.

In 2020 Starbucks worked with Microsoft to develop a blockchain similar to the one we discussed above for fish. It enables you to see where the coffee beans you have begun their life, and it can also take you to where they were roasted. It can in the future even tell you if the grower gets a good return for selling to Starbucks, so you can think about whether you should rather write your book from an independent café that ensures the grower gets a better return. It would be remiss of this chapter to not point out the reporting that Starbucks does on human rights, according to the Corporate Human Rights Benchmark (CBHR), is not very good at all. They scored 8.5 out of 100 (CHRB, 2019). Benchmarking companies on their human rights, environment, social, and governance policies will increase through the decade.

Art and comics

Art sales are often hidden behind moneyed anonymity. *Driven to Abstraction*, a film that premiered in late 2020, looked at the inside story of a US$60 million art forgery hoax by Knoedler & Company (founded 1846), one of New York's prestigious galleries over the 15 years that it sold forged paintings.

Blockchain offers security to guarantee of the authenticity of a picture, statue, or art piece. It ensures over time that a history of an art piece, of all transactions in its sale, and its ownership are all preserved. If a transaction is in a block ledger, and its tag is removed, when the piece is put up for sale a red light would show that it might be fake or stolen.

Blockchain also enables an ongoing income for an artist who might sell the artwork for US$1000, only to see the same piece sold ten years later to someone else for US$40,000. The original sale might include a percentage of the resale value. Blockchain would enable this to be possible. It might also be possible for different people to own a percentage of an artwork, because with blockchain this could be guaranteed.

The rise of digital art is also supported by blockchain. Limited 'digital art' is already available, and by 2030 these digital art pieces may be contracted for limited use. If you want to use it in your AR/VR or as an organic light-emitting diode (OLED) wallpaper, then it may cost more per different uses. This potentially builds in an additional income for the artists over time. John Zettler of the Revitalizing Art Reinventing Emotion (R.A.R.E), a digital art marketplace based on blockchain states:

> 'I think blockchain verified art is in the very first pitches of the first inning', Zettler said further on blockchain's impact on art, 'Long term, I see a world where life is full of digital interfaces, whether it's augmented reality, virtual reality, OLED wallpaper, or some other technology that blurs the line between the physical & digital worlds'.
>
> *(Haley, 2020)*

In 2019, Spiderman #25 was published with the additional story titled 'Robo-Helpers'. A year later, the news came out that the story was actually written by Keaton Patti's AI bot. The bot read all Spiderman comics and came out with 'one of the greatest and most hilarious short Spidey stories of all time' (Erdmann, 2020).

With COVID-19, the comics industry, like many other industries, took a huge hit. As it starts to recover and look for cost savings, AI bots may become an increasing part of writing comics. Comics have in the past been available at local convenience stores and then comic shops. More recently, comics have also become part of online publishing to be read on your Kindle, laptop, or phone. Like they do with music, big data and analytics will recommend what comics you might like based on your previous buying. If you are still interested in having a physical comic, blockchain will offer 100 per cent traceability for your comic from buying to production to buying to delivery.

> Sustainable Development Goal 12: Ensure sustainable consumption and production patterns.

Fashion

> We believe that the future of fashion is circular – it will be restorative and regenerative by design and the clothes we love never end up as waste.
>
> *(McCartney, 2020)*

Putting fashion in entertainment seems a little strange, but for a significant portion of the population, it is something they follow, buy, and enjoy. As mentioned in Chapter 3: Home life, 3-D printers will play an important role in enabling you to print your clothes, the latest fashion either at home or at a fashion house that can guarantee the quality and deliver it to you by drone by the next morning (SDG12). Or as mentioned again in Chapter 3: Home life, you will be able to rent the clothes for a day, a week at a fraction of the cost.

There has been an increasing understanding that, like any activity, the impacts of fashion on the planet need to be considered. Environmental understanding in fashion started in the late 1980s with two companies, Patagonia and Esprit. Company owners Yvon Chouinard and Doug Tompkins were both environmentally conscious outdoor people. They developed products that were termed at the beginning 'eco fashion'. They looked at the lifecycle of a product, initially focusing on organic cotton and on reducing consumption. Patagonia even commissioned an advertisement for their own product with the headline 'Don't buy this jacket'. It was an attempt to make people think before overconsuming.

Their leadership inspired a sustainable fashion industry which accepted that fashion had to consider environmental, social, and ethical issues in producing their products. The use of water, material, energy, and greenhouse gas (GHG) emissions have become increasingly part of the sustainable fashion world. One cotton shirt takes 2,700 litres of water to produce, which would be enough water for one person to drink for two-and-a-half years. As far as GHG emissions, a polyester shirt produces 5.5 kg (12.1 lbs.) (Drew and Yehounme, 2017).

There are several leading designers that are promoting sustainable textile brands. They include Ryan Jude Novelline, Lucy Tammam, Amal Kiran Jana, and Stella McCartney. Innovations have already been happening with recycling polyester, growing cotton with climate-positive practices, viscose made with cleaner processing. Building on these innovations now with the use of hemp, bamboo, spider silk, and other sustainable fabrics is creating choice and direction for fashion. Brands like Wrangler that use denim have focused on using foam instead of water to dye the denim. This change results in 100 per cent less water used and 60 per cent less energy. They also use nanobubble technology to ensure minimum water and zero discharge from the process while producing a soft and natural feel (Wrangler, 2020).

On 14 March 2019 the United Nations Environment Programme (UNEP) launched the UN Alliance for Sustainable Fashion. Its assessment of the fashion industry noted that:

> The industry is the second-biggest consumer of water, generating around 20 percent of the world's wastewater and releasing half a million tons of synthetic microfibers into the ocean annually. The average consumer buys 60 percent more pieces of clothing than 15 years ago. Each item is only kept for half as long.
>
> *(UNEP, 2019)*

Gambling and gaming

Perhaps an unusual pairing, the difference of course is one is based on luck and the other on skill.

The online betting industry has grown – since it was started in 1994 by the Liechtenstein International Lottery the industry now stands at around US$40 billion globally.

It is probably not surprising that gambling has been using VR since 2016, when the first virtual reality roulette game came out.

> The online gambling industry is growing at an exponential rate due to the emergence of new technologies such as hybrid games, virtual reality (VR), and augmented reality (AR). Casino operators use these technologies to differentiate themselves from their competitors and succeed in this highly competitive industry.
>
> *(Business Research Company, 2020)*

The pandemic of 2020/21 has accelerated the use of online gambling and gambling using VR. From your home, you can now enter a virtual casino and even talk to other players as you place your bet. The casinos can be staffed with live dealers to make the experience more real and more entertaining. To engage through streaming, the gambler will need a high-speed Internet connection, something that will be possible with 5G or even 6G by 2030.

In 2021 virtual casinos are still in early development, but by working with the video game sector they are benefiting from the advances being made there.

Gaming has come a long way since Atari captured so many people with Space Invaders in 1978.

Pokémon GO's use of AR has also opened the opportunities for AR to develop and mix experiences with real life as far as gaming is concerned. The development of gaming will expand to all media platforms, and the game console of today may be like Space Invaders, a quaint footnote for history.

The integration of facial recognition into both gambling and gaming is not far off. It will not stop there: With AI and big data, the casino or gaming platform will know a lot of your personal data. With your VR headset you will be walking into a world that will seem so real and where the AI (deep learning) will have remembered any previous visits and people you might have met there. It will open up new opportunities for celebrities to be guest stars in your game or even your favourite poker player 'in theory' playing against you. Perhaps you would like to be playing against Taylor Swift or Chris Hemsworth (dressed as Thor), provided those celebrities have licensed their respective images to play the games. Or perhaps the game or casino will be on the Moon or Mars or on a space station orbiting Krypton (home planet of Superwoman and Superman) as it explodes if you lose the game.

As you will have surmised from what we have already said about it, blockchain will be an integral part of gaming by 2030 as you buy a digital currency to enable you to build your virtual world. In 2017, the rock band Muse teamed up with Dapper Labs and created the first blockchain game. The player buys assets known as 'non-fungible tokens' and the game limits by the number of cats sold and bred, creating value in the blockchain.

> The blockchain allows them to sell their profile to others on a secure platform if they want. They can also take their profile with them into a new game. There have been experiences in incorporating the blockchain on games. For example, Beyond the Void, a space strategy game, was built on the Ethereum blockchain. Imagine playing Call of Duty in a Grand Theft Auto map using World of Warcraft weapons. This is what will be possible when everything goes onto the blockchain.
>
> *(Coinjournal Press Team, 2018)*

The gaming world has had too many violent games and too few positive ones. For those older gamers who wanted to be more creative there was always Sim City, and more recently for younger gamers, games like Angry Birds, LEGO Creator Islands, or Big Brain Academy.

A key challenge for game creators with a more socially concerned youth is producing more positive games that people enjoy playing and which support a more sustainable world. There have been positive sides to gaming, including bringing simulated activities to people with disabilities and providing a safe recreational outlet for people who struggle with mental health issues.

One of the Angry Birds became an Honorary UN Ambassador for the International Day of Happiness in 2016. As part of the responsibilities, the Angry Bird went on a virtual world tour highlighting the way to take action on climate change. UN Secretary General Ban Ki-moon waxed enthusiastic:

> We are proud to give Red a reason to go Green. … There is no better way to mark the International Day of Happiness than to have our animated ambassador raise awareness about the importance of addressing climate change to create a safer, more sustainable and happier future for all.
>
> *(UN, 2016)*

Angry Bird was the first gaming character to be a UN Honorary Ambassador, but not the only fictional character to be a Honorary UN Ambassador. In 2009, in preparation for the UN Climate Summit in Copenhagen, Tinker Bell was used to promote environmental awareness among children. Positive gaming by 2030 will become more of the narrative for children growing up and will be interactive through VR.

Extended reality, a term being used to cover VR, AR, and mixed reality, will enable due to the advances in other technology:

> Super-fast networking, that will let us experience VR as a cloud service just like we currently consume music and movies. And artificial intelligence (AI) will provide us with more personalized virtual worlds to explore, even giving us realistic virtual characters to share our experiences with.
>
> *(Marr, 2020)*

A final thought for those *Star Trek* fans who know well the Holodeck where those participating may engage in different virtual reality experiences. That may not be in our homes by 2030 but may be in our shopping centres. Already prototypes by the company Sandbox VR exist licensed by Star Trek Disney, who are franchising the idea out in 2020.

Sex

By 2030, our sex life will have expanded with the use of disruptive industries.

Porn has come a long way since Hugh Hefner launched Playboy in December 1953 with Marilyn Monroe on the cover. By the way, Playboy had bought the rights to use a Tom Kelley photo of Marilyn from the John Baumgarth Calendar Company. When they were shot Marilyn did not know where they would appear.

When porn went online, it was no longer restricted to occupying the magazine rack in the top shelf of newsagent stands. In 2014, Ela Darling became the first VR adult actress. So, what is the experience that people have with VR?

For those who have not yet experienced virtual reality porn, it's a completely immersive way to consume adult content. There are 180-degree and 360-degree porn websites available which allow you to explore the environment you're in, which can include exotic locations around the world or fantasy locations that don't exist in real life.

(Bell, 2020)

The leading VR Company (2021) for sex is KIIROO with their Titan VR which enables the first interactive vibrating stroker (Futurism, 2020). This can be used by partners who are in different locations or in the same room – there are also over 4000 VR videos and counting which are available if you do not have a partner. With these, you can test out sex acts that you would not normally try or might be embarrassed to ask a partner to try. It may give you and your partner a platform to see what it would look and feel like. Big data and AI systems will by 2030 learn what you like and tailor experience to your interests.

Another frontier (not the Final Frontier!) will expand the use of robots for sex.

In 2020, the actress Anna Kendrick starred in a hilarious Quibi series called *Dummy*. Quibi is the film version of Twitter with episodes at ten minutes long. *Dummy* tells the story of Cody's (Anna's) boyfriend in the series where she finds out that he has a sex doll named Barbara. Barbara can speak, at least to Cody – the series is at times in a kind of updated *Thelma and Louise* with Cody travelling around with Barbara. It explores the relationship between Cody and Barbara – seeing Barbara as a real person and by doing so, as the writer Cody Heller (she used her own name) said,

Humanizing her and feeling jealous, asking myself: Do I live up to her? Am I as pretty as her? What does she look like? What is she like? I became obsessed with this doll, and it was taking up a lot of my mental space.

(Roth, 2020)

A short story by Eta Hoffmann called *The Sandman* (1817) explored the idea of a sex robot, as did Philip K. Dick's novel *Do Androids Dream of Electric Sleep?* (1968) which became the film *Blade Runner*. Margaret Atwood's book *The Heart Goes Out* (2016) has sex robots that look like Elvis. Atwood is known by many for her dystopian fantasy *The Handmaid's Tale*.

HBO's *Westworld* (2016–20) viewed the subject of sex robots as something for popular discussion. It was set in 2053, operating like a theme park, and each area is hosted by androids that look like humans. A similar idea was promoted in Barry J. Hutchinson's *Space Team: Planet of the Japes* (2017) though it is more focused on out-of-control robotic space clowns on a planet that had different themed areas that could appeal to whatever you wanted to.

The pandemic, in addition to everything else, has had an impact on sexuality and relationships. This has resulted in the need for social distance and longer periods of confinement – often by yourself – particularly for those in the high-risk categories. Consequently, there has also been an increased use of cybersex, including kinky parties broadcast over Zoom video feeds.

Sex robots are already available in 2021 and are developing quickly; it is expected within the next few years that the advanced versions will have a 'heartbeat' and seem to breathe (Best, 2020).

By 2030 with smart assistants (Siri or Alexa) the interaction will be linked to your AI robot and they will be able to flirt with you, they will be able to talk romantically to you, they will offer a different experience for particularly lonely people but also for those wanting to try new things.

3-D printing will enable most sex toys to be printed at home. 3-D printing of sex toys has been available since 2011 though the quality was not too good. In 2021 high-quality 3-D printable sex toys are available in a wide choice of 3-D designs.

There are a couple of reasons why people might want to 3-D print these – the first being discretion as people worried about even a package with their name on it going through the mail. The second reason involves being able to offer the chance for personalisation of what you might like to print as a sex toy. The software to do this is already available as a free download which allows you to change the parameters of your sex toy. As of 2020 the 3-D-printed sex toy has not taken off to the level expected. Some of the reasons for this is the cost of a good 3-D printer but also the quality of the product and concerns about whether its safety.

> However, as titillating as all these options may have been for some people, 3-D-printable sex toys were faced with some of the same problems that 3D-printed silverware and flatware models have seen. Anything that comes in contact with a person's insides has to be made such that they aren't prone to growing potentially dangerous bacteria.
>
> *(Molitch-Hou, 2020)*

One additional problem is that it is another way for plastic to get into the waste stream which finds its way into landfills or the oceans. In a circular economy would you be returning the plastic toys to the producer to be reused? Esty has become the platform to go to have a tailored sex toy created. It is still possible to hope that the development and expansion of 3-D printers to people's homes by 2030 may not be driven by sex toys but by other products such as clothing and household goods.

References

Agence France-Presse (2016) First Recording of Computer-Generated Music – Created by Alan Turing – Restored, The Guardian. Available online at: https://www.theguardian.com/science/2016/sep/26/first-recording-computer-generated-music-created-alan-turing-restored-enigma-code

Bell, J. (2020) What is the Viewing Experience of VR Porn Really Like? Big Think. Available online at: https://bigthink.com/partnerships/virtual-reality-porn-reality-lovers?rebelltitem=1#rebelltitem1

Best, S. (2020) Lifelike Sex Robots that 'Have a Heartbeat' and 'Breathe' Could Go on Sale This Year, Mirror. Available online at: https://www.mirror.co.uk/tech/lifelike-sex-robots-have-heartbeat-22009064

Burgess, M. (2020) Porn Sites Still Won't Take Down Nonconsensual Deepfakes, WIRED. Available online at: https://www.wired.com/story/porn-sites-still-wont-take-down-non-consensual-deepfakes/

Business Research Company (2020) The Growing Gambling Industry: Forecasts, Technologies, and Trends, Business Research Company. Available online at: https://blog.marketresearch.com/the-gambling-industry-forecasts-and-trends

Channel 4 (2020) Deepfake Queen to Deliver Channel 4 Christmas Message, BBC. Available online at: https://www.bbc.com/news/technology-55424730

Cheesborough, C. (2020) FIFA Planning to Introduce ROBOT Referees for Offside Decisions at 2022 World Cup … and they will take into Account the Length of Different Players' FEET to Cut Out Controversial Calls, MAILONLINE. Available online at: https://www.dailymail.co.uk/sport/football/article-8486311/FIFA-planning-introduction-ROBOT-referees-offside-decisions-2022-World-Cup.html

Chow, R.A. (2020) 'There's a Wide-Open Horizon of Possibility.' Musicians Are Using AI to Create Otherwise Impossible New Songs, Time. Available online at: https://time.com/5774723/ai-music/

Civil Eats (2019) Exploring a Decade of Big Changes in Local Food, Civil eats. Available online at: https://civileats.com/2019/11/19/exploring-a-decade-of-big-changes-in-local-food/

Codemasters (2020) Formula 1 Launches Virtual Grand Prix Series to Replace Postponed Races, Codemasters. Available online at: https://www.codemasters.com/formula-1-launches-virtual-grand-prix-series-to-replace-postponed-races/

Congress (1995) Section 230 of the Communications Decency Act, US Congress. Available online at: https://www.eff.org/issues/cda230

Coinjournal Press Team (2018) How Blockchain is Changing the Rules of the Game, Coinjournal Press Team. Available online at: https://coinjournal.net/news/how-blockchain-is-changing-the-rules-of-the-game/

Corporate Human Rights Benchmark (2019) Corporate Human Rights Benchmark 2018 Company Scoresheet – Starbucks. Available online at: https://www.corporatebenchmark.org/sites/default/files/2018-11/Starbucks%20CHRB%202018%20Results%20on%2020181026%20at%20173526.pdf

Diamandis, P. (2019) The Future in Entert[AI]nment – Part 1, Diamandis. Available online at: https://www.diamandis.com/blog/future-of-entertainment-part-1

Drew, D. and Yehounme (2017) The Appeal Industry's Environmental Impact in 6 graphics, World Resources institute. Available online at: https://www.wri.org/blog/2017/07/apparel-industrys-environmental-impact-6-graphics#:~:text=Water%20use%20and%20pollution%20also,million%20Olympic%2Dsized%20swimming%20pools.

Erdmann, K. (2020) A Spider-Man Comic was Written By A.I. and the Result is Madness, Screenrant. Available online at: https://screenrant.com/spider-man-story-written-by-ai/

FoodPrint (2020) The Problem of Food Waste, FoodPrint. Available online at: https://foodprint.org/issues/the-problem-of-food-waste/

Formula 1 (2019) Formula 1 announces plan to be Net Zero Carbon by 2030, Formula 1. Available online at: https://www.formula1.com/en/latest/article.formula-1-announc es-plan-to-be-net-zero-carbon-by-2030.5IaX2AZHyy7jqxl6wra6CZ.html

Futurism (2020) Realistic, Interactive VR Sex is Finally Here, and It's Affordable VR Sex is no Longer Just a Hypothetical, Futurism. Available online at: https://futurism. com/vr-sex-kiiroo-titan-headset-vibrating-stroker

Golliver, B. (2017) Interview with NBA Vice President of Global Media Distribution Jeff Marsilio in the NBA's Tantalizing and Terrifying Future in Virtual Reality, The Crossover. Available online at: https://www.si.com/nba/2017/11/07/nba-virtual-reality-future-cameras-technology-lebron-james

Haley, S.M. (2020) 'Digital Art' Framed and Collected on Blockchain, Forbes. Available online at: https://www.forbes.com/sites/michaelhaley/2020/01/30/digital-art-framed-and-collected-on-blockchain/#523b7b7b8d90

Hogan Lovells, H., Thornton, P., Fromlowitz, P., Sylla, A., Shelbourne Fleeson, R. and Kathryn Pennisi, M. (2020) Deepfakes: An EU and U.S. perspective, Lexology. Available online at: https://www.lexology.com/library/detail.aspx?g=8f038b17-a124-46b2-85dc-374f3ccf9392

Hou-Molitch, M. (2020) Where are They Now: 3D-Printed Sex Toys, 3Dprint .com. Available online at: https://3dprint.com/261832/where-are-they-now-3d-p rinted-sex-toys/

IBM (2019) IBM, Raw Seafoods Collaborate to Use Blockchain to Help Improve Seafood Traceability and Sustainability While Addressing Fraud, IBM. Available online at: https://newsroom.ibm.com/2019-10-17-IBM-Raw-Seafoods-Collabo rate-to-Use-Blockchain-to-Help-Improve-Seafood-Traceability-and-Sustainability-While-Addressing-Fraud

Job-applications.com (2020) Restaurant Job Salaries, Job-applications.com. Available online at: https://www.job-applications.com/restaurant-jobs/restaurant-salaries/

Keegan, R. (2020) A.I. Robot Cast in Lead Role of $70M Sci-Fi Film, Hollywood reporter. Available online at: https://www.hollywoodreporter.com/news/ai-robot-cast-lead-role-70m-sci-fi-film-1300068

Kollen, R. (2019) Jay Leno quote in Southern California Football Association, Kollen Bulletin. Available online at: http://www.sccfoa.org/kollenbulletin11142019.asp

Lund University (2020) World's First Live Concert with '3D-Printed Band', Lund University. Available online at: http://www.lunduniversity.lu.se/article/worlds-first-live-concert-3d-printed-band

Marr, B. (2020) The Future of Virtual Reality, LinkedIn. Available online at: The Future Of Virtual Reality (VR) | LinkedIn.

McCartney, S. (2020) Circularity, McCartney. Available online at: https://www.ste llamccartney.com/experience/en/sustainability/circularity-2/

Miller, R. (2018) Walmart is betting on the blockchain to improve food safety, Tech Cruch. Available online at: https://techcrunch.com/2018/09/24/walmart-is-betting-on-the-blockchain-to-improve-food-safety/

Modern Restaurant Management (2020) Decade of Disruption: Restaurant Insiders Dish What's on the Plate, Modern Restaurant Management. Available online at: https:/ /modernrestaurantmanagement.com/decade-of-disruption-restaurant-insiders-dish-whats-on-the-plate/

National Restaurant Association (2019) Restaurant Industry 2030: Actionable Insights for the Future, National Restaurant Association. Available online at: https://restaur ant.org/research/reports/restaurant-industry-2030

Parkin, S. (2019) The Rise of the Deepfake and the Threat to Democracy, The Guardian. Available online at: https://www.theguardian.com/technology/ng-interactive/2019/jun/22/the-rise-of-the-deepfake-and-the-threat-to-democracy

Restaurant Brands International (2020) Our Approach, RBI. Available online at: https://www.rbi.com/IRW/CustomPage/4591210/Index?KeyGenPage=472710

Robb, D. (2020) SAG-AFTRA Expects NY Gov. Andrew Cuomo to Sign Law Banning "Deepfake" Porn Face-Swapping, Deadline. Available online at: https://deadline.com/2020/07/deepfakes-sag-aftra-expects-andrew-cuomo-to-sign-law-banning-face-swapping-porn-1202997577/

Roth, D. (2020) What Anna Kendrick fans don't know about Dummy, Looper. Available online at: https://www.looper.com/228372/what-anna-kendrick-fans-dont-know-about-dummy/?utm_campaign=clip

Schlehuber, R. (2019) Is it time for robots to take over NFL officiating? Daily News. Available online at: https://thedailynews.cc/articles/is-it-time-for-robots-to-take-over-nfl-officiating/

Tassi, P. (2020) An 'Avengers' Deepfake Puts MCU Actors in the Upcoming Game, Forbes. Available online at: https://www.forbes.com/sites/paultassi/2020/08/27/an-avengers-deepfake-puts-mcu-actors-in-the-upcoming-game/#2530e0bc4955

The Presidents (2019) Deepfakes – The Presidents, YouTube. Available on: https://www.youtube.com/watch?v=rvF5IA7HNKc

Vuksic, G. (2020) Virtual Reality Concerts powered by AI, DEVPOST. Available online at: https://devpost.com/software/vr-concerts-powered-by-ai

Wrangler (2020) Indigood Sustainable Denim, Wrangler. Available online at: https://eu.wrangler.com/uk-en/indigood-sustainable-denim.html

United Nations (2016) UN appoints Red from the 'Angry Birds' as Honorary Ambassador for International Day of Happiness, UN. Available online at: https://news.un.org/en/story/2016/03/524812-un-appoints-red-angry-birds-honorary-ambassador-international-day-happiness

United Nations Environment Programme (2019) UN Alliance for Sustainable Fashion addresses damage of 'fast fashion, UNEP. Available online at: https://www.unenvironment.org/news-and-stories/press-release/un-alliance-sustainable-fashion-addresses-damage-fast-fashion

7
SOCIAL LIFE

Introduction

At the start of 2021, there were 4.2 billion social media users worldwide. That is about 53 per cent of the world's current population (Kemp, 2021). Looking ahead to 2030, recent statistics only point toward the rapid growth of social media usage around the world. From January 2020 to January 2021, there were 490 million new social media users. You can frame that statistic as 13 per cent year-on-year growth, with an average of 1.3 million people joining social media every day (in 2020), or about 15.5 new users every second (Kemp, 2021).

We Are Social, a global digital marketing company, reported in their annual social media 'State of Digital' report that the typical social media user now spends around two hours and 25 minutes on social media each day. Broken down by country, Filipinos are the largest consumers of social media, with an average of four hours and 15 minutes a day using it, while the Japanese are on the other end of the scale with about 51 minutes a day.

As of 2021, about 66.6 per cent of the world's population uses a mobile phone, and the majority of phone time is spent on social communication apps (44 per cent), with the remaining amount of time spent on video and entertainment (26 per cent), gaming (9 per cent), and other apps (21 per cent) (Kemp, 2021). Globally, We Are Social predicts that in 2021, if we were to add up the total amount of time spent by all social media users, we would spend 3.7 trillion hours on social media within the year.

So, what can people expect to be spending so much of their time doing on social media apps? Almost everything.

DOI: 10.4324/9781003045496-7

Social media platforms and usage trends

Currently, the top ten social media platforms are Facebook, YouTube, WhatsApp, Facebook Messenger, Instagram, Weixin/WeChat, TikTok, QQ, and Douyin (Kemp, 2021). It's hard to say what the future holds for these platforms. Policy and regulation around privacy and big data, new platforms emerging, and users' desire for de-centralisation may drastically shift the landscape of social media over the next ten years. However, how people actually use social media seems more predictable.

There have been shifts in what people share on social media from the days of MySpace to the ingenious content developed on TikTok. However, as Jay Owens explained in an article for Medium about trends on social media:

> 'People still want to tell the truth about their lives and the world – absolutely nothing has changed there'. While it's more likely that people are sharing idealistic versions of their lives rather than the full truth and transparency, Owens does argue that what is changing, 'are the cultural formats people are using for discussion – the carrier waves for this signal', however, at the core of all our social media engagement, people are still fundamentally 'seeking to communicate their deepest personal truths: their values, hopes, and fears, with each other'.
>
> *(Owens, 2018)*

Some experts predict that people will share less outside content like memes and articles to focus instead on relationships by emphasising personal posts, photographs, and small, intimate connections (Kulkarni, 2017). In this scenario, social media users want their profiles to create an 'ongoing time capsule, a living record of their lives', says Chirag Kulkarni in '11 Ways Social Media Will Evolve in the Future' (Kulkarni, 2017). Kulkarni speculates that rather than create bursts of single-moment content, users will create content that is a:

> Multi-faceted, interactive diary involving many writers, all telling pieces of their own and others' stories.
>
> *(Kulkarni, 2017)*

IOT, the Internet of Things, will likely facilitate some people's desire to share the minutiae of daily life, further integrating social media into our everyday lives. Home devices, cars, exercise apps, etc., can all be connected to social media, furthering our ability to share, bond, and connect over everyday activities.

Other experts see a trend toward people sharing less personal information on the top social media platforms. This school of thought anticipates that we will instead prefer watching videos, killing time, and sharing events or observations to connect with friends (Awan, 2019). Either way, there seems to be consistency in the idea that video will be the primary way of sharing content on social media. As of 2019, 56 per cent of Internet users watch videos on Facebook, Twitter, Snapchat, or Instagram each month (Awan, 2019).

Medium writer Asad Awan wrote in his article, 'Social Media in 2030 (and how it will affect YOU)', that the opportunity for social video has just begun. He observed in that article that teens are using less and less text to message each other and instead are communicating via audio snippets, live video messages, and augmented reality filters. As GlobalWebIndex puts it in their latest social video report, 'video positions social media as the go-to destination for anything from music consumption to online shopping and live sports broadcast and commentary' (Awan, 2019). You need to look no further than TikTok for an example of how video will play a role in our social lives.

By the end of 2020, TikTok was the most downloaded app of the year (Galer, 2020). With 880 million active users, the video-sharing app has garnered the attention of billions around the world and dramatically changed how people consume and create content. Created by Beijing-based company ByteDance, TikTok was the fastest app in the history of social media to reach a billion user downloads (Galer, 2020). While YouTube enabled many people to become content creators through their computers, TikTok is turning even more people into content creators via their phones. People shoot and edit their videos in the app. As Sophia Smith Galer, a writer for the BBC, explains, TikTok is like 'colour-by-numbers content creation' (Galer, 2020). The burden of making social media videos look like professional videography is gone. Users create short 60-second clips of people lip-syncing, practising a comedy routine, dancing, or even teaching a science lesson.

As described in a Medium article, TikTok has:

> 'Created a new generation of bona fide celebrities famous for entertaining people in under a minute'. (McGowan, 2020). While the app has indeed created several Gen Z and millennial celebrities like Charli D'Amelio, Addison Rae, and Spencer X, it also creates a space for ordinary, normal people. It may mean that the days of hyper-curated content are gone. App users come to see ordinary and relatable individuals. Galer says, 'If Instagram gave us the IG [Instagram] model, TikTok's given us our talented next-door neighbor' (Galer, 2020). This has had a particularly huge impact on the music industry. Luke Durac McGowan wrote in a Medium article, 'There's no hierarchy – you don't have to be an "influencer" for content you make to go viral on the app. As long as you have a funny idea, or can sing, or possess some other talent that people are willing to sacrifice 15 seconds to watch, you can enjoy your time in the limelight'
>
> *(McGowan, 2020).*

The app has been career-changing for artists and creators during the COVID-19 pandemic. Record labels lost the ability to find new talent in their normal venues, so they turned to TikTok (Garcia-Navarro, 2020). During the pandemic, there were tens of millions of people stuck at home creating hit songs. The app shows you an endless roll of videos, so once a song starts to gain popularity, then people are constantly making videos with that song. In an interview with NPR, *Los Angeles Times* pop music critic Mikael Wood said:

> You could hear the same song in five different videos in five minutes, which is a kind of exposure that you would never get on Top 40 radio.
>
> *(NPR, 2020)*

For example, Lil Nas X's 'Old Town Road' was one of the first big songs to come out of TikTok (Garcia-Navarro, 2020). It didn't take long for other celebrities to catch on. Canadian rapper Drake released 'Toosie Slide' in April 2020. In its first 25 seconds, the song instructs you to follow a set of dance moves basic enough for anyone to learn. This established the Toosie Slide Dance Challenge on TikTok, and resulted in the song being streamed over 350 million times on Spotify (McGowan, 2020). McGowan's Medium article notes that:

> It isn't about the quality of the music on TikTok anymore. It's about how quickly it can capture the rapidly shrinking attention spans of Gen Zs.
>
> *(McGowan, 2020)*

It's not just music. TikTok has highlighted activism occurring around the globe.

> Sustainable Development Goal 16. Promote peaceful and inclusive societies for sustainable development, provide access to justice for all and build effective, accountable, and inclusive institutions at all levels.

TikTok had a prominent role in the Black Lives Matter (BLM) movement, promoting BLM as a trend on its Discover page. The hashtag gained more than 23 billion views as people like Kareem Rahma posted scenes in Minneapolis to the tune of songs like Post Malone's remix of Childish Gambino's, 'This Is America' (Galer, 2020).

However, there are serious questions about how TikTok is moderated and what political and social content makes it to the app's users. The company employs internal censors, and has modified its policies in deference to requests from the Chinese government. For example, the app deleted 17-year-old Feroza Aziz's TikTok after trying to bring attention to China's internment of millions of minority Muslims in concentration camps (Zhong, 2019). While the BLM protests received billions of views, the widely covered protests in Hong Kong were suspiciously scarce from TikTok (McGowan, 2020). Moderation documents released in March 2020 exposed the strict policies the app maintains with respect to user appearance and general aesthetics. McGowan's article observed that anyone deemed to have an 'abnormal body shape' or regarded as too thin, too fat, or too ugly is suppressed by moderators. Similarly, videos that appear to be filmed in 'dilapidated or run-down' areas are filtered from the 'For You' page (McGowan, 2020).

While those questions continue to be explored and challenged, it is clear that the app isn't going anywhere anytime soon. As Galer writes in her BBC article:

> While platforms like Instagram increasingly become arenas where only the biggest brands with their marketing budgets get any screentime at the expense of newer, smaller talent, TikTokkers with powerful messages – for now – are free to run amok, defiant in their power to take on the algorithm, the internet, and the world beyond.
>
> *(Galer, 2020)*

The algorithm Galer mentions is the fundamental difference between TikTok and other social media platforms. The algorithm built into the app is extremely intelligent and is more integrated within TikTok than other social media apps. TikTok is unique in that the app chooses the content you see, not you. As McGowan explains:

> It studies you. It learns what you like – and more importantly, what you don't. How long you watch, what you like, how quickly you swipe off a video – all of these markers are collected, stored, and analysed to give users the most pleasurable experience and to keep them watching for as long as possible.
>
> *(Galer, 2020)*

This generates a 'For You' page displaying videos tailored to people's specific tastes. Other social media platforms like Facebook and YouTube use algorithms, but the user ultimately decides what to watch. That's not the case on TikTok. In addition to their unique algorithm, the app enables users to scroll endlessly, populating video after video, playing automatically. Users never have to decide what's next.

Politics

Sophisticated algorithms and massive amounts of data collection by virtually all social media platforms enable these applications to learn a lot about their users. Some people even say that Facebook knows you better than you know yourself, based on your historical habits and likes.

Daniel Hulme, chief executive officer of Satalia, an AI technology company, shared with The Drum his thoughts about the world in 2030:

> I saw a really great TED talk recently where it was predicted you could build a digital avatar of yourself. It will ask you questions about how you feel about certain political issues, and pull in all your data. Instead of us having to elect politicians to decide what policies are created, our digital avatars could vote on them. It would mean we could get rid of politicians...
>
> *(McCarthy, 2020)*

For now, politicians and political debates riddle people's online lives. But an article written in *The Atlantic*, 'Bots Are Destroying Political Discourse As We Know It', by Bruce Schneier, forecasts the drowning out of real human political debate. As Schneier writes, one of the biggest threats on the horizon is that 'Artificial personas are coming, and they're poised to take over political debate'. He explains that the threat comes from the combination of artificial-intelligence-driven text generation and social media chatbots. This is not a new phenomenon. Chatbots have been influencing social media discourse for years. The article suggests that:

> About a fifth of all tweets about the 2016 presidential election was published by bots, according to one estimate, as were about a third of all tweets about that year's Brexit vote.
>
> *(Schneier, 2020)*

Schneier says these bots:

> 'Overwhelm actual political speech' because the overwhelming number of fake, bot-generated posts can 'distort people's sense of public sentiment and their faith in reasoned political debate'. Over time, algorithmic bots have developed fake names, bios, and even photos generated by AI.
>
> *(Schneier, 2020)*

Schneier says bots are making it harder for researchers to detect their presence. He fears they will soon embed themselves in human social groups more seamlessly:

> Soon, AI-driven personas will be able to write personalized letters to newspapers and elected officials, submit individual comments to public rule-making processes, and intelligently debate political issues on social media. They will be able to comment on social media posts, news sites, and elsewhere, creating persistent personas that seem real even to someone scrutinizing them.
>
> *(Schneier, 2020)*

Another writer posits, "As AI insinuates itself more fully into our lives, we may yet require a new social contract—one with machines rather than with other humans." (Christakis, 2019)

Against the ultimate concern that these bots will drown out any actual debate on the Internet, the hope is that social networks can keep up with the obfuscation technology and verify that an actual person is behind a social media account – unless or until social media company executives decide that they have a financial interest in aiding and abetting obfuscation, in which case the bots win.

The Internet, and social media, in particular, have made humankind more connected than ever. While social media has expanded our networks and allowed us to engage with an endless number of people, experts suggest that social media also fosters more extreme levels of social grouping than we may experience in our offline lives, which leads to increased polarisation. With social media, we can separate who we share our thoughts, feelings, and information with. You can allow certain people to see posts about your life, while a separate set of people can see your political posts (Kulkarni, 2017). You can form even more exclusive friend groups, followers, or networks with people who have shared beliefs and interests. However, experts who shared their predictions in a Pew research study warned that these groupings can be highly polarising, especially when it comes to politics (Anderson et al., 2020).

Shopping and marketing

Social media platforms have already become mediums for virtual markets and will increasingly do so in the future. In an opinion piece for The Drum, Lore Oxford noted that:

> Instagram feels like a virtual mall. A place where teens come to social-ize and fawn over brands they want to buy into; where new homeowners come to peruse bed frames and lampshades; where beauty lovers, gamers and streetwear nerds can come to pick up the latest drop.
>
> *(Oxford, 2020)*

And who will be pushing those products? Meet Miquela (Instagram handle @ liliquela), an artificial intelligence 'influencer'. With 3 million Instagram followers, she's no different than the human fashion bloggers who have immaculately planned posts, themed feeds, and endless advice to share … except for the fact that she's fake (Davis, 2018). Miquela has even collaborated with Prada for Milan Fashion Week in 2018. She posted 3-D-generated gifs of herself at the Milan show venue wearing their latest collection, and on Instagram, she gave Prada followers a tour of the space. Also, in 2018, fashion brand Balmain announced its 'Balmain Army' featuring three CGI models, including the first digital supermodel 'Shudu'. Shudu has been fea-tured in magazines like Hypebeast, V Magazine, and Vogue, and in 2018 was named one of the most influential people on the Internet by Time. Jessica Davis wrote in a Harper's Bazaar article, 'How artificial intelligence models are taking over your Instagram feed', that CGI models are becoming more common. They even have recourse to a dedicated modelling agency, The Digitals (Davis, 2018).

By 2030 we will see even more people searching for products via social media. In a world where everyone has a mobile phone, and thus a camera, many experts believe that visual search, rather than text-based queries, will be the default way to look up products and information (Wiggers, 2019). In 2017, Pinterest launched Lens – a visual search tool that lets users search for products or inspiration using uploaded photos. As data journalist James Le explains in a Medium article:

> I spot something out in the world that looks interesting, but when I try to search for it online later, words fail me. I have this rich, colorful picture in

my mind, but I can't translate into the words I need to find it. Pinterest's Visual Lens is a way to discover ideas without having to find the right words to describe them first.

(Le, 2018)

You simply click the camera in the search bar, snap, or upload a photo, and see what results you get. Point Lens at a pair of shoes and a 'Shop' tab with a feed of shoppable Pins based on in-stock products will appear. Additionally, every Product Pin links directly to the checkout page on the retailer's site. Not sure what outfit to wear with those shoes? Pinterest will recommend outfit ideas that match your search. Take a picture of someone on the street with an outfit you like, and Lens will show you similar products and outfit inspiration based on your search. You can even point Lens at the ingredients you have lying around your kitchen to discover a range of useful recipes.

Pinterest utilises machine learning algorithms and technologies from the growing field of 'computer vision'. Pinterest started this venture in 2014 when it acquired VisualGraph, an image-recognition startup, and established its computer vision team (Le, 2018). In the same Medium article, Le explains that:

Computer vision is a field of computer science and subfield of machine learning that works on enabling computers to see, identify and process images in the same way that human vision does, and then provide the appropriate output. It is like imparting human intelligence and instincts to a computer.

(Le, 2018)

For example, one major component of Lens is query understanding, where Pinterest draws information from the image by analysing visual features to detect objects, compute salient colours, recognise lighting, and assess image quality. With visual feature analysis, it can also compute annotations and categories (Le, 2018).

Pinterest revealed that Lens can now recognize more than 2.5 billion objects across home and fashion Pins, including tattoos, nails, sunglasses, cats, wedding dresses, plants, quilts, brownies, natural hairstyles, home decor, art, food, and more. For comparison, that is 1.5 billion more products than Google Lens, Google's AI-powered analysis tool, could recognize in December 2018.

(Wiggers, 2019)

Pinterest has what most analysts conclude is the biggest data set in the world to train computers to see images. The company has billions of photos of furniture, food, and clothing, that have been labelled by their users for years (Le, 2018).

Virtual companionship

Current social media limits user engagement to whatever chat options it offers. However, 'social VR' will allow people to connect on a more personal level. Today most people access social media via smartphones and tablets, but many experts predict that, in the future, this will be done via a VR helmet (Watson, 2019). Tracy Watson from Skywell Software says:

CARTOON 7.1 Mom is sitting in a common space of the family's house and dad is getting onto an exercise bike with a large screen in front. The kids walk in through the front door of their home, presumably after school. The two kids start walking away in different directions (headed toward their rooms)

In a virtual social network, gamers can create their avatars, put on a headset and walk around in the game environment that can also be customized by the users themselves. This way, they are able to connect on a much more personal level, and the games become much more fun.

(Watson, 2019)

Social VR will not be limited to gaming but will also infiltrate our business and personal worlds. For example, in the future, you won't need to physically be in a meeting, because you can conduct it virtually where it feels like everyone is in the same 'conference room' even if you are spread across the world. You will even be able to send your colleagues a VR message with everything you need to say (Watson, 2019).

Outside of work, people will be able to engage virtually on a more personal and immersive experience. Social VR will provide users the freedom and creativity to portray themselves online. John McCarthy at The Drum says in 2030 we can expect to see:

A lot of experimentation with how to add sensory layers to online experiences. What started off as a very Gen Zed trend in gaming, buying skins or digital clothing and digital makeup, is now going to be the norm. With virtual backgrounds, interiors and realities, virtual calls will become more immersive.

(McCarthy, 2020)

People can interact on social VR apps which are programmes that allow multiple users to congregate in a virtual space. McCarthy says it's the simulated presence these apps offer that distinguishes them from other digital communication tools (McCarthy, 2020).

For example, with VR it would be possible to sit with your friends and family from the other side of the world in a VR cinema and watch a movie together, something that is not possible with applications like Zoom. AltSpaceVR fosters a virtual town square where groups of people can gather to hold concerts, play games, and talk to one another. Nature Treks VR enables users to explore meadows and beaches while a soothing soundscape plays in the background, while another app lets you walk around a 3-D rendering of Zion National Park. An app called Real VR Fishing simulates lakes and rivers while people fish for prize-winning catches (Roose, 2020).

Mark Zuckerberg, the chief executive of Facebook, has called VR 'the next major computing and communication platform' and other VR leaders have predicted that we will eventually use it for everything from workplace collaboration to sex (Roose, 2020). While major companies like VRChat, Snapchat, YouTube, and Facebook already have VR applications that users can access today, VR currently remains a niche of ultra-gamers (Roose, 2020). Time will tell if social VR becomes more accessible and mainstream.

> Sustainable Development Goal 3. Ensure healthy lives and promote well-being for all at all ages.

Throughout the COVID-19 global pandemic, anxiety and loneliness were on the rise. As reported in *The Guardian*, millions of people turned to 'AI friends' for companionship during these isolated times. These AI friends 'listen and support' you when you're feeling down. You can even name them, pick a gender, their voice, and their appearance.

A San Francisco-based startup called Replika created one of the growing numbers of chatbots using AI to support people's need for companionship. Replika currently has 7 million users and saw a 35 per cent increase in traffic since Covid (Balch, 2020). As described by a piece written for The Verge:

> Imagine a computer that talks like a human but has the knowledge of the internet and the patience and flexibility of a machine. Imagine if it sounded like your favorite celebrity or even someone you knew and loved.
>
> *(Vincent, 2018)*

We are a long way away from achieving AI with that level of sophistication; however, researchers are working toward creating AI with such depth.

AI products like Replika are stand-in friends, but others are designed as virtual doctors and therapists. Woebot, for example, is a therapy chatbot that Stanford University found reduces symptoms of anxiety and depression. Alison Darcy, co-founder of Woebot, explains that:

> Part of our endeavor was to make whatever we created so emotionally accessible that people who wouldn't normally talk about things would feel safe enough to do so.
>
> *(Balch, 2020)*

However, as this technology becomes more sophisticated, experts worry that emotive AI can confuse people who may mistake the programmed bots for real humans. As emotive AI develops and usage increases, companies must make sure to clarify that these are not real humans that people are communicating with (Adams, 2018; Outing, 2017).

Dating

The future of virtual companionship goes far beyond AI therapists and chatbots. A range of technologies will help uncover behaviours, preferences, and values in the hope of finding our perfect romantic companions. According to the online dating service eHarmony, in 2040, 70 per cent of couples are expected to meet online (eHarmony, 2020). By 2031, the company predicts just over half of relationships will have started online – 38 per cent from online dating or matchmaking services and 12 per cent through other types of websites (eHarmony, 2020).

Online dating is decades old but rapidly grew with the release of the first smart-phone in 2007 (Beckman, 2019). Apps like Match, eHarmony, Grindr, Tinder, and Bumble have brought millions to online dating. As Hesam Hosseini, CEO of online dating brand Match, frames it:

> I feel like we've solved the volume problem. How do you solve the quality part of that volume equation? If we're going on a lot of dates, great, but are we really on a better path to finding a partner?
>
> *(Beckman, 2019)*

However, despite how jaded people have become about online dating, eHar-mony and many others predict that online dating will become even more inte-grated into people's lives. Many of today's online dating companies believe they have the next solution to the quantity v quality predicament.

Dawoon Kang, co-founder and co-CEO of Coffee Meets Bagel, thinks machine learning and AI may be able to help. As she sees it:

> People, a lot of times, don't know what they want. They may say they want certain things, but they don't actually want that.
>
> *(Beckman, 2019)*

Kang believes that improved machine learning could select matches based on your actions rather than what you say your preferences are (Beckman, 2019). Better suited matches could be found with AI that considers how much time you spend in a dating app, the profiles you're looking at and for how long, the content of your chats, how you tend to swipe, how long it takes you to respond to certain messages, and whether you initiate chats (Beckman, 2019). It doesn't have to stop there.

Let AI access the depths of your phone and it can analyse if you pay your bills on time, what websites you visit, what type of news you read, and what shows you binge-watch. With photodetection and facial recognition, AI could access your camera roll and determine your 'type'. The dating app, Badoo, uses facial recognition to match people with others who look like their favourite celebrity. Maybe you are interested in someone who likes to hike, swim, and run just as much as you. Through your smartphone, AI can consider people's Fitbit or Apple activity to match exercise preferences (Beckman, 2019).

Loveflutter, a UK dating app, uses tweets to determine various personality traits to match people. The app also plans to use AI to analyse people's chats and coach them through meeting in-person. There is also the dating tool AIMM. Think of a Siri that helps you find your next significant other. The voice-acti-vated dating app asks you questions for a week and then sends matches. AIMM can curate personalised photo tours and audio snippets of you and your potential match sharing embarrassing stories, or descriptions of their ideal date. The app even tries to pick up on people's values throughout various conversations. For example, if someone talks about their family all of the time, the app could infer that family is important to them. It's likely that other digital assistants will suggest daily matches and dating tips (Beckman, 2019).

As if the depths of our phone aren't personal enough, maybe gene matchmaking will be the key to finding the perfect pair. Pheramor, DNA Romance, and Instant Chemistry have been trying their hand at biological matchmaking, and see it as the next best step for the future of dating. These companies analyse users' DNA and as described in a Mashable article:

> Propose that certain genes connected to your immune system, known as the major histocompatibility complex (MHC), govern who you're attracted to.
> *(Mansky, 2018)*

As the saying goes, opposites attract – people with dissimilar MHC are expected to like each other. While there is some science that backs up the companies' claims, experts caution the validity of this type of matchmaking (Mansky, 2018).

Unsurprisingly AR and VR will likely play a role in the future of dating. From the comfort of their home or thousands of miles apart, couples will be able to go on virtual dates where they play games or travel to a favourite destination. Some predict that in 20 years we could have AR glasses that show us who is single and display a compatibility score above their heads (Beckman, 2019). It's possible that you could point your phone at people in the distance and see their dating profile. This will be increasingly possible as facial recognition technology is on the rise (Beckman, 2019).

References

Adams, T. (2018) The Charge of the Chatbots: How Do you Tell Who's Human Online?, The Guardian. Available online at: https://www.theguardian.com/technology/2018/nov/18/how-can-you-tell-who-is-human-online-chatbots

Anderson, J., Rainie, L., & Vogels, E. (2020) The Innovations these Experts Predict by 2030, Pew Research Study. Available online at: https://www.pewresearch.org/internet/2020/06/30/innovations-these-experts-predict-by-2030/

Awan, A. Social Media in 2030 (and how it will affect YOU), Medium. Available online at: https://medium.com/@asadxawan/social-media-in-2030-and-how-it-will-affect-you-4f937ab32a4e

Balch, O. (2020) AI and Me: Friendship Chatbots are on the Rise, But is There a Gendered Design Flaw?, The Guardian. Available online at: https://www.theguardian.com/careers/2020/may/07/ai-and-me-friendship-chatbots-are-on-the-rise-but-is-there-a-gendered-design-flaw

Beckman, B. (2019) What Will Online Dating be Like in 2030?, Mashable. Available online at: https://mashable.com/article/future-online-dating/

Christakis, N. (2019) How AI Will Rewire Us, The Atlantic. Available online at: https://www.theatlantic.com/magazine/archive/2019/04/robots-human-relationships/583204/

Davis, J. (2018) How Artificial Intelligence Models are Taking over Instagram – the Rise of CGI Robot Influencers, Harpers Bazaar. Available online at: https://www.

harpersbazaar.com/uk/fashion/fashion-news/a22722480/how-artificial-intelligence-models-are-taking-over-your-instagram-feed/

eHarmony (2020) Over 50 Percent of Couples Will Meet Online by 2031, eHarmony. Available online at: https://www.eharmony.co.uk/dating-advice/online-dating-unplugged/over-50-of-couples-will-meet-online-by-2031#.XF-EAc9KhTZ

Galer, S. (2020) How TikTok changed the world in 2020, BBC. Available online at: https://www.bbc.com/culture/article/20201216-how-tiktok-changed-the-world-in-2020

Garcia-Navarro, L. (2020) How TikTok has Changed the Music Industry, NPR. Available online at: https://www.npr.org/2020/09/27/917424879/how-tiktok-has-changed-the-music-industry

Kemp, S. (2021) Digital 2021: The Latest Insights into the 'State of Digital', We are Social USA. Available online at: https://wearesocial.com/us/blog/2021/01/digital-2021-the-latest-insights-into-the-state-of-digital

Kulkarni, C. (2017) 11 Ways Social Media Will Evolve in the Future, Entrepreneur. Available online at: https://www.entrepreneur.com/article/293454

Last name, first initial. (date) title, website title or newspaper. Available online at: URL

Le, J. (2018) Pinterest's Visual Lens: How Computer Vision Explores Your Taste, Medium. Available online at: https://medium.com/cracking-the-data-science-interview/pinterests-visual-lens-how-computer-vision-explores-your-taste-47d591b42d7c

Mansky, J. (2018) The Dubious Science of Genetics-Based Dating, Smithsonian Magazine. Available online at: https://www.smithsonianmag.com/science-nature/dubious-science-genetics-based-dating-180968151/

McCarthy, J. (2020) Fact or Fantasy? Futurists Predict A Better World for 2030, The Drum. Available online at: https://www.thedrum.com/news/2020/06/29/fact-or-fantasy-futurists-predict-better-world-2030

McGowan, L. (2020) How TikTok is Influencing Minds and Changing Culture, Medium. Available online at: https://medium.com/the-innovation/how-tiktok-is-influencing-minds-and-changing-culture-123c532a764b

Outing, S. (2017) Is There a Robot 'Friend' in Your Future?, Forbes. Available online at: https://www.forbes.com/sites/nextavenue/2017/10/04/is-there-a-robot-friend-in-your-future/?sh=75762f74516f

Owens, J. (2018) The Age of Post-Authenticity and the Ironic Truths of Meme Culture, Medium. Available online at: https://medium.com/s/story/post-authenticity-and-the-real-truths-of-meme-culture-f98b24d645a0

Oxford, L. (2020) Instagram at 10: What Does Its Future Look Like?, The Drum. Available online at: https://www.thedrum.com/opinion/2020/10/06/instagram-10-what-does-its-future-look

Roose, K. (2020) This Should Be V.R.'s Moment. Why is It Still So Niche?, The New York Times. Available online at: https://www.nytimes.com/2020/04/30/technology/virtual-reality.html

Schneier, B. (2020) Bots are Destroying Political Discourse As We Know It, The Atlantic. Available online at: https://www.theatlantic.com/technology/archive/2020/01/future-politics-bots-drowning-out-humans/604489/

NPR (2020) How TikTok has Changed the Music Industry, NPR. Available online at: How TikTok Has Changed The Music Industry : NPR

Vincent, J. (2018) Inside Amazon's $3.5 million competition to make Alexa chat like a human, The Verge. Available online at: https://www.theverge.com/2018/6/13/17453994/amazon-alexa-prize-2018-competition-conversational-ai-chatbots

Watson, T. (2019) VR Social Media: Is it the Future of Social Interaction?, Skywell Software. Available online at: https://skywell.software/blog/vr-social-media-future/

Wiggers, K. (2019) Pinterest's Lens can now recognize 2.5 billion home and fashion objects, VentureBeat. Available online at: https://venturebeat.com/2019/09/17/pinterests-lens-can-now-recognize-2-5-billion-home-and-fashion-objects/

Zhong, R. (2019) TikTok Blocks Teen Who Posted About China's Detention Camps, The New York Times. Available online at: https://www.nytimes.com/2019/11/26/technology/tiktok-muslims-censorship.html

8

LIVING AROUND THE GLOBE

The Fourth Industrial Revolution around the globe

The Fourth Industrial Revolution (4IR) has birthed promising technologies that have the potential to revolutionise our lives. Throughout the book, we have discussed the different fronts in which new and emerging technologies could shape various industries and our lives by 2030: From the homes that would need to be more flexible to accommodate the nature of remote working and connected Internet of Things (IoT) devices, to the further development of autonomous technologies, and the revolutionary power of data analytics and artificial intelligence.

As discussed in Chapter 1, the term 'Fourth Industrial Revolution' was coined in 2016, when Klaus Schwab, Founder and Executive Chairman of the World Economic Forum, popularised it. According to Schwab, a technological revolution is underway:

> Characterized by a fusion of technologies that is blurring the lines between the physical, digital, and biological sphere.
>
> *(Schwab, 2016)*

This period that we are currently living is driven by technological advances such as blockchain, cloud computing, AI, big data and analytics, the IOT, 3-D printing, virtual reality, and other emerging technologies that are changing the way we live, work, travel, and relate to one another.

It is clear that the 4IR is among us and the pandemic is blurring on its way the boundaries between the physical, digital, and biological. The COVID-19 pandemic of 2020–2021 forced us to heavily rely on digital technologies not only for work but also for our social and economic interactions. Many of us find ourselves

DOI: 10.4324/9781003045496-8

CARTOON 8.1 The family travels to Ecuador to visit Antonio's mom Victoria where she is a landowner and owns a vast plantain and fruits plantation for exports

video chatting with our grandparents and our friends even when they live just around the corner. In some countries shift from the use of hard cash and ATMs to digital payments and credit cards, and online shopping was heavily encouraged. The pandemic brought to light our interconnectivity and reliability on technology.

COVID-19 brought insecurity to our lives and affected everybody regardless of who or where you were. It radically disrupted the execution of pre-arranged plans and projects. Even if you belong to the 1percent, your liberties and your ability to plan for the future and even for a vacation were challenged by the pandemic. Even if you were Jeff Bezos and increased your wealth during this period of widespread unemployment and economic insecurity, some area of your life was impacted. Yet the pandemic also created a space for innovation and problem-solving, and new opportunities to create economic value.

The pandemic could not go unnoticed. It seemed at first sight that besides all the tragedies it brought, it also worked as a powerful force that put all of humanity in the same boat, kind of like a 'great equaliser'. But as the pandemic developed, even though we were all on boats at sea, each boat seemed quite different. And suddenly, some people found themselves in yachts; others in inflatable boats, rafts, or drowning. COVID-19 brought to light inequalities within and between countries. It has always been obvious that economic inequalities existed between the 'developed' and the 'developing' world, yet the pandemic exposed these differences, potentially serving as a call to rethink the social, cultural, and economic future of humanity.

The pandemic and the policy responses to try containing the virus left us in a global economic recession, leaving many economies shattered and citizens without a stable source of income. For example, many middle- and low-income countries that rely on tourism were hard hit. Many developing nations already suffer from high inflation and do not have the means to provide economic recovery packages with direct cash assistance, as was the policy in many developed nations.

Most of the policies adopted around the world, like strict lockdowns (to help save lives and contain the virus), were, to some degree, 'developed' nation-centric because these types of policies do not take into full account the informal economy and other challenges that developing economies face.

A report by the International Labour Organization (ILO) found that more than 60 per cent of the world's employed population work in some way as part of the informal economy (ILO, 2018). Most of these two billion people are in the emerging and developing economies, and they lack social protection, workers' rights, and decent working conditions (ILO, 2018). This means that while some part of the population could work from home or attend in-person work safely, the options for someone working in the informal economy were quite different. Many people participating in the informal economy were out of work without compensation, had no social security or insurance during the pandemic, or had to work in unsafe conditions that increased their potential exposure to the virus, and therefore also the potential exposure of their families.

Sustainable Development Goal 3: Ensure healthy lives and promote well-being for all at all ages.

Nevertheless, for many developing countries, the pandemic also served as a wakeup call to modernise and diversify their economies. We do not know yet how what economic recovery or depression will actually look like. The COVID-19 pandemic could serve as an inflexion point to power developing nations into the 4IR. As we enter the 4IR and are faced with the potential disruptions it is important to address challenges from the perspective of the 2030 Agenda for Sustainable Development, its Sustainable Development Goals (SDGs), and the Paris Agreement to ensure that we have a common goal to work towards and use emerging technologies to achieve a more sustainable, equitable, and inclusive world.

The 2030 Agenda and its 17 Sustainable Development Goals (SDDGs) are a comprehensive and ambitious framework set by Member States of the United Nations which calls for urgent action and designs a 'pathway' to create a better, inclusive, and sustainable future for all. A report by the World Economic Forum found that the technologies emerging from the 4IR could 'fast track' 70 per cent of the SDGs (Cann, 2020).

This means that these technologies have the potential to address the inequalities that were so clearly exposed during the pandemic and set us straight to achieve the 2030 Agenda, the Paris Agreement, and to equally enjoy the benefits of the 4IR around the world.

Sustainable Development Goal 7: Ensure Access to affordable, reliable, sustainable, and modern energy for all.

Sustainable Development Goal 9: Build resilient infrastructure, promote inclusive and sustainable industrialisation, and foster innovation.

4IR technologies that are already in use today could particularly help address issues of health (SDG3), clean energy (SDG7), and industry and infrastructure (SDG9) (Cann, 2020). The 4IR also has the potential to raise global income levels and improve the quality of life around the world (Schwab, 2016). However, the gap between where we are and where we want to be is rather significant and requires an international effort that ensures no one will be left behind and that there is a just transition.

Despite its great potential, if efforts are not directed correctly and the right policies and partnerships are not put in place, the 4IR could also increase inequalities within and between countries as it disrupts labour markets around the world and automates jobs. In fact, economic inequality represents one of the greatest threats associated with the 4IR, and if not addressed properly, it could trigger future uprisings. As such, we must move beyond idolising these technologies, their potential, and the so-called 'Tech for Good' ethos to action and implementation where technologies are used directly to address societies' biggest challenges, such as the implementation of the 2030 Agenda.

To ensure that developing nations participate in and reap the benefit of the 4IR, we need first to understand the current state of these technologies. For instance, just ten nations (the US, Japan, Germany, China, Taiwan, France, Switzerland, the UK, the Republic of Korea and the Netherlands) account for 90 per cent of all global patents, and 70 per cent of the exports associated with advanced digital technologies powering the 4IR (Arthur, 2020). And only 40 other countries are actively engaged in these technologies, while the rest of the world is largely excluded from 4IR technologies such as AI and robotics, big data and analytics, cloud computing, IoT, and additive manufacturing (3-D printing) (Arthur, 2020).

This means that most developing nations are not participating – at least not in a meaningful and impactful way – in the development of these technologies. As these technologies not only have the power to help deliver the SDGs but also the potential to revolutionise, in every corner of the world, the way we work, live, and interact, inclusivity and participation in their development is essential to ensure they serve everyone. To achieve the 2030 Agenda, and a more equal and sustainable society, it is essential that developing nations and their citizens are included in the process of technological development, adoption and policy development to ensure that better decisions are made, and new perspectives and ideas are brought to the table.

All that being said, the question remains: What may technological adoption look like in different regions of the world by 2030? In the following sections we will explore each of the industries we have discussed throughout the book so we can image how these technologies might be adopted in the developing countries, and what questions and policy implications we need to be thinking about today to shape a better future for everyone.

The future of home life around the globe

In Chapter 3, we discussed the impact that technologies such as AI, big data, and analytics, 3-D printing, and IoT, among others, could have on our homes, from the bathroom and bedroom to the living room and the kitchen. Nevertheless, as we will continue to argue throughout this chapter, technological development and adoption may look different in different parts of the world. In the developing world, the adoption of 4IR technologies in the home may occur while technologies from the Third Industrial Revolution (3IR) like broadband Internet and digitalisation, are still being adopted by many. For example, broadband adoption, a technology from the 3IR is still not mass adopted in most countries of the developing world. The share of the population using the Internet in 2017 shows this clearly (Figure 8.1), yet they may have a smartphone with a virtual assistant.

Sustainable Development Goal 1: End poverty in all of its forms everywhere.

First and foremost, technological adoption in the home will not only look different between the 'Global North' and the Global South' but within and among countries. Even though income inequality within some regions of the developing world like Latin America and the Caribbean has been falling in the last three decades, developing regions of the world continue to have the highest levels of income inequality (United Nations, 2021). As of 2017, 689 million people lived below the poverty line of US\$ 1.90 a day, and almost half of the world's population have no access to at least one social protection cash benefit (United Nations, 2021; World Bank, 2021). Most of these people reside in the developing world, particularly in Southern Asia and Sub-Saharan Africa.

Fixed broadband subscriptions (per 100 people), 2017

Fixed broadband subscriptions refers to fixed subscriptions to high-speed access to the public Internet (a TCP/IP connection), at downstream speeds equal to, or greater than, 256 kbit/s.

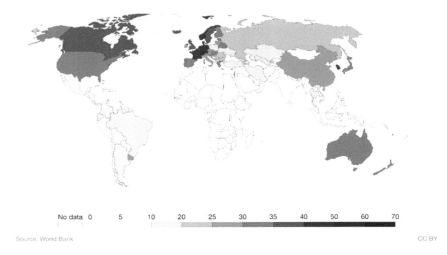

No data 0   5   10   20   25   30   35   40   50   60   70

Source: World Bank

FIGURE 8.1 Broadband adoption around the world, 2017 (World Bank, 2018)

As such, it is hard to imagine that smart homes will be widespread in developing nations where 'favelas' and 'villas' or slums are commonplace. To ensure the equitable adoption of 4IR technologies we must resolve issues related to poverty and inequality (SDG1). Yet, if properly exploited, 4IR technologies could bring significant improvements to the quality of life for many people as they decrease the cost of living.

Today over one billion people live without access to adequate shelter, and it is estimated that this number will significantly rise (New Story Charity, 2021). Technologies such as additive manufacturing or 3-D printing have the potential to reduce the cost of homeownership, and therefore may present an opportunity. Not only will you be able to print a house faster and cheaper than you can otherwise build one, but 3-D printing may democratise access to homes for many. Organisations like New Story Charity already are taking advantage of this technology to build houses for different communities around the world.

Like its predecessor, the 4IR could yield greater insecurity and inequality if these technologies are not thoughtfully implemented. If policy and privacy protections are not put in place the 'haves' will control most of the information and data, giving them a significant advantage over the 'have-nots'. Business with such access and control of data will also have a significant advantage compared to those who do not have such sophistication.

The 'haves' will own IoT devices to help secure their homes to avoid robberies and break-ins, with security cameras connected to the Internet and their phones to monitor their homes, while the 'have-nots' may not have the opportunity to leverage IoT devices in their homes. Some people in the developing world may have smart fridges that can check to see whether they have all the ingredients for a particular meal and even connect with nearby grocery stores to arrange for food delivery to the doorsteps of their well-appointed homes. And just like it will be in many homes of the developed world, IoT will also be used to monitor water usage and optimise energy use. Other people in the developing world will not have access to grocery stores, smart refrigerators, or even access to electricity.

When it comes to energy use and adoption of renewable energy in the home, solar power and batteries present a big opportunity for many households in the developing world (SDG7). In the 1990s, around 30 per cent of the world population lacked access to electricity and by 2018 that figured decreased to almost 10 per cent (The World Bank, 2018). By 2030, most households in the developing world may take advantage of decentralised energy resources, including advanced batteries and solar panels.

Despite the great benefits of 4IR technologies and the improvement in quality of life at home that they can bring, homes and cities in the developing world face a major challenge: They often lack the proper infrastructure and an enabling policy environment to implement these technologies (SDG9). Infrastructural gaps in homes, buildings, and cities may inhibit the technological adoption of IoT devices, renewable energy, and robotics.

When we are talking about infrastructure, we not only mean physical infrastructure but also cybersecurity and governance infrastructure that ensures the protection of privacy of individuals, their homes, and the protection against hacks. As mentioned in Chapter 3 the data generated by IoT devices will be leveraged by companies and used to give you better recommendations and 'teach' machines. The home of 2030 will also need to accommodate remote working, as more people work from home, the need for stronger network security increases. Many developing nations are nowhere close to where they need to be to accommodate for these changes in life, leaving the privacy of many individuals and the security of many homes compromised, sometimes by design.

While the hype for 4IR technologies is evident, technologies are being rolled out at an exponential rate without proper thought about the infrastructure needed to support their adoption, so developing nations will be left particularly exposed as they seek to exploit these new technologies for their economic growth. In this context, for many developing nations, data breaches are not only a matter of data privacy but also represent human security issues, particularly for those with weak democratic institutions.

In July of 2019, a major electricity supplier in Johannesburg was hacked, leaving millions without power, and in August of 2019 a UN Security Council report found that South Africa is among several countries targeted by North Korean hackers who infiltrated cryptocurrency exchanges (Allen, 2019). Africa is the home to many young democracies and many still have relatively weak democratic institutions. This condition leaves their citizens vulnerable to exploitation and manipulation, making privacy issues of particular concern.

The lack of infrastructure is not only a problem of security, but it will also inhibit technological adoption in the developing world. Whether or not people in the developing world can or cannot afford 4IR technologies at home, lack of infrastructure may deter people from enjoying these technologies, thus slowing industrial development and innovation. Even though people may be able to acquire a smart fridge that orders directly to your grocery, many countries in the developing world lack the broader infrastructure to support 4IR technologies, proper postal systems, and have unnamed streets, making the grocery delivery process complicated. This mundane example reflects the broader digital divide between the developed and developing worlds, and the need to upgrade Internet, cybersecurity, and physical infrastructure to have all people participating and enjoying the benefits of the 4IR. The 4IR has the power to bring many innovations to the home that could be enjoyed both in the developed and the developing parts of the world. Nonetheless, this prospect, particularly in the developing world that lacks the infrastructure to support these developments, makes it urgent for politicians and policymakers to begin thinking about the blind spots in technological adoption, and address inequality to realise the full power of 4IR technologies.

The future of mobility around the globe

Mobility has become a necessary part of human life. Many of us have long dreamed of flying cars, self-driving vehicles, and even teleportation. Even though we will not be teleporting by 2030, advancements taking place today in the mobility industry indicate that our incumbent mobility system is being challenged by the emergence of 4IR technologies. From self-driving cars to new sources of energy, the future of mobility brings hopes for smarter cities, less traffic and pollution, and increased ease of travel.

In Chapter 4, we explored what the future of mobility may look like by 2030, from commuting to work and moving within and between cities to travelling abroad and to space. However, as we continue our journey around the world, we notice that mobility systems are likely to develop differently in different parts of the world, particularly with reference to urban mobility.

The evolution of mobility around the world by 2030 will vary from city to city, and the systems that prevail will do so partly as a result of policy-making and environmental factors. For example, the evolution of mobility in San Francisco, a city that is famous for its steep hills, will look quite different than mobility in Panama City, a city that is known for its very warm and humid weather. Various social, environmental, economic, and technological trends will disrupt the incumbent mobility models. Each country and city will face different challenges, so it will be up to local policymakers to work closely together with urban planners if they are to leverage 4IR technologies that will enhance mobility in their cities and improve people's quality of life.

SDG13: Take urgent action to combat climate change and its impacts.

In many cities, traffic and air pollution from cars are health hazards. Traffic jams and long commutes have been associated with higher stress levels, while air pollution accounts for an estimated 4.2 million deaths annually due to stroke, heart disease, lung cancer, and acute and chronic respiratory diseases (WHO, 2021). Our carbon-based mobility systems have not only directly affected our health (and that of our planet) by being one of the biggest contributors of CO_2 and hence a driver of climate change (SDG3, SDG13). They also make our cities noisy and congested. Currently, the transportation sector contributes 23 per cent of global energy-related greenhouse gas emission, and 18 per cent of all manmade emissions (The World Bank, 2017).

Mobility patterns are already changing with electrification, connectivity, autonomy, and share mobility at the forefront. Companies like Uber and its ride-sharing system are thriving all around the world. And, with the growth of 'megacities', conditions are ripe for change if we are to leverage 4IR technologies in our cities.

A report by McKinsey found that congested metropolitan areas in developing countries will likely adopt a 'clean and shared' mobility model by 2030 (Hannon et al., 2016). These cities already suffer from congestion and poor air quality, with Delhi suffering from one of the highest levels of air pollution. Given the overpopulation of these cities, rather than owning self-driving vehicles, by 2030 a person from Mexico City or Mumbai will most likely log in into their phones and order a self-driving taxi:

> By 2030 shared vehicles could account for almost half of passenger miles due to a combination of greater utilization and more passengers per trip.
> *(Hannon et al., 2016)*

Business models like that of City Bikes could also thrive in this environment. By 2030 public transportation in cities will need to improve if they are to move millions of people from point A to B. A person in Delhi may be able to commute in the public Hyperloop to get to work faster. Cities with already congested mobility will benefit from developing integrated mobility systems. A person in Mexico City could take a super train to get the nearest station and then complete the last mile of the trip by calling a self-driving car from an app, using a monowheel, or grabbing a shared bike. These options for mobility will also be embedded within apps to show you not only the best route on public transport but also other possible options for commuting.

SDG11: Make cities and human settlements inclusive, safe, resilient, and sustainable.

The mass adoption of electric vehicles in developing countries, while possible, also presents a challenge because many people in the developing world have older cars that are not even close to current standards of CO_2 emission. However, acquiring new, 0 km, electric cars could be expensive, so policy makers need to create the proper incentives to facilitate a transition to cleaner cities (SDG11). In addition, in most cases the infrastructure to have electric vehicles like charging stations are not in place in most parts of the world. If we want to decarbonise our transportation system by 2030 these issues need to be addressed.

In addition, getting electric vehicles to rural communities that may not even have access to electricity will be a challenge. Yet increasing mobile connectivity between rural areas of the developing world will significantly help in their economic development as they will have greater access to markets and education.

If we close the transport access gap in rural areas (The World Bank, 2017) one billion more people would be connected to education, health, and jobs. If this gap is to be addressed through providing green energy, facilitating transportation will not be enough but also the infrastructure to make this system work.

In Africa, 450 million people, that is, more than 70 per cent of the region's rural population, lack proper transportation. This deprives them of access to jobs, education, and healthcare services (The World Bank, 2017). The Global Mobility Report by The World Bank explains that transitioning to sustainable mobility – that is in the sense of social, environmental, and climate impact – will not only help more rural people to access services and jobs, but it will allow regions like Africa to become food self-sufficient and create a regional food market worth 1 US trillion by 2030 (The World Bank, 2017).

In Chapter 4, we discussed the benefits that 4IR technologies like self-driving, new energy sources, big data and analytics, and IoT could bring to our mobility systems. The disruption of current mobility systems could bring enormous benefits to developing countries by 2030. These technologies present a big opportunity to make cities more sustainable and more inclusive, ensuring that all residents have access to basic needs, a voice in governance and planning.

Nevertheless, just as it is the case with home life, for developing nations to take advantage of these technologies and transform their mobility systems to a more integrated and sustainable model, they need to overcome physical and digital infrastructural challenges. These infrastructural challenges for mobility should support the production of e-vehicles, electricity charging stations, and the overall development of reliable electricity system. As well, as we further move to implement 4IR technologies and apply automation, quantum computer and cloud computing to our mobility systems, cybersecurity infrastructure is essential. For instance, self-driving cars may increase security due to fewer crashes, yet if digital infrastructure is not protected against cyber-attacks, the security of cars can be compromised, and so can that of people. It is without doubt that most developing countries lack the cybersecurity needed to protect their systems against attacks, and as such it is essential, they put plans in place to upgrade their infrastructure.

The future of education, work, and health around the globe

SDG4: Ensure inclusive and equitable quality education and promote lifelong learning opportunities for all.

Given the COVID-19 pandemic and the disruptions it brought to the way we work and study, changes to education, work, and health are at the forefront of our lives. Many of us will look at the pandemic as a pivotal moment, where a paradigm shift began. The pandemic saw 850 million children worldwide shut out of schools (Beard, 2020). Millions of people were forced out of their jobs or forced to work from home. Health and access to medicine became the priority in the world's agenda and the process for vaccine approval was revolutionised as scientists brought vaccines to market in about a year, redefining the vaccine-making process thanks to an unprecedented public-private partnership.

For education, work, and health, 2020 and 2021 have been all but ordinary, with the foundations of our lives shaken up. These changes were felt all over the world. Nevertheless, the ease with which countries were able to move from place-based to remote working and schooling, and the pace with which vaccines are being distributed, varies greatly.

As discussed in Chapter 5, technologies such as AI and analytics, virtual reality, automation, and blockchain have the potential to revolutionise the workplace, the school, and the various tiers of the health care system. The workforce of 2030 will be more entrepreneurial, flexible, and perhaps free-lance-based. For a person to thrive in the workplace in 2030 there will be a constant need for re-education and skills such as leadership and 'growth mindset', which can be defined as the belief that intelligence is not fixed but rather learned.

Education in 2030 around the globe

During the COVID-19 pandemic, the divide between rural and urban areas within countries, and between developing and developed nations, became much clearer. A report by UNICEF and the International Telecommunications Union (ITU) found that two-thirds of the world's school-age children, that is 1.4 billion kids aged 3 to 17 years old, do not have an Internet connection in

CARTOON 8.2 The rest of the family stand there with a thinking/concerned face

their home (UNICEF, 2021). This means that of the 850 million children that were sent home due to COVID-19, many were not able to continue their education online. Access to the Internet is essential for children to learn and thrive in the current economy, and it will be essential for their economic inclusion by 2030.

'That so many children and young people have no internet at home is more than a digital gap – it is a digital canyon', said Henrietta Fore, UNICEF Executive Director:

> Lack of connectivity doesn't just limit children and young people's ability to connect online. It prevents them from competing in the modern economy. It isolates them from the world. And in the event of school closures, such as those currently experienced by millions due to COVID-19, it causes them to lose out on education. Put bluntly: Lack of Internet access is costing the next generation their futures.
>
> *(UNICEF, 2021)*

The generation that will be most impacted by the changes brought by the 4IR are the young children of today. Consequently, it is essential that the digital divide existing today is addressed if we want these kids to thrive in the hyper-connected and technological world of 2030. The digital divide is leaving children from developing countries, particularly from poorer households and rural areas, with few opportunities to thrive. Currently, less than 1 in 20 school-age children from low-income countries have Internet connections at home, compared with nearly 9 in 10 from high-income countries (UNICEF, 2021). Not only are many children lacking Internet access, limiting their educational opportunities, but many children, 262 million, are out of school altogether (UNESCO, 2021).

For children and parents to enjoy the 4IR technologies, inequality must be addressed. By 2030 4IR technologies have the potential to bring education to the doorstep for many children. Many children that currently do not attend school are in that situation because the nearest school is too far, and they may not have access to it. Yet if the Internet is brought to rural areas and computers distributed in communities, children will have the opportunity to connect, learn, and participate in the economies of 2030.

Moreover, as discussed in Chapter 5, education in schools of 2030 will be more personalised, and technology will become an essential part of it. These children will have the opportunity to connect through a VR set to a classroom and received personalised education from afar or in person. 4IR technologies could help bridge the digital divide and be the solution for the same disruptions in education that they're bringing.

Education is changing not only at the primary school level but also in the trends that we see emerging in universities and higher education that could also open the door for creating a highly educated pool of talent around the world. Universities in the developed world are often expensive, and so their 3- or 4-year degree programmes pose a financial challenge. But the emergence of 'boot camps' and online education provides a cheaper alternative that will give greater access to high-skill jobs for people around the world.

Working life

Technological advances like AI, automation, big data and analytics, cloud computing, and IoT will drive economic development by 2030. Currently, we understand economic development in terms of GDP, yet this measure does not fully account for the picture of economic development that encompasses things like the health of our children, the quality of education, and the prevalence or absence of general well-being.

For developing countries to take advantage of 4IR to drive their economies they will need to address their economic development not only from the perspective of GDP but also of happiness and wellness, where not only monetisation is considered but also the quality of work, education, and purpose. There are numerous indexes, such as the Human Development Index, the Social Progress Index, and the World Happiness Report, that attempt to quantify human development based on various factors. For example, an analysis from the World Happiness Reports correlates happiness with economy and GDP, health, family, government trust, freedom, and generosity found that often the poorest countries and regions of the world also performed the worst in terms of overall happiness and well-being.

Regions with the most developed nations score the highest (Australia, New Zealand, North America, Western Europe). This may suggest that there is a link between economic development and happiness – yet it is not the only factor but might include factors such as generosity, freedom, trust and happiness, health, family and GDP. However, it is interesting to see (Table 8.1) that Costa Rica is the only country in the world to abolish its army and finds itself as the highest developing country at 15 in the top 25 in the 2020 World Happiness Report, while their GDP puts them at 78.

TABLE 8.1 World Happiness Report 2020 – Top 25 countries (SDSN, 2020)

	Country	Region	Wellness score	GDP world position
1	Finland	Western Europe	7.80	44
2	Denmark	Western Europe	7.64	38
3	Switzerland	Western Europe	7.55	20
4	Iceland	Western Europe	7.50	109
5	Norway	Western Europe	7.48	30
6	Netherlands	Western Europe	7.44	17
7	Sweden	Western Europe	7.35	24
8	New Zealand	North America and ANZ	7.29	52
9	Austria	Western Europe	7.29	28
10	Luxembourg	Western Europe	7.23	72
11	Canada	North America and ANZ	7.23	10
12	Australia	North America and ANZ	7.22	13
13	United Kingdom	Western Europe	7.16	6
14	Israel	Middle East and North Africa	7.12	31
15	Costa Rica	Latin America and Caribbean	7.12	78
16	Ireland	Western Europe	7.09	32
17	Germany	Western Europe	7.07	4
18	United States	North America and ANZ	6.93	1
19	Czech Republic	Central and Eastern Europe	6.91	46
20	Belgium	Western Europe	6.86	23
21	United Arab Emirates	Middle East and North Africa	6.79	29
22	Malta	Western Europe	6.77	126
23	France	Western Europe	6.66	7
24	Mexico	Latin America and Caribbean	6.46	15
25	Taiwan	East Asia	6.45	No data

Reviewing the reports and looking at the data it can be concluded that for poorer countries to be fully 'happy' economic development must be address so as it trickles in other areas of life like family and healthcare, contributing to overall well-being. Table 8.2 looks at the bottom 20 countries where there is data in the 2020 World Happiness Report. As we can see, most come from Sub-Saharan Africa countries, many of which are classed as least developed with the most vulnerable populations and ones that will be hit most by the climate changes we will see in the 21st century.

Even though GDP appears to hold the strongest relation to happiness, other factors like health and family play a significant role.

The COVID-19 pandemic significantly changed the way we work, sending us to work from home. Many tech companies are changing their policies to accommodate remote working permanently. Companies like Shopify announced that it was now a 'digital-by-default' company and that most of their employees will be working remotely (Kauk, 2021). As has been argued throughout the chapter, many developing countries do not have the physical or digital infrastructure

TABLE 8.2 World Happiness Report 2020 – Bottom 20 countries where data exists (SDSN, 2020)

	Country	Region	Wellness score	GDP world position
130	Mauritania	Sub-Saharan Africa	4.37	130
131	Sri Lanka	South Asia	4.32	68
132	Congo (Kinshasa)	Sub-Saharan Africa	4.31	89
133	Swaziland	Sub-Saharan Africa	4.30	162
134	Myanmar	Southeast Asia	4.30	77
135	Comoros	Sub-Saharan Africa	4.28	191
136	Togo	Sub-Saharan Africa	4.18	159
137	Ethiopia	Sub-Saharan Africa	4.18	64
139	Madagascar	Sub-Saharan Africa	4.16	129
139	Egypt	Middle East and North Africa	4.15	40
140	Sierra Leone	Sub-Saharan Africa	3.92	163
141	Burundi	Sub-Saharan Africa	3.77	173
142	Zambia	Sub-Saharan Africa	3.75	111
143	Haiti	Latin America and Caribbean	3.72	128
144	Lesotho	Sub-Saharan Africa	3.65	175
145	India	South Asia	3.57	5
146	Malawi	Sub-Saharan Africa	3.53	148
147	Yemen	Middle East and North Africa	3.52	112
148	Botswana	Sub-Saharan Africa	3.47	116
149	Tanzania	Sub-Saharan Africa	3.47	76
150	Central African Republic	Sub-Saharan Africa	3.47	176
151	Rwanda	Sub-Saharan Africa	3.31	144
152	Zimbabwe	Sub-Saharan Africa	3.29	113
153	South Sudan	Sub-Saharan Africa	2.81	No data
154	Afghanistan	South Asia	2.56	115

neither to maintain a large force of people working from home, and a great part of the population works in the informal sector, where jobs require physical presence.

The nature of remote working will change life in cities as many companies will not require large offices, and many people may choose to live in cheaper countries. By 2030 paying rent in 'Global North' cities like NYC, San Francisco, Tokyo, and London may not be as expensive as the tech exoduses from these hubs reduces prices for real estate there. These new changes to how people work present a challenge for companies and governments to adapt to a more nomadic workforce.

Developing countries lag behind in the adoption of 4IR technologies not only because they often lack the requisite infrastructure but also because they lack a skilled work force. Educating people for the changing market of 2030 is essential. Many developing nations do not have the high-skill workers to satisfy current needs, for example, in fields like data analytics and machine learning. And, if they do not commit to capacity building for the future, they will face an even bigger skills gap (Asghar, Rextina, Ahmed, & Tamimy, 2020).

Educating the workforce for the jobs of 2030 will be necessary to minimise job loss due to automation. There are two parts of the story: Some believe that 4IR will create permanently high unemployment, while others believe that the technology will create new jobs that keep pace with those destroyed. But even if the latter theory is correct, a significant portion of the workforce will be disrupted, forced to transition from shrinking and possibly obsolete occupations and industries to new and growing ones. In addition, technology will increasingly be embedded in the workplace, meaning that all workers – even those in growing industries – will need to learn the skills to interact with these new technologies. New jobs created during the 4IR will probably demand some level of sophisticated skill, and they may not resolve the issue with low-skill work (Harari, 2018). As a result, we might end up with an even more unequal world with the workforce divided into low-skill, low-pay jobs and high-skill, high-pay jobs (Harari, 2018). To address the potential issues, we must rethink our political, social, and economic structures to better suit modern life and the challenges of the 4IR.

For centuries, developing nations have been 'exporters of wealth', first through colonialism and later through neoliberalism and neo-colonialism. Developing countries and low-skilled workers around the world have long been exploited. The 4IR has the potential to change this dynamic, creating a world where low-skill workers and developing countries are not suffering from exploitation anymore but could still be threatened by economic irrelevance (Harari, 2018).

Despite the challenges and the potential dangers that the 4IR could bring, there are also many opportunities that can be exploited if developing countries increase their commitment and policy development to better leverage these technologies. With proper initiatives in place, by 2030, many of the factory workers in the developing world might be retrained to satisfy the needs of the smart factories of the future (Asghar et al., 2020).

By 2030, farmers may host their own e-commerce websites, bringing sold goods to a nearby market for pick up the next day. Online farmers markets, where you can pick the fruits and vegetables with a VR set, could help farmers address bigger markets and get more revenue. Farm trucks will be able to use a road that was 3-D-printed from recycling material. Farmers would also be able to leverage IoT to monitor and control their crops from their phones.

Of course, there are many developing nations, such as India and even Panama, that have service-based economies rather than manufacturing or agricultural economies. These economies urgently need to train their work force for the future, creating cloud computing experts, data analysts and machine learning experts. Most importantly, these nations need to work hard in cyber security to prevent their service industry, farmers, and factories from being hacked and endangering people.

On a positive note, the IoT does enable individual produces of goods such as fabrics, glass, or other handmade work to sell directly to the buyer in another country or within their own country. This could enable villages in remote areas to sell without a middle person and therefore to make more money … provided there is an infrastructure to ensure that what they produce arrives at the buyers in a reasonable time period.

Health

With the COVID-19 pandemic, health became a central issue in our lives. 4IR technologies like IoT, nanotechnology, and big data and analytics have the capacity to revolutionise our health systems around the world and give more access to people. Yet as the race for vaccines demonstrated, world inequalities are excluding many from accessing medicine. If we want to exploit the benefits of 4IR and technological advancements by 2030, increased access to health care must be addressed first.

As discussed in Chapter 5, 4IR technologies like IoT and data analytics give us the opportunity to enjoy preventative medicine, to be connected easily with our doctors, and receive medical advice. People living in rural areas can teleconference with their doctors. IoT and data analytics can save the lives of many by providing health information in real time.

Currently, however, half of the workforce lacks access to essential healthcare, and 100 million people are still pushed into extreme poverty because of health expenses (WHO, 2017). So once again, to exploit the power of 4IR in the healthcare system, many countries still need to address issues of access to Internet, cyber security, and infrastructure.

In addition, IoT health-related devices that are tracking and monitoring your health, while useful, also pose a significant data privacy challenge. Health data is extremely sensitive, and it could be exploited for insurance companies to drive up prices. Safe servers and infrastructure will be essential to protect people's data.

Entertainment & social life

Entertainment and socialising are a central part of human life. Depending on where we are in the world, we experience entertainment and socialisation in different ways. Consequently, the beauty of our differences will most likely result in different implementations of 4IR technologies in our lives.

By 2030, online content will be our main source of entertainment if it is not already so. In Chapter 6 we discussed the potential danger of 'deepfakes' as you can impersonate public figures, for example. Currently, there is software to detect content manipulated that way. But by 2030 with the advancement of AI, deepfakes may become more prominent and real. This technology could represent the biggest threat to newer and weaker democracies in the developing world by propagating fake news. Politicians around the world need to step up their policy game to respond to these types of content.

Besides, online content streaming services for movies and videos will become commonplace. In the past five years, we have seen companies like Netflix revolutionise the movie industry and completely challenge the Hollywood model. Netflix opened the door to indie movies and developed localised content. By 2030, this trend will likely keep growing, giving access to a greater pool of content from different countries and diverse backgrounds.

Food plays a key role in our entertainment and social life. By 2030, there will be 8.5 billion mouths to feed, putting increased pressure on farmers around the world. It is well-known that there are exploitative practices in our current food chain with the environment and poor farmers in the developing world paying the price. However, technologies such as blockchain have the power to improve conditions for many farmers because this technology can increase the transparency, traceability, and verification of data.

Finally, during 2020 we saw an emerging popularity of social media trend with the app 'Clubhouse', an audio-based social media app by invitation only. As social media has become increasingly crowded and overpopulated by companies and advertisements, people are trying to find new ways to connect. However, this app signals a troubling trend: invitation only. If by 2030 inequality rises, and low-skill low-pay, high-skill high-pay jobs become the norm, 'invitation only' apps may contribute to further isolation from people who are different than us, by excluding others based on their skill levels or economic and social circles.

It is clear that 4IR technologies will continue to shape our lives by 2030. However, it is unclear what direction these developments will take us. The intention of this chapter was to raise questions about the potential impact of these technologies around the world given the socio-political economic system that we have inherited – one based on economic inequalities. It is necessary to discuss how these technologies and advances fit within the global political economy so we can better understand how developments impact us and how can we use them to the advancement of society.

What it is clear is that there are many issues that countries need to prioritise and address to exploit the positive power that 4IR technologies can bring to our lives. In this chapter we emphasised issues of physical and digital infrastructure. Nevertheless, one of the biggest challenges that both developing and developed nations need to address is their political toolkit: As the world continues to change, political and policy-making processes also need to change, to catch up with current needs and to better serve the lives of people of the 21st century.

References

Allen, K. (2019) Africa Should not be Too Quick to Embrace the Fourth Industrial Revolution, The Guardian. Available online at: https://www.theguardian.com/global-development/2019/sep/16/africa-should-not-be-too-quick-to-embrace-the-fourth-industrial-revolution

Arthur, C. (2020) Fourth Industrial Revolution: How Latecomers and Laggards Can Catch up, United Nations Industrial Development Organization. Available online at: https://www.unido.org/stories/fourth-industrial-revolution-how-latecomers-and-laggards-can-catch

Asghar, S., Rextina, G., Ahmed, T., & Tamimy, M. (2020). The Fourth Industrial Revolution in the Developing Nations: Challenges and Road Map. Commission on Science and Technology for Sustainable Development in the South (COMSATS), Research Paper 102, South Center. Available online at: https://www.southcentre.int/research-paper-102-february-2020/

Beard, A. (2020) Can Computers Ever Replace the Classroom, The Guardian. Available online at: https://www.theguardian.com/technology/2020/mar/19/can-computers-ever-replace-the-classroom

Cann, O. (2020) Fourth Industrial Revolution Tech Can Fast Track 70 Percent of Sustainable Development Goals. World Economic Forum. Available online at: https://www.weforum.org/press/2020/01/fourth-industrial-revolution-tech-can-fast-track-70-of-

Sustainable Development Goals. World Economic Forum. Available online at: https://www.weforum.org/press/2020/01/fourth-industrial-revolution-tech-can-fast-track-70-of-sustainable-development-goals

Hannon, E., McKerracher, C., Orlandi, I., & Ramkumar, S. (2016) An Integrated Perspective on the Future of Mobility, McKinsey and Company. Available online at: https://www.mckinsey.com/business-functions/sustainability/our-insights/an-integrated-perspective-on-the-future-of-mobility#

Harari, Y. N. (2018) 21 Lessons for the 21st Century. Penguin Random House Group.

International Labour Organization (2018) More than 60 Per cent of the World's Employed Population are in the Informal Economy, ILO Newsroom, Informal Economy. Available online at: https://www.ilo.org/global/about-the-ilo/newsroom/news/WCMS_627189/lang--en/index.htm#:~:text=Apercent20newpercent20ILOpercent20reportpercent20shows,workpercent20andpercent20decentpercent20workingpercent20conditions.

Kauk, S. (2021) What Does Working Remotely Mean for the Planet? Shopify. Available online at: https://www.shopify.com/blog/working-remotely-for-the-planet

New Story Charity (2021) We're Tackling One of the World's Biggest Problems: Homelessness, New Story. Available online at: https://newstorycharity.org/about-us/

Schwab, K. (2016) In *The Carrier's Role in the Fourth Industrial Revolution*, Verizon. Available online at: itw_industrial_revolution (verizon.com)

Sustainable Development Solutions Network (2020) The World Happiness Report, SDSN. Available online at: https://worldhappiness.report/ed/2020/

The World Bank (2017) Technology Adoption, World Bank. Available online at: www.OurWorldInData.org

The World Bank (2017) Global Mobility Report 2017, World Bank. Available online at: https://sustainabledevelopment.un.org/content/documents/2643Global_Mobility_Report_2017.df

The World Bank (2018) Share of the Population Using the Internet 2017, World Bank. Available online at: www.OurWorldInData.org

The World Bank (2021) Poverty Overview, World Bank. Available online at: https://www.worldbank.org/en/topic/poverty/overview

The World Bank. (2018) Access to Electricity (%of population). Available online at: https://data.worldbank.org/indicator/EG.ELC.ACCS.ZS?view=chart

UNESCO (2021) Leading SDG 4 – Education 2030, UNESCO. Available online at: https://en.unesco.org/themes/education2030-sdg4

UNICEF (2021) Two Thirds of the World's School-Age Children have No Internet Access at home, New UNICEF-ITU Report says. UNICEF. Available online at: https://www.unicef.org.uk/press-releases/two-thirds-of-the-worlds-school-age-children-have-no-internet-access-at-home-new-unicef-itu-report-says/

United Nations (2021) Ending Poverty, UN. Available online at: https://www.un.org/en/global-issues/ending-poverty

United Nations (2021) Inequality – Bridging the Divide, UN. Available online at: https://www.un.org/en/un75/inequality-bridging-divide

WHO (2017) World Bank and WHO: Half the World Lacks Access to Essential Health Services, 100 Million Still Pushed into Extreme Poverty Because of Health Expenses, World Health Organization. Available online at: https://www.who.int/news/item/13-12-2017-world-bank-and-who-half-the-world-lacks-access-to-essential-health-services-100-million-still-pushed-into-extreme-poverty-because-of-health-expenses

WHO (2021) Air Pollution, WHO. Available online at: https://www.who.int/news-room/air-pollution

9
BEYOND 2030

Introduction

> Any sufficiently advanced technology is indistinguishable from magic.
> *(Arthur C. Clarke, 1973)*

We hope you have found our insights into what life might be like in 2030 to be interesting, thought-provoking, and at times amusing. Our aim was to offer a positive view of 2030 while at the same time giving you, the reader, some idea of how those changes would help ensure we live more sustainably on this planet while delivering on the Sustainable Development Goals and the Paris Climate Agreement of keeping the world under a 2 degree C (preferably 1.5 degree C) rise in temperature by 2100.

While writing this book we have noticed the increased media coverage on nearly all the disruptive industries that we have focused on. They will become part of our lives over the next ten years and in many cases will improve those lives wherever we live.

In 2021 we are in the process of vaccinating the world's population to address the COVID-19 pandemic and hopefully as a byproduct setting up health services worldwide to be robust for any future pandemic.

Countries are introducing stimulus packages to support their citizens and deciding on the elements of their recovery packages. It looks like these will have to include a sizable amount of funding for what has been termed 'Green New Deals'. Underpinning these 'New Deals' is funding for new greener technologies, some of which have been covered in these pages.

According to Vivid Economics (Harvey, 2021), spending on low carbon projects and clean technology are already around 12 per cent of the stimulus packages (March 2021). As countries emerge from the pandemic there will also need

DOI: 10.4324/9781003045496-9

to be recovery packages aimed at getting people back to work and more of that will focus on clean and green technologies.

The world of 2050

> We won't experience 100 years of progress in the 21st century – it will be more like 20,000 years of progress (at today's rate).
>
> *(Kurzweil, 2001)*

So, what would the world of 2050 be like? This is where we could find ourselves more in the science fiction genres of a book shop rather than the non-fiction section.

In 2030 the SDGs will be revised, and a new set of goals agreed to which will take us up to 2050.

On the climate front, the reduction in CO_2 emissions will need to be around 45 per cent by 2030 and reach net zero by 2050. We are far from that being a reality – yet.

By 2030 some of the issues that are raised in the Sustainable Development Goals may no longer be such a priority. The SDGs aim for governments to support eradicating extreme poverty by 2030 and this is attainable, and we hope will be achieved. Other significant drivers – population, urbanisation and climate change – will still be critical to address, though we hope that some progress will have been made. Here is our top ten for 2030 ... though we are sure there will be others.

1. Climate change (SDG13).
2. Health – pandemics (SDG3).
3. Food availability (SDG2).
4. Sustainable cities and communities (SDG 11).
5. Water availability (SDG6).
6. Employment – livelihood challenge (SDG8).
7. Inequity (SDG10).
8. Biodiversity loss (SDG15 and SDG14).
9. Education (SDG4).
10. Governance (expanded to include technology) (SDG16).

Within the next set of 'goals' up to 2050, there are several technology problems that researching this book have highlighted. This is not to say that others will not emerge, but these ten, we believe, will need to be included in some form of multilateral agreements:

1. Deepfake.
2. Cybersecurity.
3. Privacy.

4. AI robot police and soldiers.
5. Drone weaponisation.
6. 3-D printing of weapons.
7. Use of personal data for political repression.
8. Use of social media to promote hate and racism.
9. The move to freelancing to reduce salaries and benefits.
10. The use of microchip technology in a person to monitor them or control them.

What role multilateralism and the UN will have in addressing these challenges will be critical to the kind of world we might live in. Will it be open or closed? Will it be for everyone or just for the few? Will it be green and sustainable or moving towards disaster and conflict?

> Ultimately, in looking to the future, we must consider the human element, and how technology can ensure that no one is left behind. The future of digital cooperation must include voices from around the world, particularly from developing countries, in the dialogue on global digital cooperation, so that the models we build are representative of the world, and the hopes and aspirations of all people. If technology is changing the relationship between governments and citizens, it is on governments to drive a positive, empowering change.
>
> *(Alhashimi, 2021)*

Final thoughts

Before we know it, 2030 will be here and this will be a history book, perhaps quoted in future publications about how wrong we were. We hope if that is the case that we were wrong in the right direction, and our world is in a much better place than our predictions.

In the large arc of history, the next ten years may not seem long, but as the quote from Kurzweil above recognised at the turn of the century, we are in a time of massive progress and that will bring social change at a speed we have never had to deal with before. Generally, people do not like change – they want stability in their lives. So, helping this next generation to be more entrepreneurial and to expect more change in their lives is part of the challenge of this cohort of politicians who will have to shepherd in those changes.

The decisions in 2015 to adopt the Sustainable Development Goals and targets, and the Paris Climate Agreement, gave us the roadmap to reducing greenhouse gases, and their momentum offers us the right foundations to build upon. Only time will tell if we took those opportunities.

This book is supported by a website (www.tomorrowspeople2030.com), with which we hope to continue the discussion with the reader and enable them to put forward their thoughts on what our world in 2030 and 2050 might look like.

We would like to hear your thoughts on potential personal challenges, and what political action should be considered to ensure that these disruptive industries have the maximum positive impact and the minimum negative impact on individuals, communities, countries, and our planet.

> Yesterday is not ours to recover but tomorrow is ours to win or lose.
>
> *(Johnson, 1963)*

References

Alhashimi, H. (2021) Future of Digital Cooperation in the Future of Diplomacy after COVID -19, Routledge

Clarke, A.C. (1973) Profiles of the Future: An Inquiry into the Limits of the Possible, Harper & Row.

Harvey, F. Global Green Recovery Plans Fail to Match 2008 Stimulus Report Shows, The Guardian. Available online at: https://www.theguardian.com/environment/2021/feb/12/global-green-recovery-plans-fail-to-match-2008-stimulus-report-shows

Johnson, B.L. (1963) Speech by President Lydon Johnson on the November 28, 1963.

Kurzweil, R. (2001) The law of accelerating returns, Kurzweil acceleration intelligence. Available online at: https://www.kurzweilai.net/the-law-of-accelerating-returns Also, Consider What Would be the Difference Between the World of 2050 and 1950 https://www.npr.org/2020/06/14/876887695/an-elevator-to-the-stars-encore

ANNEX 1

Sustainable Development Goals
(United Nations, 2015)

Goal 1. End poverty in all its forms everywhere.

Goal 2. End hunger, achieve food security and improved nutrition, and promote sustainable agriculture.

Goal 3. Ensure healthy lives and promote well-being for all at all ages.

Goal 4. Ensure inclusive and equitable quality education and promote lifelong learning opportunities for all.

Goal 5. Achieve gender equality and empower all women and girls.

Goal 6. Ensure availability and sustainable management of water and sanitation for all.

Goal 7. Ensure access to affordable, reliable, sustainable, and modern energy for all.

Goal 8. Promote sustained, inclusive, and sustainable economic growth, full and productive employment and decent work for all.

Goal 9. Build resilient infrastructure, promote inclusive and sustainable industrialisation and foster innovation.

Goal 10. Reduce inequality within and among countries.

Goal 11. Make cities and human settlements inclusive, safe, resilient, and sustainable.

Goal 12. Ensure sustainable consumption and production patterns.

Goal 13. Take urgent action to combat climate change and its impacts.*

Goal 14. Conserve and sustainably use the oceans, seas, and marine resources for sustainable development.

Goal 15. Protect, restore, and promote sustainable use of terrestrial ecosystems, sustainably manage forests, combat desertification, and halt and reverse land degradation and halt biodiversity loss.

Goal 16. Promote peaceful and inclusive societies for sustainable development, provide access to justice for all and build effective, accountable, and inclusive institutions at all levels.

Goal 17. Strengthen the means of implementation and revitalise the global partnership for sustainable development.

★ *Acknowledging that the United Nations Framework Convention on Climate Change is the primary international, intergovernmental forum for negotiating the global response to climate change.* (UN, 2015)

Reference

United Nations. (2015) *Transforming Our World: The 2030 Agenda for Sustainable Development*. UN. Available online at: https://sdgs.un.org/2030agenda

ANNEX 2

Key aspects of the Paris Agreement

(Summary taken from the UN Framework on Climate Change Convention web site [UNFCCC], 2015)

At COP 21 in Paris, on 12 December 2015, Parties to the UNFCCC reached a landmark agreement to combat climate change and to accelerate and intensify the actions and investments needed for a sustainable low carbon future. The Paris Agreement builds upon the Convention and – for the first time – brings all nations into a common cause to undertake ambitious efforts to combat climate change and adapt to its effects, with enhanced support to assist developing countries to do so. As such, it charts a new course in the global climate effort.

The Paris Agreement's central aim is to strengthen the global response to the threat of climate change by keeping a global temperature rise this century well below 2 degrees Celsius above pre-industrial levels and to pursue efforts to limit the temperature increase even further to 1.5 degrees Celsius. Additionally, the agreement aims to increase the ability of countries to deal with the impacts of climate change, and at making finance flows consistent with low GHG emissions and climate-resilient pathway. To reach these ambitious goals, appropriate mobilization and provision of financial resources, a new technology framework and enhanced capacity-building is to be put in place, thus supporting action by developing countries and the most vulnerable countries, in line with their own national objectives. The Agreement also provides for an enhanced transparency framework for action and support.

The Paris Agreement requires all Parties to put forward their best efforts through "nationally determined contributions" (NDCs) and to strengthen these efforts in the years ahead. This includes requirements that all Parties report regularly on their emissions and on their implementation efforts. There will also be a global stock take every five years to assess the collective progress towards achieving the purpose of the agreement and to inform further individual actions by Parties.

The Paris Agreement opened for signature on 22 April 2016 – Earth Day – at UN Headquarters in New York. It entered into force on 4 November 2016, 30 days after the so-called "double threshold" (ratification by 55 countries that account for at least 55% of global emissions) had been met. Since then, more countries have ratified and continue to ratify the Agreement, reaching a total of 125 Parties in early 2017. The current number of ratifications can be found here.

In order to make the Paris Agreement fully operational, a work programme was launched in Paris to develop modalities, procedures and guidelines on a broad array of issues. Since 2016, Parties work together in the subsidiary bodies (APA, SBSTA and SBI) and various constituted bodies. The Conference of the Parties serving as the meeting of the Parties to the Paris Agreement (CMA) met for the first time in conjunction with COP 22 in Marrakesh (in November 2016) and adopted its first two decisions. The work programme is expected to be completed by 2018.

The Paris Agreement, adopted through Decision 1/CP.21, addresses crucial areas necessary to combat climate change. Some of the key aspects of the Agreement are set out below:

- **Long-term temperature goal (Art. 2)** – The Paris Agreement, in seeking to strengthen the global response to climate change, reaffirms the goal of limiting global temperature increase to well below 2 degrees Celsius, while pursuing efforts to limit the increase to 1.5 degrees.
- **Global peaking and 'climate neutrality' (Art. 4)** –To achieve this temperature goal, Parties aim to reach global peaking of greenhouse gas emissions (GHGs) as soon as possible, recognizing peaking will take longer for developing country Parties, so as to achieve a balance between anthropogenic emissions by sources and removals by sinks of GHGs in the second half of the century.
- **Mitigation (Art. 4)** – The Paris Agreement establishes binding commitments by all Parties to prepare, communicate and maintain a nationally determined contribution (NDC) and to pursue domestic measures to achieve them. It also prescribes that Parties shall communicate their NDCs every five years and provide information necessary for clarity and transparency. To set a firm foundation for higher ambition, each successive NDC will represent a progression beyond the previous one and reflect the highest possible ambition. Developed countries should continue to take the lead by undertaking absolute economy-wide reduction targets, while developing countries should continue enhancing their mitigation efforts, and are encouraged to move toward economy-wide targets over time in the light of different national circumstances.

- **Sinks and reservoirs (Art.5)** –The Paris Agreement also encourages Parties to conserve and enhance, as appropriate, sinks and reservoirs of GHGs as referred to in Article 4, paragraph 1(d) of the Convention, including forests.
- Voluntary cooperation/Market- and non-market-based approaches (Art. 6) – The Paris Agreement recognizes the possibility of voluntary cooperation among Parties to allow for higher ambition and sets out principles – including environmental integrity, transparency and robust accounting – for any cooperation that involves internationally transferal of mitigation outcomes. It establishes a mechanism to contribute to the mitigation of GHG emissions and support sustainable development and defines a framework for non-market approaches to sustainable development.
- **Adaptation (Art. 7)** – The Paris Agreement establishes a global goal on adaptation – of enhancing adaptive capacity, strengthening resilience and reducing vulnerability to climate change in the context of the temperature goal of the Agreement. It aims to significantly strengthen national adaptation efforts, including through support and international cooperation. It recognizes that adaptation is a global challenge faced by all. All Parties should engage in adaptation, including by formulating and implementing National Adaptation Plans, and should submit and periodically update an adaptation communication describing their priorities, needs, plans and actions. The adaptation efforts of developing countries should be recognized.
- **Loss and damage (Art. 8)** – The Paris Agreement recognizes the importance of averting, minimizing and addressing loss and damage associated with the adverse effects of climate change, including extreme weather events and slow onset events, and the role of sustainable development in reducing the risk of loss and damage. Parties are to enhance understanding, action and support, including through the Warsaw International Mechanism, on a cooperative and facilitative basis with respect to loss and damage associated with the adverse effects of climate change.
- **Finance, technology and capacity-building support (Art. 9, 10 and 11)** – The Paris Agreement reaffirms the obligations of developed countries to support the efforts of developing country Parties to build clean, climate-resilient futures, while for the first time encouraging voluntary contributions by other Parties. Provision of resources should also aim to achieve a balance between adaptation and mitigation. In addition to reporting on finance already provided, developed country Parties commit to submit indicative information on future support every two years, including projected levels of public finance. The Agreement also provides that the Financial Mechanism of the Convention, including the Green Climate Fund (GCF), shall serve the Agreement. International cooperation on climate-safe technology development and transfer and building capacity in the developing world are also strengthened: a technology framework is established under the Agreement and capacity-building activities will be strengthened

through, inter alia, enhanced support for capacity building actions in developing country Parties and appropriate institutional arrangements. Climate change education, training as well as public awareness, participation and access to information (Art 12) is also to be enhanced under the Agreement.

- Climate change education, training, public awareness, public participation and public access to information (Art 12) is also to be enhanced under the Agreement.
- **Transparency (Art. 13), implementation and compliance (Art. 15)** – The Paris Agreement relies on a robust transparency and accounting system to provide clarity on action and support by Parties, with flexibility for their differing capabilities of Parties. In addition to reporting information on mitigation, adaptation and support, the Agreement requires that the information submitted by each Party undergoes international technical expert review. The Agreement also includes a mechanism that will facilitate implementation and promote compliance in a non-adversarial and non-punitive manner, and will report annually to the CMA.
- **Global Stocktake (Art. 14)** – A "global stocktake", to take place in 2023 and every five years thereafter will assess collective progress toward achieving the purpose of the Agreement in a comprehensive and facilitative manner. It will be based on the best available science and its long-term global goal. Its outcome will inform Parties in updating and enhancing their actions and support and enhancing international cooperation on climate action.

Decision 1/CP.21 also sets out a number of measures to enhance action prior to 2020, including strengthening the technical examination process, enhancement of provision of urgent finance, technology and support and measures to strengthen high-level engagement. For 2018 a facilitative dialogue is envisaged to take stock of collective progress towards the long-term emission reduction goal of Art 4. The decision also welcomes the efforts of all non-Party stakeholders to address and respond to climate change, including those of civil society, the private sector, financial institutions, cities and other subnational authorities. These stakeholders are invited to scale up their efforts and showcase them via the Non-State Actor Zone for Climate Action platform (http://climateaction.unfccc.int). Parties also recognized the need to strengthen the knowledge, technologies, practices and efforts of local communities and indigenous peoples, as well as the important role of providing incentives through tools such as domestic policies and carbon pricing. (UNFCCC, 2015)

Reference

United Nations Framework Convention on Climate Change. (2015) *Key Aspects of the Paris Agreement*. UNFCCC. Available online at: https://unfccc.int/process-and-meetings/the-paris-agreement/the-paris-agreement/key-aspects-of-the-paris-agreement

INDEX

Page numbers in *italics* represent figures, while page numbers in **bold** represent tables.